AF527147

TERRORISM AND KASHMIR

TERRORISM AND KASHMIR

N K Verma

MD PUBLICATIONS PVT LTD
NEW DELHI
www.mdppl.com

Copyright © 2010 by MD Publications Pvt Ltd.

All rights reserved. No part of this book may be reproduced or utilized in any form or by any means, electronically or mechanically, including photocopying, recording, or by any information storage and retrieval system, without the prior permission in writing from the publisher.

Published by :

MD Publications Pvt Ltd
"MD House", 11, Darya Ganj,
New Delhi - 110 002
Phone : +91-11-45355555
E-mail : contact@mdppl.com
Website: www.mdppl.com

ISBN: 978-81-7533-303-1

Published and Printed by Mr. Pranav Gupta on behalf of **MD Publications Pvt Ltd** at Times Press, Delhi.

PREFACE

The genesis of the bloody dispute dates back to the events of 1947 when India and Pakistan became independent from British Rule. The State of Jammu and Kashmir (J&K) was ruled by a much-hated tyrant Hari Singh who was oppressive against the majority Muslim population. Kashmiris had begun a liberation movement in 1931 under the leadership of the charismatic leader Sher-i-Kashmir (Lion of Kashmir) Sheikh Abdullah which marked the beginning of a strong Kashmiri Nationalism. The vacillating Hari Singh was compelled to accede to India under threat of invasion from Pathan tribesmen backed by Pakistan.

In theory, the rulers of the Princely States were allowed to accede their States to either India or Pakistan, irrespective of the wishes of their people; but as a practical matter, they were encouraged to accede to the geographically contiguous Dominion, taking into account the wishes of their people and in cases where a dispute arose, it was decided to settle the question of accession by a plebiscite, a scheme proposed and accepted by India. Being a Muslim majority State and contiguous to Pakistan, Kashmir was expected to accede to Pakistan; since the Hindu ruler acceded instead to India, a dispute arose in the case of Kashmir.

India is fighting the terrorists in Kashmir since 1989. Pakistan fought three wars on Kashmir- 1947-48, 1965, and 1971. But his every attempt to snatch Kashmir from India becomes futile. Pakistan army understood the edge of Indian army over Pakistan army in conventional warfare. So change their modus operandi and wage proxy war against India. Pakistan support trained and financed the local Kashmiri youth for jihad against India. Though there had been instances of sporadic conflict in many regions for many years, intensified attacks occurred in the late 1980s, when the 1987 state elections were rigged although disputed ; had resulted in some of the 'states legislative assembly' 'formed militant wings' later on after the election forming and creating the catalyst for the insurgency.

Kashmir militancy phase from 1995 to now comprises mostly foreign terrorists from Afghanistan, Pakistan etc. They were funded, armed and trained by Pakistan and pushed into the Indian Kashmir for jihad against Indian army. These foreigner mercenaries or terrorist get monthly salary and even lump sum payment to there family on death, so called martyr. These foreigner mercenaries launch fidayeen or suicidal attack on the security forces for maximum damage. These tactics used to boost the morale the new recruit terrorists.

India frequently asserts that most of the separatist militant groups are based in Pakistan and Pakistan-administered Kashmir (also known as Azad Kashmir). Some like the All Parties Hurriyat Conference and the Jammu and Kashmir Liberation Front demand an independent Kashmir. Other militant groups such as Lashkar-e-Toiba and Jaish-e-Mohammed favour a Pakistani-Kashmir.

India has always taken the stand that Kashmir is an internal issue and that it will not permit third party mediation. Over twenty years of militancy has vitiated the atmosphere so much in the valley. Kashmir is no longer a territorial dispute, but is a part of the global fight against Islamic fundamentalism. Also, the only resolution that will be acceptable to Pakistan is accession to Pakistan. India should continue to resist any outside interference in Kashmir.

I am very grateful to Mr. Pranav Gupta, Director of MD Publications Pvt Ltd, New Delhi, for his kind cooperation and support for this book.

N K Verma

CONTENTS

1

Terrorism and Kashmir
An Introduction

Insurgency in Kashmir has existed in various forms, both on the Indian administrated side of the disputed territory of Jammu and Kashmir and Pakistan-administered Kashmir. Kashmir has been the target of a campaign of militancy by all sides in the conflict. Thousands of lives have been lost since 1989 due to the intensified insurgency. Casualties include civilians, Indian Armed Forces, and Kashmiri and foreign militants. The Inter-Services Intelligence of Pakistan has been accused by India of supporting and training *Mujahideen* to fight in Jammu and Kashmir. While, International Human Right Groups have accused Indian army of committing grave Human rights violations in Indian-administered Jammu and Kashmir.

MILITANCY AND MILITARY

Though there had been instances of sporadic conflict in many regions for many years, intensified attacks occurred in the late 1980s, when *Mujahideen* fighters from Afghanistan slowly infiltrated the region, with Pakistan's help, following the end of the Soviet-Afghan War in 1989. Since then, violence has increased significantly in strength. Many separatists have carried out attacks on local Hindus, Indian civilians and Indian army installations in response to what they see as Indian army occupation.

India frequently asserts that most of the separatist militant groups are based in Pakistan and Pakistan-administered Kashmir (also known as Azad Kashmir). Some like the All Parties Hurriyat Conference and the Jammu and Kashmir Liberation Front, demand an independent Kashmir. Other militant groups such as *Lashkar-e-Toiba* and *Jaish-e-Mohammed* favour a Pakistani-Kashmir. These groups have contacts with Taliban and Bin Laden. Both the organisations no longer operate under these names after they were banned by the Indian and Pakistani government, and by other countries including the US and UK.

Of the larger militant groups, the Hizbul *Mujahideen,* a militant organisation based in Indian administered Kashmir, unlike other groups, has only kept its name. Despite casualties, the militants are still believed to number thousands rather than hundreds. Several new separatist organizations have also emerged. According to US Intelligence, *Al-Qaeda* also has a main base in Pakistani Kashmir and is helping to foment terrorism in Jammu and Kashmir. However India, Pakistan and the separatist organizations call this as hoax. Inspector General Police, Kashmir range also referred this as a hoax.

It is hard to determine the total number of casualties. According to a report by the Government of India in the year 2000, 31,000 Indian civilians had lost their lives due to the insurgency. Human rights groups and local NGOs put the total figure at more than 84,000 (2005 figure). Militancy had reached its peak in 1994 when the region saw more than 6,043 incidents and has since declined. However, Kashmir continues to remain as the most volatile region in the world with an average of 2,500 incidents every year. According to an Indian estimate in 2005 there were about 2,000 militants in the Kashmir valley alone; 1,200 of them belong to the Hizbul *Mujahideen.*

Not all Kashmiri separatists and militant organizations share the same ideology. Some fight in the name of religion, some are openly pro-Pakistan and some favour an independent Kashmir. Due to the presence of the numerous anti-Indian insurgent groups India has been compelled to deploy massive number of troops in the Indian administered Jammu and Kashmir for the task of counter insurgency. New Delhi has never made an official count, but military analysts estimate that anywhere from 30,000 to nearly 33,000 security personnel are most likely involved, supported by thousands of Indian paramilitary groups such as the Rashtriya rifles, and the Romeo Force (all a part of Indian army). Stimson.org notes of the Indian Armed forces in Kashmir that:

Some reports estimate that India deploys approximately 400,000 combined army and paramilitary forces in Kashmir, most of which are stationed in the interior, 80,000 of which are deployed along the LoC. Pakistani forces deployed along the LoC are reported to number in the 40,000-50,000 range. *Times Online* reports that around 250,000 Indian troops are stationed in Kashmir, while Pravda.RU, a widely read Russian News source notes that 350,000-600,000 troops may be deployed in Kashmir.

MILITANT GROUPS

Over the last two years, a militant group, *Lashkar-e-Toiba* has split into two factions: *Al Mansurin* and *Al Nasirin*. Another new group reported to have emerged is the Save Kashmir Movement. Harkat-ul-*Mujahideen* (formerly known as Harkat-ul-Ansar) and *Lashkar-e-Toiba* are believed to be operating from Muzaffarabad, Azad Kashmir and Muridke, Pakistan respectively. Other less well known groups are the Freedom Force and Farzandan-e-Milat. A smaller group, Al-Badr, has been active in Kashmir for many years and is still believed to be functioning.

All Parties Hurriyat Conference, an organization that uses moderate means to press for the rights of the Kashmiris, is often considered as the mediator between New Delhi and insurgent groups. Not much is known about collaboration between the various groups, but most say they are members of an alliance known as the United Jihad Council (UJC). The two groups which India says were behind the December 2001 attack on the Indian parliament in New Delhi – known then as *Jaish-e-Mohammed* and *Lashkar-e-Toiba* are believed to be members of the *UJC*.

India says that it was *Jaish-e-Mohammed* that attacked the Jammu and Kashmir State Assembly in Srinagar in October 2001. It is also known that the *Jaish-e-Mohammed* was responsible for the hijacking of Indian Airlines Flight IC-814 to Kandahar, which forced the Government of India to release Maulana Masood Azhar, the chief of the *Jaish-e-Mohammed*. Recruits from various parts of the world have been sent to Pakistan-administered Kashmir for training and advice.

INDIA AND PAKISTAN

A 1994 report by *Human Rights Watch* group lends support to both Indian and Pakistani charges. In support of Indian claims, it states that "There is compelling evidence that elements of the Pakistani government have sponsored a significant flow of arms to Kashmiri militants from arms bazaars in the North West Frontier Province, as well as an extensive training program."

While in support of Pakistani claims, it states that "the human rights record of the Indian government in Punjab and Kashmir is appalling. Abuses in Kashmir are clearly on the rise." The US government has also supported the claim that anti-India terror groups exist in India. India claims that there are also other Afghan, Egyptian, Yemeni and Bangladeshi terrorists active in Jammu and Kashmir. The Council on Foreign Relations states that Pakistan's military and Inter-Services Intelligence (ISI) both include personnel who sympathize with-or even assist-Islamist militants adding that "ISI has provided covert but well-documented support to terrorist groups active in Kashmir, among other outfits."

In a recent infiltration bid, a Pakistan Army officer was shot dead, with India citing that this was clear and conclusive evidence of Pakistani involvement in the insurgency. The UN Security Council has also confirmed the existence of terrorist groups based in [Pakistani] Kashmir and urged Pakistan to crack down on terrorist groups which had been operating in

Kashmir and killing innocent people. Pakistan describes the separatists as "freedom fighters" and says that it supports their effort for the cause of the Kashmiris only morally and diplomatically. Pakistan however admits that there has been 'cross border infiltration of militants' across the Line of Control. In 2008, Pakistani President Asif Ali Zardari said India has never been a threat to Pakistan, and that militants in Kashmir are terrorists. In 2002, Pakistani president Pervez Musharraf tried to clamp down on the militants operating from Pakistan.

India, however, claims that Islamabad supports these groups financially and militarily. Sources have maintained that Pakistan's intelligence organisation, Inter Services Intelligence, is the main supplier of funds and arms to these groups; a claim that Islamabad has dismissed. According to the Indian news site Rediff.com, British Government had stated in 2002 that there is a 'clear link' between Pakistan's Inter Services Intelligence and three major militant groups An article in The Guardian had uncovered evidence that Pakistani militants were openly raising funds and training new recruits and that the ISI's Kashmir Cell was instrumental in funding and controlling the militant outfits. Richard Bennett, a British military and intelligence analyst states that the ISI has armed and trained generations of Islamist extremists and has directed many of their attacks both within the Kashmir and in India's major cities.

Indian sources also allege that there are between 2,600 to 3,000 militants receiving training in camps across Pakistan and Pakistan Administered Kashmir. During a peace summit between former Pakistani President Pervez Musharraf and Indian former-Prime Minister Atal Bihari Vajpayee in January 2004, Islamabad assured India that it would do everything possible to curb the activities any training camps on its territory. However, violence has continued in Kashmir despite a 3 year long peace process between India and Pakistan. There were as many as 166 incidents in June 2005 alone in which some 201 people have died.

According to Indian sources there are about 37 training camps in Pakistan, 49 in Azad Kashmir and 22 in Afghanistan. The FBI also has produced images of camps operating in

Pakistan. India claims that every year thousands of armed insurgents infiltrate into Indian-administered Kashmir and carries out attacks against Indian Security Forces and Kashmiri civilians. In June 2005, the Indian Army had foiled at least 72 infiltration attempts along the Line of Control in Kashmir.

India alleges that despite the commitments made by Pervez Musharraf, Islamabad has done little to stop the training camps on its soil. According to India, most of the militants in Kashmir come from Pakistan, Afghanistan, Egypt, Yemen and Bangladesh.

Not all Kashmiri separatists and militant organizations share the same ideology. Some fight in the name of religion, some are pro-Pakistan and some favour an independent Kashmir. While the vast majority of militants are Muslims, one report indicated a minority of fighter (40 to 50) are Hindu militants who have either taken up arms or provided safe cover for militants.

INDIAN CLAIMS

The following statistics were compiled by Indian Army:

1. Number of civilians killed in Kashmir since 1988: 65,000 to 1,00,000
2. Number of Kashmiri militant camps in Pakistan-administered Kashmir: 49
3. Total number of Kashmir militant camps in Pakistan: 37
4. Number of Kashmiri militant camps in Afghanistan: 22 (During Taliban rule)
5. Number of militants* operating in Jammu and Kashmir: 800 (2009 estimate)
6. Number of Kashmiri Militants in Indian jails: 125
7. Number of explosions carried out by the Militants* in India: 4,730
8. Total number of Kashmiri Pandits displaced from the state: over 750,000
9. Amount of explosives recovered from Kashmiri Militants in India: 60 tons or 30,000 kg (estimate)

Major Kashmiri Militant training camps:

Location of major Militant camps	
Muridke (near Lahore)	Punjab, Pakistan
Kotli	Pakistan-administered Kashmir
Mużaffarabad	Pakistan-administered Kashmir
Skardu	Northern Areas, Pakistan
Gultari	Northern Areas, Pakistan
Tarkuti	Northern Areas, Pakistan
Batrasi	North West Frontier Province, Pakistan
Sufaida	North West Frontier Province, Pakistan
Tanda Allabyar	Sindh, Pakistan

Note: Pakistan denies the existence of such training camps on their territory, and the existence of such camps is a matter of controversy.

HUMAN RIGHTS VIOLATIONS

HUMAN RIGHTS VIOLATIONS BY INDIA

A 1996 Human Rights Watch report accuses the Indian military and Indian-government backed paramilitaries of "committ[ing] serious and widespread human rights violations in Kashmir." One such alleed massacre occurred on January 6, 1993 in the town of Sopore. *TIME Magazine* described the incident as such: "In retaliation for the killing of one soldier, paramilitary forces rampaged through Sopore's market setting buildings ablaze and shooting bystanders. The Indian government pronounced the event 'unfortunate' and claimed that an ammunition dump had been hit by gunfire, setting off fires that killed most of the victims."

In addition to this, there have been claims of disappearances by the police or the army in Kashmir by several human rights organizations. Many human rights organizations such as Amnesty International and the Human Rights Watch (HRW) have condemned human rights abuses in Kashmir by Indians such as "extra-judicial executions","disappearances", and torture; the "Armed Forces Special Powers Act", which "provides impunity for human rights abuses and fuels cycles of violence.

The Armed Forces Special Powers Act (AFSPA) grants the military wide powers of arrest, the right to shoot to kill, and to occupy or destroy property in counterinsurgency operations. Indian officials claim that troops need such powers because the army is only deployed when national security is at serious risk from armed combatants. Such circumstances, they say, call for extraordinary measures." Human rights organizations have also asked Indian government to repeal the Public Safety Act, since "a detainee may be held in administrative detention for a maximum of two years without a court order."

HUMAN RIGHTS VIOLATIONS BY PAKISTAN

Human rights violations have also been reported in Pakistan-administered Kashmir. A 2-day conference on Gilgit Baltistan was held on April 8-9, 2008 at the European Parliament in Brussels under the auspices of International Kashmir Alliance. Here several members of the European Parliament (MEPs) expressed concern over the human rights violation in Gilgit Baltistan and urged the government of Pakistan to establish democratic institutions and rule of law in this area of northern Kashmir. Abdul Hamid Khan, Chairman Balawaristan National Front speaking at the same conference said "no democratically elected representative (from Gilgit Baltistan) was included when Karachi Agreement was signed between Pakistan and Muslim Conference leaders in 1949."

On April 25, 2007 European Union published a report entitled 'on Kashmir: present situation and future prospects'. Section 2 of the noted the absence of democracy in Gilgit Baltistan region and in section 32 deplored the human rights violations in this region. A 2008 report by the United Nations High Commissioner for Refugees determined that Pakistan administered Kashmir, was 'Not Free'.

It also criticized the Pakistani Government saying 'The appropriation of land in the Northern Areas by non-Kashmiri migrants from elsewhere in Pakistan, with the tacit encouragement of the federal government and army, has led to dwindling economic opportunities for the local population and an increase in sectarian tension between the majority Shia Muslims and a growing number of Sunnis.' The same report determined that the Indian administered Jammu and Kashmir was 'Partly Free'. Parties like Balawaristan National Front are fighting for independence of Pakistan-administered Kashmir from Pakistan.

HUMAN RIGHTS VIOLATIONS BY MILITANTS

Islamic militants are accused of violence against the Kashmir populace. Thousands of civilian Kashmiri Hindus have been killed in Kashmir over the past 10 years by Islamic militants' organisations. Human rights organisations put the figure of the number of civilians killed between Jan 1, 1999 and December 31, 1999 at about 9,733. Tens of thousands of Kashmiri Pandits have emigrated as a result of the violence. Estimates of the displaced vary from 170,000 to 700,000. Thousands of Pandits have to move to Jammu because of terrorism.

On February 15, 2006 United States Congressman Frank Pallone introduced a resolution in United States House of Representatives condemning the violation of Human rights of Kashmiri Pandits. He stated that an ethnic cleansing campaign was being run by Islamic terrorists to convert Kashmir into a Muslim state and 400,000 Kashmiri Pandits had either been murdered or displaced from their homes.

The resolution was passed by the House (with Senate concurring) and stated that :

1. Congress condemns the human rights violations committed against Kashmiri Pandits in the strongest terms;

2. It is the sense of Congress that the Government of the Republic of India and the State Government of Jammu and Kashmir should take immediate steps to remedy the situation of the Kashmiri Pandits and should act to ensure the physical, political, and economic security of this embattled community; and
3. Congress supports mutual discussions between the Government of India and the State Government of Jammu and Kashmir to achieve a peaceful and equitable solution to the Kashmiri conflict that is acceptable to the Kashmiri Pandits while ensuring that they are a part of the ongoing dialogue.

MILITANT ACTS IN J&K

July and August 1989 - 3 CRPF personnel and politician Mohd. Yusuf Halwai of NC/F was killed.

1989 kidnapping of Rubaiya Sayeed daughter of the then Home Minister of India Mufti Sayeed.

1995 kidnapping of western tourists in Jammu and Kashmir 6 foreign trekkers from Anantnag district were kidnapped by Al Faran, One was beheaded later, one escaped and other four remain untraced presumable killed.

Sangrampora Killings - On March 22, 1997, 7 Kashmiri Pandits were killed in Sangrampora village in the Budgam district.

Wandhama Massacre - In January 1998, 24 Kashmiri Pandits living in the village of Wandhama were massacred by Pakistani militants. According to the testimony of one of the survivors, the militants dressed themselves as officers of the Indian Army, entered their houses and then started firing blindly. The incident was significant because it coincided with former US president Bill Clinton's visit to India and New Delhi used the massacre to present a case against the alleged Pakistan-supported terrorism in Kashmir.

1998 Prankote massacre - 26 Hindu villagers of Udhampur district were killed by militants.

1998 Champanari massacre - 25 Hindu villagers killed on June 19, 1998 by Islamic militants.

2001 terrorist attack on Jammu and Kashmir legislative assembly On October 1, 2001, a bombing at the Legislative Assembly in Srinagar killed 38.

2003 Nadimarg Massacre - 24 Hindus killed in Nadimarg, Kashmir on March 23, 2003 by *Lashkar-e-Taiba* militants.

Qasim Nagar Attack - On July 13, 2003, armed militants believed to be a part of the *Lashkar-e-Toiba* threw hand grenades at the Qasim Nagar market in Srinagar and then fired on civilians standing nearby killing 27 and injuring many more.

July 20, 2005 Srinagar Bombing - A car bomb exploded near an armoured Indian Army vehicle in the famous Church Lane area in Srinagar killing 4 Indian Army personnel, one civilian and the suicide bomber. Militant group Hizbul *Mujahideen,* claimed responsibility for the attack.

Budshah Chowk attack - A militant attack on July 29, 2005 at Srinigar's city centre, Budshah Chowk, killed 2 and left more than 17 people injured. Most of those injured were media journalists.

Assassination of Ghulam Nabi Lone - On October 18, 2005 suspected Kashmiri militants killed Jammu and Kashmir's then education minister Ghulam Nabi Lone. Militant group called Al Mansurin claimed responsibility for the attack. Abdul Ghani Lone, a prominent All Party Hurriyat Conference leader, was assassinated by unidentified gunmen during a memorial rally in Srinagar. The assassination resulted in wide-scale demonstrations against the Indian forces for failing to provide enough security cover for Mr. Lone.

On May 3, 2006 militants massacred 35 Hindus in Doda and Udhampur districts in Jammu and Kashmir.

On June 12, 2006 one person was killed and 31 were wounded when terrorists hurled three grenades on Vaishnodevi shrine-bound buses at the general bus stand.

June 2, 2009: 17-year-old Nigeen Awan was shot and killed at her residence by Militants.

June 16, 2009: 45-year-old Rashma Jan died when terrorists barged into her house at Sopore on June 16 and fired indiscriminately.

RECENT DEVELOPMENTS

Violent activities in the region declined in 2004. There are two main reasons for this: warming of relations between New Delhi and Pakistan which consequently lead to a ceasefire between the two countries in 2003 and the fencing of the LOC being carried out by the Indian Army. Moreover, coming under intense international pressure, Islamabad was compelled to take actions against the militants' training camps on its territory. In 2004, the two countries also agreed upon decreasing the number of troops present in the region.

Under pressure, Kashmiri militant organisations have made an offer for talks and negotiations with New Delhi, which was accepted by India. India's Border Security Force blamed the Pakistani military for providing cover-fire for the militants whenever they infiltrated into Indian Territory from Pakistan. However, ever since the ceasefire has come into action, the militants have received no back-up from Pakistani Military, which has contributed significantly to the decline in *cross-border terrorism* in the state. Even the recently elected Pakistani President, Asif Ali Zardari admitted that the militants operating in Kashmir were indeed terrorists.

2008

According to Govt. of India Home Ministry, 2008 marks the lowest civilian casualties in 20 years with 89 deaths, compared to highest of 1,413 in 1996. 85 security personnel died in 2008 compared to 613 in 2001. Human right situation improved with only 1 custodial death and no custodial disappearance.

2009

Hizbul Mujahideen founder, considered founder of terrorism in Kashmir, Ahsan Dar was arrested on Jan 14th.

Feberuary 21, 2009: Bomai Killing: Army kills two devotees in an indiscriminate firing incident by 22nd Battalion of Rashtriya Rilfes in Bomai, Sopore which results in massive valley wide protests?

March 6, 2009: Nowhatta Killing: A CRPF vehicle killed one youth and crushed another at Nawhatta during a protest. The killing triggered violent protests across the city and Authorities' clamed curfew for continuously for four days.

Separatists and workers of a political party were believed to be behind stone a pelting incident which generally leads to retaliatory fire by the police. Autorickshaw laden with stones meant for distribution was seized by the police in 11 March, 2009.

March 18, 2009: Rajpora killing: Barely a few hours after the union home minister, P Chidambaram, assured action against troopers found guilty for Bomai killings, 181 bn of paramilitary CRPF troopers shot dead a carpenter, Ghulam Mohiudin Malik son of Muhammad Akbar Malik, at Khaigam Pakherpora in south Kashmir's Pulwama district.

May 31, 2009: Shopian rape and murder case: Protests over rape and murder of two young women allegedly by Indian Armed Forces. Pro-freedom leaders arrested and police and paramilitary forces resorted to firing at protesters in several places, including Shopian, Baramulla and Srinagar killing one person and injuring hundreds.

Militancy in the disputed region of Kashmir has been major fuel for discord between India and Pakistan since the 1980s. Attacks in the region began to increase in scale and intensity following the Soviet invasion of Afghanistan, when foreign insurgents flooded the region to join the Afghan Mujahadeen.

The majority Muslim region has its own local militant groups, but experts believe most of the recent Kashmir and Kashmir-based terrorism has been the work of foreign Islamists who seek to claim the region for Pakistan. A spate of Islamist cross-border attacks into Indian-held territory, the December 2001 storming of the Indian parliament in New Delhi, and the 2008 Mumbai attacks have all reinforced

Kashmir's standing as the significant bone of contention between India and Pakistan. Both states have nuclear weapons, making Kashmir one of the world's most dangerous flashpoints.

ORIGINS OF THE CONFLICT

Kashmir has been a constant source of tension since 1947, when the British partitioned their imperial holdings in South Asia into two new states, India and Pakistan. For Pakistan, incorporating the majority Muslim province of Kashmir is a basic national aspiration bound up in its identity as an Islamic state. Islamabad's official line on Kashmir, which the United States echoed as recently as June 2009, is that incorporation into either India or Pakistan must be determined by Kashmiris. Meanwhile, India sees the province as vital to its identity as a secular, multiethnic state.

Movements for an independent Kashmiri state, such as the Kashmir Freedom Movement and the Jammu Kashmir Liberation Front, also exist and have many supporters. India now holds about two-thirds of the disputed territory, which it calls Jammu and Kashmir. Pakistan controls about one-third, which it calls Azad (meaning "free") Kashmir. China also controls two small sections of northern Kashmir. India and Pakistan fought two wars over the region in 1947 and 1965, and a limited conflict in 1999. At least fifty thousand people have died in political violence in Kashmir since 1989.

Though flare-ups have occurred on both sides of the line, violence in Kashmir has decreased dramatically. According to the Indian Home Ministry, the number of violent incidents in 2008 was the lowest in twenty years (AFP) at seven hundred, a 40 per cent drop compared to the number of incidents reported in 2007. The South Asia Terrorism Portal reports that 2008 also marks the first time civilian casualties have been under one hundred since 1990.

TERRORIST GROUPS

The U.S. State Department lists three Islamist groups active in Kashmir as foreign terrorist organizations: *Harakat ul-*

Mujahideen, Jaish-e-Mohammed, and *Lashkar-e-Taiba.* The first group has been listed for years, and the other two were added after the December 2001 Indian parliament attack. All three groups have attracted Pakistani members as well as Afghan and Arab veterans who fought the 1980s Soviet occupation of Afghanistan.

Harakat ul-Mujahideen (HUM) was established in the mid-1980s. Based first in Pakistan and then in Afghanistan, it has several hundred armed supporters in Pakistan and Kashmir. The group is responsible for the December 1999 hijacking of an Indian airliner and numerous attacks on Indian troops and civilians in Kashmir. Jammu Kashmir Liberation Front Harakat members have participated in insurgent and terrorist operations in Myanmar, Tajikistan, and Bosnia.

Jaish-e-Mohammed (JEM) was founded in 2000 by Maulana Masood Azhar, a Pakistani cleric. The group seeks to incorporate Kashmir into the state of Pakistan and has openly declared war on the United States. JEM has carried out attacks on Indian targets, the Pakistani government, and various sectarian minority groups within Pakistan. Acts of terrorism attributed to the group include the 2001 attack on the Indian Parliament and a series of assaults in 2002 on Christian sites in Pakistan. The Pakistani government has also implicated JEM for the two assassination attempts on former Pakistani President Pervez Musharraf. According to the U.S. State Department, the group has at least several hundred armed supporters as well as tens of thousands of followers.

Lashkar-e-Taiba (LeT), active since 1993, was formed as the military wing of the well-funded Pakistani Islamist organization Markaz-ad- Dawa-wal-Irshad. The group, one of the largest and most proficient of the Kashmir-based terrorist groups, has claimed responsibility for a number of high-profile attacks on Indian targets in Jammu and Kashmir, as well as within India. India says that over the last several years the group has split into two factions, al-Mansurin and al-Nasirin. There is wide speculation that LeT was responsible for the July 11, 2006 string of bombings on

Mumbai's commuter railroad, though a spokesman for the group denied any involvement. The Indian government alleges that LeT was responsible for coordinating the 2008 Mumbai attacks.

Since Pakistan outlawed these groups, attacks in Kashmir and Pakistan have been carried out under other guises as a tactic to avoid detection while still maintaining the same leadership and ideology. Often times these groups pose as charitable organizations to avoid government sanctions. One group calling itself *al-Qanoon* or *Lashkar-e-Omar* is thought to be a coalition of members of *Jaish-e-Mohammed, Lashkar-e-Taiba,* and other Pakistan-based Islamist groups, including the anti-Shia Lashkar-e-Jhangvi organization.

LINKS TO THE PAKISTANI STATE

India has long accused Pakistan's premier intelligence service, Inter-Services Intelligence (ISI), of arming, training, and providing logistical support to militants in Kashmir. Pakistan denies any ongoing collaboration between the ISI and militants, stressing a change of course after September 11, 2001. After the December 2001 attack on India's parliament, former Pakistani President Pervez Musharraf promised to crack down on terrorist groups active in Kashmir and purge ISI officials with ties to these groups.

However, the Indian government implied the ISI's involvement in a July 2008 attack on the Indian embassy in Kabul, and again in the November 2008 attacks in Mumbai. But as this Backgrounder points out, some experts believe the relationship between the Pakistani military and some Kashmiri groups has turned with the rise of militancy within Pakistan.

Shuja Nawaz, author of *Crossed Swords: Pakistan, its Army, and the Wars Within,* says the ISI "has certainly lost control" of Kashmiri militant groups. According to Nawaz, some of the groups trained by the ISI to fuel insurgency in Kashmir have been implicated in bombings and attacks within Pakistan, therefore making them army targets.

THE AL-QAEDA CONNECTION

Many terrorists active in Kashmir received training in the same *madrasas*, or Muslim seminaries, where Taliban and *Al-Qaeda* fighters studied, and some received military training at camps in Taliban-ruled Afghanistan. Leaders of some of these terror groups also have *Al-Qaeda* connections.

The long-time leader of the *Harakat ul-Mujahideen* group, Fazlur Rehman Khalil, signed al-Qaeda's 1998 declaration of holy war, which called on Muslims to attack all Americans and their allies. Maulana Masood Azhar, who founded the *Jaish-e-Mohammed* organization, traveled to Afghanistan several times to meet Osama bin Laden. Azhar's group is suspected of receiving funding from al-Qaeda, U.S. and Indian officials say. In 2006, *Al-Qaeda* claimed to have established a wing in Kashmir.

OBSTACLE TO PEACE

Despite a resumption of formal peace talks between India and Pakistan in 2004, militant attacks continue to hinder progress towards a sustainable deal on Kashmir. After New Delhi and Islamabad agreed to launch a landmark bus service in February 2005 across the cease-fire line, militants vowed to target the service. In April of the same year, one bus survived a grenade attack.

In March 2008, seventeen were wounded when a bomb exploded on a highway overpass in Indian-controlled Kashmir. A week later a gun battle erupted between Indian security forces and militants during a search-and-cordon operation, killing five. Both India and Pakistan have been accused of committing human rights violations in Kashmir, exacerbating the antagonism and mutual distrust both states have for one another. Talks were effectively put on hold in 2008 after India accused the ISI and Pakistani authorities of being complicit in the Mumbai attacks.

2

Historical Survey of Jammu and Kashmir

According to legend, Jammu was founded by Raja Jamboolochan in the 14th century BCE. During one of his hunting campaigns he reached the Tawi River where he saw a goat and a lion drinking water at the same place. The king was impressed and decided to set up a town after his name, *Jamboo*. With the passage of time, the name was corrupted and became "Jammu". According to folk etymology, the name "Kashmir" means "desiccated land" (from the Sanskrit: *Ka* = water and *shimeera* = desiccate). In the *Rajatarangini,* a history of Kashmir written by *Kalhana* in mid-12th century, it is stated that the valley of Kashmir was formerly a lake.

According to Hindu mythology, the lake was drained by the great *rishi* or sage, Kashyapa, son of Marichi, son of Brahma, by cutting the gap in the hills at Baramulla (*Varaha-mula*). When Kashmir had been drained, Kashyapa asked Brahmans to settle there. This is still the local tradition, and in the existing physical condition of the country, we may see some ground for the story which has taken this form. The name of Kashyapa is by history and tradition connected with the draining of the lake, and the chief town or collection of dwellings in the valley was called *Kashyapa-pura,* which has been identified with *Kao-1r6.nupos* of Hecataeus (*apud* Stephen of Byzantium) and *Kaspatyros* of Herodotus (3.102, 4.44). Kashmir is also the count:y meant by Ptolemy's *Kao-ir, pta.*

Cashmere is an archaic spelling of Kashmir, and in some countries it is still spelled this way. Kashmir was one of the major centres of Sanskrit scholars. According to the Mahabharata, the Kambojas ruled Kashmir during the epic period with a Republican system of government from the capital city of of *Karna-Rajapuram-gatva-Kambojah-nirjitastava.*, shortened to Rajapura, which has been identified with modern Rajauri. Later, the Panchalas are stated to have established their sway. The name *Peer Panjal,* which is a part of modern Kashmir, is a witness to this fact.

Panjal is simply a distorted form of the Sanskritic tribal term Panchala. The Muslims prefixed the word 'peer' to it in memory of Siddha Faqir and the name thereafter is said to have changed into Peer Panjal. The Mauryan emperor Ashoka is often credited with having founded the city of Srinagar. Kashmir was once a Buddhist seat of learning, perhaps with the Sarvâstivâdan school dominating. East and Central Asian Buddhist monks are recorded as having visited the kingdom. In the late 4th century AD, the famous Kuchanese monk Kumârajîva, born to an Indian noble family, studied Dîrghâgama and Madhyâgama in Kashmir under Bandhudatta.

He later becoming a prolific translator who helped takes Buddhism to China. His mother Jîva is thought to have retired to Kashmir. Vimalâksa, a Sarvâstivâdan Buddhist monk, travelled from Kashmir to Kucha and there instructed Kumârajîva in the *Vinayapitaka*. In the 14th century, Islam gradually became the dominant religion in Kashmir, starting with the conversion in 1323 of Rincana, the first king of a new dynasty from Ladakh. The Muslims and Hindus of Kashmir lived in relative harmony, since the Sufi-Islamic way of life that ordinary Muslims followed in Kashmir complemented the Rishi tradition of Kashmiri Pandits.

This led to a syncretic culture where Hindus and Muslims revered the same local saints and prayed at the same shrines. The famous Sufi saint Bulbul Shah was able to persuade the king of the time Rinchan Shah from Ladakh to adopt the Islamic way of life, and the foundation of Sufiana composite culture was laid when Muslims, Hindus and Buddhists were co-existing. Several Kashmiri rulers, such as Sultan Zain-ul-Abidin, were tolerant of all religions in a manner comparable to Akbar. However, several Muslim rulers of Kashmir were intolerant to other religions.

Sultãn Sikandar Butshikan of Kashmir (AD 1389-1413) and his (former Brahmin) minister Saif ud-Din is often considered the worst of these. Historians have recorded many of his atrocities. The Tarikh-i-Firishta records that Sikandar persecuted the Hindus and issued orders proscribing the residence of any other than Muslims in Kashmir. He also ordered the breaking of all "golden and silver images". The metrical chronicle of the kings of Kashmir, called *Rajatarangini,* has (erroneousy) been pronounced by Professor H.I. Wilson to be the only Sanskrit composition yet discovered to which the appellation "history" can with any propriety be applied.

It first became known to the Muslims when, on Akbar's invasion of Kashmir in 1588, an amalgamated version was presented to the emperor. A translation into Persian was made at his order. A summary of its contents, taken from this Persian translation, is given by Abul Fazl in the *Ain-i-Akbari*. The *Rajatarangini* was written by Kalhana in the middle of the 12th century. His work, in eight books, makes use of earlier writings that are now lost. The *Rajatarangini* is the first of a series of four histories that record the annals of Kashmir. Commencing with a rendition of traditional 'history' of very early times (3102 BCE), the *Rajatarangini* comes down to the reign of Sangrama Deva, (*c.*1006 AD) and Kalhana.

The second work, by Jonaraja, continues the history from where Kalhana left off, and, entering the Muslim period, gives an account of the reigns down to that of Zain-ul-ab-ad-din, 1412. P. Srivara carried on the record to the accession of Fah Shah in 1486. The fourth work, called *Rajavalipataka,* by Prajnia Bhatta, completes the history to the time of the incorporation of Kashmir in the dominions of the Mogul emperor Akbar, 1588. By the early 19th century, the Kashmir valley had passed from the control of the Durrani Empire of Afghanistan, and four centuries of Muslim rule under the Mughals and the Afghans, to the conquering Sikh armies.

Earlier, in 1780, after the death of Ranjit Deo, the Raja of Jammu, the kingdom of Jammu (to the south of the Kashmir valley) was captured by the Sikhs under Ranjit Singh of Lahore and afterwards, until 1846, became a tributary to the Sikh power. Ranjit Deo's grandnephew, Gulab Singh, subsequently sought service at the court of Ranjit Singh; distinguished himself in later campaigns, especially the annexation of the Kashmir valley by the Sikhs army in 1819, and, for his services, was created Raja of Jammu in 1820. With the help of his officer, Zorawar Singh, Gulab Singh soon captured Ladakh and Baltistan, regions to the east and north-east of Jammu.

In 1845, the First Anglo-Sikh War broke out, and Gulab Singh "contrived to hold himself aloof till the battle of Sobraon (1846), when he appeared as a useful mediator and the trusted advisor of Sir Henry Lawrence. Two treaties were concluded. By the first the State of Lahore (*i.e.* West Punjab) handed over to the British, as equivalent for (rupees) one crore of indemnity, the hill countries between Beas and Indus; by the second the British made over to Gulab Singh for (Rupees) 75 lakhs all the hilly or mountainous country situated to the east of Indus and west of Ravi" (*i.e.* the Vale of Kashmir).

Soon after Gulab Singh's death in 1857, his son, Ranbir Singh, added the emirates of Hunza, Gilgit and Nagar to the kingdom. The *Princely State of Kashmir and Jammu* (as it was then called) was constituted between 1820 and 1858 and was "somewhat artificial in composition and it did not develop a fully coherent identity, partly as a result of its disparate origins and partly as a result of the autocratic rule which it experienced on the fringes of Empire."

It combined disparate regions, religions, and ethnicities: to the east, Ladakh was ethnically and culturally Tibetan and its inhabitants practised Buddhism; to the south, Jammu had a mixed population of Hindus, Muslims and Sikhs; in the heavily populated central Kashmir valley, the population was overwhelmingly *Sunni* Muslim, however, there was also a small but influential Hindu minority, the Kashmiri brahmins or pandits; to the northeast, sparsely populated Baltistan had a population ethnically related to Ladakh, but which practised *Shi'a* Islam; to the north, also sparsely populated, Gilgit Agency, was an area of diverse, mostly *Shi'a* groups; and, to the west, Punch was Muslim, but of different ethnicity than the Kashmir valley.

After the Indian Rebellion of 1857, in which Kashmir sided with the British, and the subsequent assumption of direct rule by Great Britain, the princely state of Kashmir came under the paramountcy of the British Crown. Ranbir Singh's grandson Hari Singh ascended the throne of Kashmir in 1925. The Maharajah Hari Singh never represented the will of his subjects, creating tension between the Hindu rulers and the Muslim population of Kashmir. Muslims in Kashmir detested him, as they were heavily taxed and had grown tired of his insensitivity to their religious concerns.

The Dogra rule (the name of the municipal governments) had excluded Muslims from the civil service and the armed services. Islamic religious ceremonies were taxed. Historically, Muslims were banned from organizing politically, which would only be tolerated beginning in the 1930s. In 1931, in response to a sermon that had tones of opposition to the government, the villages of Jandial, Makila, and Dana were ransacked and destroyed by the Dogra army, with their inhabitants burned alive.

A legislative assembly, with no real power, was created in January, 1947. It issued one statement that represented the will of the Muslim people: "After carefully considering the position, the conference has arrived at the conclusion that accession of the State to Pakistan is absolutely necessary in view of the geographic, economic, linguistic, cultural and religious conditions...It is therefore necessary that the State should accede to Pakistan". This is one of the rare instances that an elected block of the people of Kashmir had been given the chance to speak. Representing the subjects who elected them, they sought accession with Muslim Pakistan.

Prem Nath Bazaz, founder of the Kashmir Socialist Party in 1943, a reliable primary source of history, reiterated that a majority of Kashmiris were against the decision of the Maharajah in his book, *The History of the Struggle of Freedom in Kashmir*. He writes, "The large majority of the population of the State, almost the entire Muslim community and an appreciable number of non Muslims was totally against the Maharjah declaring accession to India."

This statement, and the decision reached by the legislative assembly are important because they dispel any belief that the Kashmiris' religious ties with Pakistan did not necessarily indicate a will to unite. Indeed, the ethnic bond between Kashmir and Pakistan influenced a majority of the people to seek accession with Pakistan. The Hindu Maharajah would not listen, and continued to delay his decision about which nation to join. Ranbir Singh's grandson Hari Singh, who had ascended the throne of Kashmir in 1925, was the reigning monarch in 1947 at the conclusion of British rule of the subcontinent and the subsequent partition of the British Indian Empire into the newly independent Union of India and the Dominion of Pakistan.

As parties to the partition process, both countries had agreed that the rulers of princely states would be given the right to opt for either Pakistan or India or-in special cases-to remain independent. In 1947, Kashmir's population was "77% Muslim and 20% Hindu" To postpone making a hurried decision, the Maharaja signed a "standstill" agreement with Pakistan, which ensured continuity of trade, travel, communication, and similar services between the two. Such agreement was pending with India. In October 1947, Pashtuns from Pakistan's North-West Frontier Province invaded Kashmir. The ostensible aim of the guerilla campaign was to frighten Hari Singh into submission. "Instead the Maharaja appealed to Mountbatten for assistance, and the Governor-General agreed on the condition that the ruler accedes to India."

Once the Maharaja signed the Instrument of Accession, "Indian soldiers entered Kashmir and drove the Pakistani-sponsored irregulars from all but a small section of the state.

The United Nations was then invited to mediate the quarrel. The UN mission insisted that the opinion of Kashmiris must be ascertained, while India insisted that no referendum could occur until all of the state had been cleared of irregulars." However, this chain of events is disputed by Pakistan, which claims that the Indian army entered Kashmir before the Instrument of Accession was signed.

The Pakistani government immediately contested the accession, suggesting that it was fraudulent, that the Maharaja acted under duress, and that he had no right to sign an agreement with India when the standstill agreement with Pakistan was still in force. According to the instruments of partition of India, the rulers of princely states were given the choice to freely accede to either India or Pakistan, or to remain independent. They were, however, advised to accede to the contiguous dominion, taking into consideration the geographical and ethnic issues.

In Kashmir, however, the Maharaja hesitated. The Maharaja, fearing pressure from Pakistan army which entered Kashmir, agreed to join India by signing the Instrument of Accession on 26 October 1947. Kashmir was provisionally accepted into the Indian Union pending a free and impartial plebiscite. This was spelled out in a letter from the Governor General of India, Lord Mountbatten, to the Maharaja on 27 October 1947. In the letter, accepting the accession, Mountbatten made it clear that the State would only be incorporated into the Indian Union after a reference had been made to the people of Kashmir.

In the last days of 1948, a ceasefire was agreed under UN auspices; however, since the plebiscite demanded by the UN was never conducted, relations between India and Pakistan soured, and eventually led to two more wars over Kashmir in 1965 and 1999. India has control of about half the area of the former princely state of Jammu and Kashmir; Pakistan controls a third of the region, the Northern Areas, or historically known as regions of Gilgit and Baltistan; and Pakistan Occupied Kashmir.

According to *Encyclopaedia Britannica,* "Although there was a clear Muslim majority in Kashmir before the 1947 partition and its economic, cultural, and geographic contiguity with the Muslim-majority area of the Punjab (in Pakistan) could be convincingly demonstrated, the political developments during and after the partition resulted in a division of the region. Pakistan was left with territory that, although basically Muslim in character, was thinly populated, relatively inaccessible, and economically underdeveloped. The largest Muslim group, situated in the Vale of Kashmir and estimated to number more than half the population of the entire region, lay in Indian-administered territory, with its former outlets via the Jhelum valley route blocked."

The UN Security Council on 20 January 1948 passed Resolution 39, establishing a special commission to investigate the conflict. Subsequent to the commission's recommendation, the Security Council ordered in its Resolution 47, passed on 21 April 1948, that the invading Pakistani army retreat from Jammu & Kashmir and that the accession of Kashmir to either India or Pakistan be determined in accordance with a plebiscite to be supervised by the UN. In a string of subsequent resolutions, the Security Council took notice of the continuing failure by India to hold the plebiscite.

However, no punitive action against India could be taken by the Security Council because its resolution requiring India to hold a Plebescite was non-binding, and the Pakistani army never left the part of the Kashmir they occupied as required by the Security Council resolution 47. The Government of India holds that the Maharaja signed a document of accession to India October 26, 1947. Pakistan has disputed whether the Maharaja actually signed the accession treaty before Indian troops entered Kashmir. Furthermore, Pakistan claims the Indian government has never produced an original copy of this accession treaty and thus its validity and legality is disputed.

However, India has produced the instrument of accession with an original copy image on its website. Alan Campbell-Johnson, the press attache to the Viceroy of India states that

"The legality of the accession is beyond doubt." The eastern region of the erstwhile princely state of Kashmir has also been beset with a boundary dispute. In the late 19th- and early 20th centuries, although some boundary agreements were signed between Great Britain, Afghanistan and Russia over the northern borders of Kashmir, China never accepted these agreements, and the official Chinese position did not change with the communist takeover in 1949.

By the mid-1950s the Chinese army had entered the north-east portion of Ladakh: "By 1956–57 they had completed a military road through the Aksai Chin area to provide better communication between Xinjiang and western Tibet. India's belated discovery of this road led to border clashes between the two countries that culminated in the Sino-Indian war of October 1962." China has occupied Aksai Chin since 1962 and, in addition, an adjoining region, the Trans-Karakoram Tract was ceded by Pakistan to China in 1965.

In 1949, the Indian government obliged Hari Singh to leave Jammu and Kashmir, and yield the government to Sheikh Abdullah, the leader of a popular political party, the National Conference Party. Since then, a bitter enmity has been developed between India and Pakistan and three wars have taken place between them over Kashmir. The growing dispute over Kashmir also leads to the rise of militancy in the state. The year 1989 saw the intensification of conflict in Jammu and Kashmir as Mujahadeens from Afghanistan slowly infiltrated the region following the end of the Soviet-Afghan War the same year.

During the 19th century rule, Kashmir was a popular tourist destination due to its climate. Formerly only 200 passes a year were issued by the government, but now no restriction is placed on visitors. European sportsmen and travellers, in addition to residents of India, traveled there freely. The railway to Rawalpindi and a road thence to Srinagar made access to the valley easier. When the temperature in Srinagar rises at the beginning of June, the residents would migrate to Gulmarg, which was a fashionable hillstation during British rule. This great influx of visitors resulted in a corresponding diminution of game for the sportsmen. Special game preservation rules have been introduced, and nullahs are let out for stated periods with a restriction on the number of head to be shot. Rawalakot and Bagh are another popular destination.

In the 1901 Census of the British Indian Empire, the population of the princely state of Kashmir was 2,905,578. Of these 2,154,695 were Muslims, 689,073 Hindus, 25,828 Sikhs, and 35,047 Buddhists. The Hindus were found mainly in Jammu, where they constituted a little less than 50% of the population. In the Kashmir Valley, the Hindus represented "only 524 in every 10,000 of the population (*i.e.* 5.24%), and in the frontier *wazarats* of Ladhakh and Gilgit only 94 out of every 10,000 persons (0.94%)." In the same Census of 1901, in the Kashmir Valley, the total population was recorded to be 1,157,394, of which the Muslim population was 1,083,766, or 93.6% of the population. These percentages have remained fairly stable for the last 100 years.

In the 1941 Census of British India, Muslims accounted for 93.6% of the population of the Kashmir Valley and the Hindus constituted 4%. In 2003, the percentage of Muslims in the Kashmir Valley was 95% and those of Hindus 4%; the same year, in Jammu, the percentage of Hindus was 67% and those of Muslims 27%. In the same Census of 1901, four divisions were recorded among the Muslims of the princely state: Shaikhs, Saiyids, Mughals, and Pathans. The Shaikhs were the most numerous, with clan names (known as *krams*) including "Tantre," "Shaikh," "Mantu," "Ganai," "Dar," "Damar," "Lon" etc. The Saiyids, it was recorded "could be divided into those who follow the profession of religion and those who have taken to agriculture and other pursuits. Their *kram* name is "Mir." While a Saiyid retains his saintly profession Mir is a prefix; if he has taken to agriculture, Mir is an affix to his name."

The *Mughals* who were not numerous were recorded to have *kram* names like "Mir" (a corruption of "Mirza"), "Beg," "Bandi," "Bach," and "Ashaye." Finally, it was recorded that the Pathans "who are more numerous than the Mughals... are found chiefly in the south-west of the valley, where Pathan colonies have from time to time been founded. The most interesting of these colonies is that of Kuki-Khel Afridis at Dranghaihama, who retain all the old customs and speak Pashtu."

The Hindu population of Kashmir Valley in 1901 was recorded to be 60,641. Among the Hindus of *Jammu* province, who numbered 626,177 (or 90.87% of the Hindu population of the princely state), the most important castes recorded in the census were "Brahmans (186,000), the Rajputs (167,000), the Khattris (48,000) and the Thakkars (93,000)."

KASHMIR

Kashmir is the northwestern region of the Indian subcontinent. Until the mid-19th century, the term "Kashmir" referred only to the valley lying between the Great Himalayas and the Pir Panjal range; since then, it has been used for a larger area that today includes the Indian administered state of Jammu and Kashmir consisting of the Kashmir valley, Jammu and Ladakh; the Pakistani-administered provinces of the Northern Areas and Azad Kashmir, and the Chinese-administered, mostly uninhabited, regions of Aksai Chin and Trans-Karakoram Tract.

In the first half of the first millennium, Kashmir became an important center of Hinduism and later of Buddhism; later still, in the ninth century, Kashmir Shaivism arose in the region. The heritage of Kashmir during this period is well documented in Rajatarangini by Kalhana. In 1349, Shah Mir became the first Muslim ruler of Kashmir and inaugurated the line *Salatin-i-Kashmir*. For the next five centuries Kashmir had Muslim monarchs, including the Mughals, who ruled until 1751, and thereafter, the Afghan Durranis, who ruled until 1820.

That year, the Sikhs under the Jat-Sikh King Ranjit Singh, annexed Kashmir. In 1846, upon the purchase of the region from the British under the Treaty of Amritsar, the Dogras-under Gulab Singh-became it's new rulers. Dogra Rule, under the 'paramountcy' (or tutelage) of the British Crown, lasted until 1947, when the former princely state became a disputed territory, now administered by three countries: India, Pakistan, and the People's Republic of China.

The *Nilamata Purana* describes the Valley's origin from the waters, *Ka* means "water" and *Shimir* means "to desiccate". Hence, Kaashmir stands for "a land desiccated from water." There is also a theory which takes Kaashmir to be a contraction of *Kashyap-mira* or *Kashyapmir* or *Kashyapmeru*, the "sea or mountain of Kashyapa", the sage who is credited with having drained the waters of the primordial lake *Satisar* that Kaashmir was before it was reclaimed.

The *Nilamata Purana* gives the name *Kaashmira* to the Valley considering it to be an embodiment of Uma and it is the Kaashmir that the world knows today. The Kaashmiris, however, call it *Kashir*, which has been derived phonetically from *Kaashmir*, as pointed out by Aurel Stein in his introduction to the *Rajatarangini*. In the *Rajatarangini*, a history of Kashmir written by *Kalhana* in the 12th century, it is stated that the valley of Kaashmir was formerly a lake. This was drained by the great rishi or sage, Kashyapa, son of Marichi, son of Brahma, by cutting the gap in the hills at Baramulla (*Varaha-mula*). Cashmere is a variant spelling of Kaashmir.

The Mauryan emperor Ashoka is often credited with having founded the city of Srinagar. Kashmir was once a Buddhist seat of learning, perhaps with the Sarvâstivâdan school dominating. East and Central Asian Buddhist monks are recorded as having visited the kingdom. In the late 4th century AD, the famous Kuchanese monk Kumârajîva, born to an Indian noble family, studied Dîrghâgama and Madhyâgama in Kashmir under Bandhudatta. He later became a prolific translator who helped take Buddhism to China. His mother Jîva is thought to have retired to Kashmir. Vimalâksa, a Sarvâstivâdan Buddhist monk, travelled from Kashmir to Kucha and there instructed Kumârajîva in the *Vinayapimaka*.

The Muslims and Hindus of Kashmir lived in relative harmony, since the Sufi-Islamic way of life that a few ordinary Muslims followed in Kashmir complemented the Rishi tradition of Kashmiri Pandits. This led to a syncretic culture where Hindus and Muslims revered the same local saints and prayed at the same shrines. Famous Sufi saint Bulbul Shah was able to convert Rinchan Shah who was then prince of Kashgar Ladakh to an Islamic lifestyle, thus founding the Sufiana composite culture. Under this rule, Muslim, Hindu and Buddhist Kashmiris generally co-existed peacefully. Over time, however, the Sufiana governance gave way to outright Muslim monarchs.

Some Kashmiri rulers, such as Sultan Zain-ul-Abidin, were tolerant of all religions in a manner comparable to Akbar. However, several Muslim rulers of Kashmir were intolerant of other religions. Sultãn Sikandar Butshikan of Kashmir (AD 1389-1413) is often considered the worst of these. Historians have recorded many of his atrocities. The *Tarikh-i-Firishta* records that Sikandar persecuted the Hindus and issued orders proscribing the residence of any other than Muslims in Kashmir. He also ordered the breaking of all "golden and silver images".

The *Tarikh-i-Firishta* further states: "Many of the Brahmins, rather than abandon their religion or their country, poisoned themselves; some emigrated from their native homes, while a few escaped. After the emigration of the Brahmins, Sikandar ordered all the temples in Kashmir to be thrown down. Having broken all the images in Kashmir, (Sikandar) acquired the title of 'Destroyer of Idols'."

POST-1948 DEVELOPMENTS

The eastern region of the erstwhile princely state of Kashmir has also been beset with a boundary dispute. In the late 19th- and early 20th centuries, although some boundary agreements were signed between Great Britain, Afghanistan and Russia over the northern borders of Kashmir, China never accepted these agreements, and the official Chinese position did not change with the communist takeover in 1949. By the mid-1950s the Chinese army had entered the north-east portion of Ladakh.

"By 1956–57 they had completed a military road through the Aksai Chin area to provide better communication between

Xinjiang and western Tibet. India's belated discovery of this road led to border clashes between the two countries that culminated in the Sino-Indian war of October 1962."

China has occupied Aksai Chin since the early 1950s and, in addition, an adjoining region almost 8% of the territory, the Trans-Karakoram Tract was ceded by Pakistan to China in 1963. Meanwhile, elections were held in Indian Jammu & Kashmir, which brought up the popular Muslim leader Sheikh Abdullah, who with his party National Conference, by and large supported India. The elected Constituent Assembly met for the first time in Srinagar on October 31, 1951. Then The State Constituent Assembly ratified the accession of the State to the Union of India on February 6, 1954 and the President of India subsequently issued the Constitution (Application to J&K) Order under Article 370 of the Indian Constitution extending the Union Constitution to the State with some exceptions and modifications.

The State's own Constitution came into force on January 26, 1957 under which the elections to the State Legislative Assembly were held for the first time on the basis of adult franchise the same year. This Constitution further reiterated the ratification of the State's accession to Union of India. However, these tidings were not recognized by Pakistan, which has continued to press for a plebiscite to ascertain the wishes of the people.

Pakistan set up its own Kashmir, called Azad Kashmir in a tiny Western chunk that it controls. The much larger region of Pakistani Kashmir in the North-West, which was a province named Northern Areas in the erstwhile state, by and large bore no mention in Pakistani laws and Constitution as being of any status, until in 1982 the Pakistani President General Zia ul Haq proclaimed that the people of the Northern Areas were Pakistanis and had nothing to do with the State of Jammu and Kashmir.

CURRENT STATUS AND POLITICAL DIVISIONS

The region is divided among three countries in a territorial dispute: Pakistan controls the northwest portion (Northern

Areas and Azad Kashmir), India controls the central and southern portion (Jammu and Kashmir) and Ladakh, and China controls the northeastern portion (Aksai Chin and the Trans-Karakoram Tract). India controls the majority of the Siachen Glacier area including the Saltoro Ridge passes, whereas Pakistan controls the lower territory just southwest of the Saltoro Ridge. India controls 141,338 km (54,571 sq mi) of the disputed territory, Pakistan 85,846 km (33,145 sq mi) and China, the remaining 37,555 km (14,500 sq mi).

Jammu and Azad Kashmir lie outside Pir Panjal range, and are under Indian and Pakistani control respectively. These are populous regions. Main cities are Jammu, Muzaffarabad and Rawalakot. The Northern Areas are a group of territories in the extreme north, bordered by the Karakoram, the western Himalayas, the Pamir, and the Hindu Kush ranges. With its administrative center at the town of Gilgit, the Northern Areas cover an area of 72,971 km^2 (28,174 mi^2) and have an estimated population approaching 1,000,000. The other main city is Skardu.

Ladakh is a region in the east, between the Kunlun mountain range in the north and the main Great Himalayas to the south. Main cities are Leh and Kargil. It is under Indian administration and is part of the state of Jammu and Kashmir. It is one of the most sparsely populated regions in the area and is mainly inhabited by people of Indo-Aryan and Tibetan descent. Aksai Chin is a vast high-altitude desert of salt that reaches altitudes up to 5,000 metres (16,000 ft). Geographically part of the Tibetan Plateau, Aksai Chin is referred to as the Soda Plain. The region is almost uninhabited, and has no permanent settlements.

Though these regions are in practice administered by their respective claimants, neither India nor Pakistan has formally recognised the accession of the areas claimed by the other. India claims those areas, including the area "ceded" to China by Pakistan in the Trans-Karakoram Tract in 1963, are a part of its territory, while Pakistan claims the entire region excluding Aksai Chin and Trans-Karakoram Tract. The two countries have fought several declared wars over the territory. The Indo-Pakistani War of 1947 established the rough boundaries of today, with Pakistan holding roughly one-third of Kashmir, and India one-half, with a dividing line of control established by the United Nations. The Indo-Pakistani War of 1965 resulted in a stalemate and an UN-negotiated ceasefire.

KASHMIR VALLEY

The Kashmir Valley or Vale of Kashmir is a valley between Himalayas and the Pir Panjal Range. It is around 135 km long and 32 km wide, formed by the Jhelum River. It was called as "Heaven on Earth" by Jahangir. It lies completely within Indian administration in the state of Jammu and Kashmir. Srinagar is its main city and also the summer capital of Jammu and Kashmir. There has been armed insurgency since 1989 due to the conflict. It has access to the rest of India through Banihal Tunnel near Qazigund on NH 1A to Jammu, which is interrupted by snowfall in winter. Other main cities are Anantnag and Baramulla.

In the 1901 Census of the British Indian Empire, Muslims constituted 74.16% of the total population of the princely state of Kashmir and Jammu, Hindus, 23.72%, and Buddhists, 1.21%. The Hindus were found mainly in Jammu, where they constituted a little less than 80% of the population. In the Kashmir Valley, Muslims constituted 93.6% of the population and Hindus 5.24%. These percentages have remained fairly stable for the last 100 years. Forty years later, in the 1941 Census of British India, Muslims accounted for 93.6% of the population of the Kashmir Valley and the Hindus for 4%.

In 2003, the percentage of Muslims in the Kashmir Valley was 95% and those of Hindus 4%; the same year, in Jammu, the percentage of Hindus was 66% and those of Muslims 30%. In the 1901 Census of the British Indian Empire, the population of the princely state of *Kashmir and Jammu* was 2,905,578. Of these 2,154,695 were Muslims (74.16%), 689,073 Hindus (23.72%), 25,828 Sikhs, and 35,047 Buddhists. Among the Muslims of the princely state, four divisions were recorded:

"Shaikhs, Saiyids, Mughals, and Pathans. The Shaikhs, who are by far the most numerous, are the descendants of Hindus, but have retained none of the caste rules of their forefathers.

They have clan names known as *krams...*" It was recorded that these *kram* names included "Tantre," "Shaikh,", "Bhat", "Mantu," "Ganai," "Dar," "Damar," "Lon" etc. The Saiyids, it was recorded "could be divided into those who follow the profession of religion and those who have taken to agriculture and other pursuits. Their *kram* name is "Mir." While a Saiyid retains his saintly profession Mir is a prefix; if he has taken to agriculture, Mir is an affix to his name."

The Hindus were found mainly in Jammu, where they constituted a little less than 80% of the population. In the *Kashmir Valley*, the Hindus represented "524 in every 10,000 of the population (*i.e.* 5.24%), and in the frontier *wazarats* of Ladakh and Gilgit only 94 out of every 10,000 persons (0.94%)." In the same Census of 1901, in the Kashmir Valley, the total population was recorded to be 1,157,394, of which the Muslim population was 1,083,766, or 93.6% and the Hindu population 60,641. Among the Hindus of *Jammu* province, who numbered 626,177 (or 90.87% of the Hindu population of the princely state), the most important castes recorded in the census were "Brahmans (186,000), the Rajputs (167,000), the Khattris (48,000) and the Thakkars (93,000)."

In the 1911 Census of the British Indian Empire, the total population of *Kashmir and Jammu* had increased to 3,158,126. Of these, 2,398,320 (75.94%) were Muslims, 696,830 (22.06%) Hindus, 31,658 (1%) Sikhs, and 36,512 (1.16%) Buddhists. In the last census of British India in 1941, the total population of Kashmir and Jammu (which as a result of the Second World War, was estimated from the 1931 census) was 3,945,000. Of these, the total Muslim population was 2,997,000 (75.97%), the Hindu population was 808,000 (20.48%), and the Sikh 55,000 (1.39%).

According to political scientist Alexander Evans, approximately 95% of the total population of 160,000-170,000 of Kashmir Brahmins, also called Kashmiri Pandits, (*i.e.* approximately 150,000 to 160,000) left the Kashmir Valley in

1990 "as militant violence engulfed the state". According to the CIA Factbook chapter on India, approximately 300,000 Kashmiri Pandits from the state of Jammu and Kashmir are internally displaced.

Culture and cuisine

Kashmiri cuisine includes dum aloo (boiled potatoes with heavy amounts of spice), tzaman (a solid cottage cheese), rogan josh (lamb cooked in heavy spices), zaam dod (curd), yakhayn (lamb cooked incurd with mild spices), hakh (a spinach-like leaf), rista-gushtava (minced meat balls in tomato and curd curry) and of course the signature rice which is particular to Asian cultures.

The traditional wazwan feast involves cooking meat or vegetables, usually mutton, in several different ways. Alcohol and Beef are not widely consumed in Kashmir. There are two styles of making tea in the region: nun chai, or salt tea, which is pink in colour and popular with locals; and kahwah, a tea for festive occasions, made with saffron and spices.

Economy

Kashmir's economy is centred on agriculture. Traditionally the staple crop of the valley was rice, which formed the chief food of the people. In addition, Indian corn, wheat, barley and oats were also grown. Given its temperate climate, it is suited for crops like asparagus, artichoke, seakale, broad beans, scarletrunners, beetroot, cauliflower and cabbage. Fruit trees are common in the valley, and the cultivated orchards yield pears, apples, peaches, and cherries. The chief trees are deodar, firs and pines, chenar or plane, maple, birch and walnut, apple, cherry.

Historically, Kashmir became known worldwide when Cashmere wool was exported to other regions and nations (exports have ceased due to decreased abundance of the cashmere goat and increased competition from China). Kashmiris are well adept at knitting and making Pashmina shawls, silk carpets, rugs, kurtas, and pottery. Saffron, too, is grown in Kashmir. Efforts are on to export the naturally grown fruits and vegetables as organic foods mainly to the Middle East. Srinagar is known for its silver-work, papier mache, wood-carving, and the weaving of silk.

The economy was badly damaged by the 2005 Kashmir earthquake which, as of October 8, 2005, resulted in over 70,000 deaths in the Pakistan-controlled part of Kashmir and around 1,500 deaths in Indian controlled Kashmir.

KASHMIR CONFLICT

The Kashmir conflict refers to the territorial dispute over Kashmir, the northwesternmost region of the Indian subcontinent. The parties to the dispute are India, Pakistan, China and the people of Kashmir. India claims the entire former Dogra princely state of Jammu and Kashmir and presently administers approximately 43% of the region including most of Jammu, Kashmir Valley, Ladakh and the Siachen Glacier. India's claim is contested by Pakistan which controls approximately 37% of Kashmir, mainly Azad Kashmir and the northern areas of Gilgit and Baltistan.

In addition, China controls 20% of Kashmir including Aksai Chin which it occupied following the brief Sino-Indian War of 1962 and the Trans-Karakoram Tract, also known as the Shaksam Valley that was ceded to it by Pakistan in 1963. India's official position is that Kashmir is an "integral part" of India. Pakistan's official position is that Kashmir is a disputed territory whose final status must be determined by the people of Kashmir. Certain Kashmiri independence groups believe that Kashmir should be independent of both India and Pakistan.

India and Pakistan have fought three wars over Kashmir: in 1947, 1965, and 1999. India and China have clashed once, in 1962 over Aksai Chin as well as the northeastern Indian state of Arunachal Pradesh. India and Pakistan have also been involved in several skirmishes over Siachen Glacier. Since the 1990s, the Indian administered Jammu and Kashmir has been hit by confrontation between Kashmiri separatists, including militants who India alleges are supported by Pakistan and the Pakistan Armed Forces, and Indian Armed Forces which has resulted in thousands of deaths.

In 1947, British rule in India ended with the creation of two new nations, the Union of India and the Dominion of Pakistan and the abandonment of British suzerainty over the 562 Indian princely states. According to the Indian Independence Act 1947, "the suzerainty of His Majesty over the Indian States lapses, and with it, all treaties and agreements in force at the date of the passing of this Act between His Majesty and the rulers of Indian States", so the states were left to choose whether to join India or Pakistan or to remain independent.

Jammu and Kashmir had a predominantly Muslim population but a Hindu ruler, and was the largest of the princely states. Its ruler was the Dogra King (or Maharaja) Hari Singh. In October 1947, Pakistani tribals from Dir entered Kashmir intending to liberate it from Dogra rule. Unable to withstand the invasion, the Maharaja signed The Instrument of Accession that was accepted by the Government of India on October 27, 1947.

INDO-PAKISTANI WAR OF 1947

The irregular Pakistani tribals made rapid advances into Kashmir (Baramulla sector) after the rumours that the Maharaja was going to decide for the union with India. Maharaja Hari Singh of Kashmir asked the Government of India to intervene. However, the Government of India pointed out that India and Pakistan had signed an agreement of non-intervention (maintenance of the status quo) in Jammu and Kashmir; and although tribal fighters from Pakistan had entered Jammu and Kashmir, there was, until then, no iron-clad legal evidence to unequivocally prove that the Government of Pakistan was officially involved.

It would have been illegal for India to unilaterally intervene (in an open, official capacity) unless Jammu and Kashmir officially joined the Union of India, at which point it would be possible to send in its forces and occupy the remaining parts. The Maharaja desperately needed the Indian military's help when the Pathan tribals reached the outskirts of Srinagar. Before their arrival into Srinagar, India argues that Maharaja Hari Singh completed negotiations for acceding Jammu and Kashmir to India in exchange for receiving military aid. The agreement which ceded Jammu and Kashmir to India was signed by the Maharaja and Lord Mountbatten of Burma.

The resulting war over Kashmir, the First Kashmir War, lasted until 1948, when India moved the issue to the UN Security Council. The UN previously had passed resolutions setting up for the monitoring of the conflict in Kashmir. The committee it set up was called the United Nations Committee for India and Pakistan. Following the set up of the UNCIP the UN Security Council passed Resolution 47 on April 21, 1948. The resolution imposed that an immediate cease-fire takes place and said that Pakistan should withdraw all presence and had no say in Jammu and Kashmir politics.

It stated that India should retain a minimum military presence and stated "that the final disposition of the State of Jammu and Kashmir will be made in accordance with the will of the people expressed through the democratic method of a free and impartial plebiscite conducted under the auspices of the United Nations". The cease fire took place. December 31, 1948. At that time, the Indian and Pakistani governments agreed to hold the plebiscite but Pakistan did not withdraw its troops from Kashmir thus violating the condition for holding the plebiscite.

Over the next several years, the UN Security Council passed four new resolutions, revising the terms of Resolution 47 to include a synchronous withdrawal of both Indian and Pakistani troops from the region, per the recommendations of General Andrew McNaughton. To this end, UN arbitrators put forward 11 different proposals for the demilitarization of the region - every one of which was accepted by Pakistan, but rejected by the Indian government. The resolutions were passed by United Nations Security Council under Chapter VI of the United Nations Charter. Resolutions passed under Chapter VI of UN charter are considered non binding and have no mandatory enforceability as opposed to the resolutions passed under Chapter VII.

SINO-INDIAN WAR

In 1962, troops from the People's Republic of China and India clashed in territory claimed by both. China won a swift victory in the war, resulting in the Chinese administration of the region called Aksai Chin, which continues to date. In addition to these lands, another smaller area, the Trans-Karakoram, was demarcated as the line of control between China and Pakistan, although parts on the Chinese side are claimed by India to be parts of Kashmir. The line that separates India from China in this region is known as the *Line of Actual Control*.

1965 AND 1971 WARS

In 1965 and 1971, heavy fighting again broke out between India and Pakistan. The Indo-Pakistani War of 1971 resulted in the defeat of Pakistan and Pakistan Military's surrender in East Pakistan (Bangladesh). The Simla Agreement was signed in 1972 between India and Pakistan. By this treaty, both countries agreed to settle all issues by peaceful means and mutual discussions in the framework of the UN Charter.

RISE OF MILITANCY SINCE 1989

In 1989, a widespread armed insurgency started in Kashmir, which continues to this day. India contends that this was largely started by the large number of Afghan *Mujahideen* who entered the Kashmir valley following the end of the Soviet-Afghan War, though Pakistan and Kashmiri nationalists argue that Afghan *Mujahideen* did not leave Afghanistan in large numbers until 1992, three years after the insurgency began. Yasin Malik, a leader of one faction of the Jammu Kashmir Liberation Front, along with Ashfaq Majid Wani and Farooq Ahmad Dar alias Bitta Karatay, was one of the Kashmiris to organize militancy in Kashmir.

However since 1995, Malik has renounced the use of violence and calls for strictly peaceful methods to resolve the dispute. He developed differences with one of the senior leader Farooq Papa for shunning the demand for independent Kashmir and trying to cut a deal with Indian Prime Minister resulting in spilt in which Bitta Karatay, Salim Nanhaji and other senior comrades joined Farooq Papa. Pakistan claims these insurgents are Jammu and Kashmir citizens, and they are rising up against the Indian Army in an independence movement. It also says the Indian Army is committing serious human rights violations to the citizens of Jammu and Kashmir. It denies that it is giving armed help to the insurgents.

India claims these insurgents are Islamic terrorist groups from Pakistan-administered Kashmir and Afghanistan, fighting to make Jammu and Kashmir part of Pakistan. It believes Pakistan is giving armed help to the terrorists, and training them in Pakistan. It also says the terrorists have been killing many citizens in Kashmir, and committing human rights violations, while denying that its own armed forces are responsible for the human rights abuses. On a visit to Pakistan in 2006 current Chief Minister of Kashmir Omar Abdullah remarked that foreign militants, who had nothing to do with Kashmir, were engaged in reckless killings and mayhem in the name of religion.

Also US Intelligence agencies believe that *Al-Qaeda* and Taliban are helping organize a terror campaign in Kashmir to foment conflict between India and Pakistan. A 2001 report 'Pakistan's Role in the Kashmir Insurgency' of US Think tank RAND corporation noted that 'More intrinsically, the nature of the Kashmir conflict has been transformed from what was originally a secular, locally- based struggle (conducted via the Jammu Kashmir Liberation Front - JKLF) to one that is now largely carried out by foreign militants and rationalised in pan-Islamic religious terms.' In July 2006 *Al-Qaeda* stated that it had established a wing in Kashmir.

The Pakistani government calls these insurgents, "Kashmiri freedom fighters", and claims that it gives only moral and diplomatic support to these insurgents, though India believes they are Pakistan-supported terrorists from Pakistan Administered Kashmir. In October 2008 President Asif Ali Zardari of Pakistan called the Kashmir separatists terrorists in an interview with The Wall Street Journal.

CONFLICT IN KARGIL

In mid-1999 insurgents and Pakistani soldiers from Pakistani Kashmir infiltrated into Jammu and Kashmir. During the winter season, Indian forces regularly move down to lower altitudes as severe climatic conditions make it almost impossible for them to guard the high peaks near the Line of Control. The insurgents took advantage of this and occupied vacant mountain peaks of the Kargil range overlooking the highway in Indian Kashmir, connecting Srinagar and Leh. By blocking the highway, they wanted to cut off the only link between the Kashmir Valley and Ladakh.

This resulted in a high-scale conflict between the Indian Army and the Pakistan Army. At the same time, fears of the Kargil War turning into a nuclear war provoked the then-US President Bill Clinton to pressure Pakistan to retreat. Faced with mounting losses of personnel and posts, Pakistan Army withdrew the remaining troops from the area ending the conflict. India reclaimed control of the peaks which they now patrol and monitor all year long.

REASONS BEHIND THE DISPUTE

The Kashmir Conflict arises from the Partition of India in 1947 into modern India and Pakistan. Both the countries have made claims to Kashmir, based on historical developments and religious affiliations of the Kashmiri people. The state of Jammu and Kashmir, which lies strategically in the Northwest of the subcontinent, bordering China and the former Soviet Union, was a princely state ruled by Maharaja Hari Singh, under the paramountcy of British India. In geographical and legal terms, the Maharaja could have joined either of the two new Dominions.

Although urged by the Viceroy, Lord Mountbatten of Burma, to determine the future of his state before the transfer of power took place, Hari Singh demurred. In October 1947, incursions and counter-incursions by Pakistan and India have taken place leading to a war, as a result of which the state of Jammu and Kashmir remains divided between the two countries. Two-thirds of the former princely state (known as the Indian state of Jammu and Kashmir), comprising Jammu, the Kashmir Valley, and the sparsely populated Buddhist area of Ladakh are controlled by India; one-third is administered by Pakistan.

The latter includes a narrow strip of land called Azad Kashmir and the Northern Areas compromising the Gilgit Agency, Baltistan and the former kingdoms of Hunza and Nagar. Attempts to resolve the dispute through political discussions were unsuccessful. In September 1965, war broke out again between Pakistan and India. The United Nations called for a yet another cease-fire, and peace was restored once again following the Tashkent Declaration in 1966, by which both nations returned to their original positions along the demarcated line.

After the 1971 war and the creation of independent Bangladesh, under the terms of the 1972 Simla Agreement between Prime Minister Indira Gandhi of India and Zulfiqar Ali Bhutto of Pakistan, it was agreed that neither country would seek to alter the cease-fire line in Kashmir, which was renamed as the Line of Control, "unilaterally, irrespective of mutual differences and legal interpretations".

Numerous violations of the Line of Control have occurred, including the infamous incursions by insurgents and Pakistani armed forces at Kargil leading to the Kargil war. There are also sporadic clashes on the Siachen Glacier, where the Line of Control is not demarcated and both countries maintain forces at altitudes rising to 20,000 ft (6,100 m).

INDIAN VIEW

The Indian claim to Kashmir centers on the agreement between Maharaja Hari Singh and the Government of India, with Prime Minister Jawaharlal Nehru and Governor General Lord Mountbatten of Burma, according to which the erstwhile Kingdom of Jammu and Kashmir joined the Union of India through the Instrument of Accession. It also focuses on India's claim of secular society, an ideology that is not meant to factor religion into governance of major policy and thus considers it irrelevant in a boundary dispute.

Another argument by India is that, in India, minorities are very well integrated, with some members of the minority communities holding positions of power and influence in India. Even though more than 80% of India's population practices Hinduism, a former President of India, A.P.J. Abdul Kalam, is a Muslim while Sonia Gandhi, the parliamentary leader of the ruling Congress Party, is a Roman Catholic. The current prime minister of India, Manmohan Singh, is a Sikh. Indian viewpoint is succinctly summarized by Ministry of External affairs, Government of India.

India holds that the Instrument of Accession of the State of Jammu and Kashmir to India, signed by the Maharaja Hari Singh (erstwhile ruler of the State) on 26 October, 1947, was completely valid in terms of the Government of India Act (1935), Indian Independence Act (1947) and international law and was total and irrevocable.

The Constituent assembly of Jammu and Kashmir had unanimously ratified the Maharaja's Instrument of Accession to India and had adopted a constitution for the state that called for a perpetual merger of the state with the Union of India. India claims that this body was a representative one, and that its views were those of the Kashmiri people at the time.

United Nations Security Council Resolution 1172 tacitly accepts India's stand that all outstanding issues between India and Pakistan and urges the need to resolve the dispute through mutual dialogue and does not call for a plebiscite.

United Nations Security Council Resolution 47 cannot be implemented since Pakistan failed to withdraw its forces from Kashmir which was the first step in implementing the resolution. Now the resolution is obsolete since the geography and demographics of the region have been permanently altered. The resolution was passed by United Nations Security Council under Chapter VI of the United Nations Charter. Resolutions passed under Chapter VI of UN charter are considered non binding and have no mandatory enforceability as opposed to the resolutions passed under Chapter VII.

The state of Jammu and Kashmir was provided significant autonomy in the Article 370 of the Constitution of India.

India does not accept the two-nation theory that forms the basis of Pakistan and argues that Kashmir, despite being a Muslim-majority state, is in many ways an "integral part" of secular India.

India points to the recent state-assembly elections held in phases in November–December 2008. High turnouts were seen in spite of calls for boycott by Kashmiri separatists. The pro-India National Conference party emerged as the winner.

Additional Indian viewpoint regarding the broader debate over the Kashmir conflict include:

India believes that the insurgency and terrorism in Kashmir is deliberately being fueled by Pakistan to create instability in the region. The Government of India has repeatedly asked the international community to declare Pakistan as a sponsor of terrorism.

Pakistan is trying to raise anti-India sentiment among the people of Kashmir by spreading false propaganda against India. According to the state government of Jammu and Kashmir, Pakistani radio and television channels deliberately spread "hate and venom" against India to alter Kashmiri opinion.

In a diverse country like India, disaffection and discontent are not uncommon. Indian democracy has the necessary resilience to accommodate genuine grievances within the framework of our sovereignty, unity and integrity. Government of India has expressed its willingness to accommodate the legitimate political demands of the people of the state of Jammu and Kashmir.

India has asked United Nations that it should not be leave unchallenged or unaddressed claims of moral, political and diplomatic support for terrorism, which were clearly in contravention of United Nations Security Council Resolution 1373 which is a Chapter VII resolution that makes it mandatory for member states to not provide active or passive support to terrorist organizations. Specifically, it has pointed out that the Pakistani government continues to support various terrorist organizations, such as Jaish-e-Mohammad and *Lashkar-e-Taiba*, in direct violation of this resolution.

India points out at various reports by human rights organizations condemning Pakistan for the lack civic liberties in Pakistan-administered Kashmir. According to India, most regions of Pakistani Kashmir, especially Northern Areas, continue to suffer from lack of political recognition, economic development and basic fundamental rights.

All differences between India and Pakistan including Kashmir need to be settled through bilateral negotiations as agreed to by the two countries when they signed the Simla Agreement on July 2, 1972.

PAKISTANI VIEW

Pakistan's claims to the disputed region are based on the rejection of Indian claims to Kashmir, namely the Instrument of Accession. Pakistan insists that the Maharaja was not a popular leader, and was regarded as a tyrant by most Kashmiris; Pakistan also maintains that the Maharaja used brute force to suppress the population. Pakistan also accuses India of hypocrisy, as it refused to recognize the accession of Junagadh to Pakistan and Hyderabad's independence, on the grounds that those two states had Hindu majorities (in fact, India occupied and forcibly integrated those two territories).

Furthermore, as he had fled Kashmir due to Pakistani invasion, Pakistan asserts that the Maharaja held no authority in determining Kashmir's future. Additionally, Pakistan argues that even if the Maharaja had any authority in determining the plight of Kashmir, he signed the Instrument of Accession under duress, thus invalidating the legitimacy of his actions. Pakistan also claims that Indian forces were in Kashmir before the Instrument of Accession was signed with India, and that therefore Indian troops were in Kashmir in violation of the Standstill Agreement, which was designed to maintain the status quo in Kashmir (although India was not signatory to the Agreement, signed between Pakistan and the Hindu ruler of Jammu and Kashmir).

From 1990 to 1999 some organizations report that Indian Armed Forces, its paramilitary groups, and counter-insurgent militias have been responsible for the deaths 4,501 of Kashmiri civilians. Also from 1990 to 1999, there are records of 4,242 women between the ages of 7-70 that have been raped. Similar allegations were also made by some human rights organizations.

In short, Pakistan holds that:

The popular Kashmiri insurgency demonstrates that the Kashmiri people no longer wish to remain within India. Pakistan suggests that this means that either Kashmir wants to be with Pakistan or independent.

According to the two-nation theory which is one of the theories that is cited for the partition that created India and Pakistan, Kashmir should have been with Pakistan, because it has a Muslim majority.

India has shown disregard to the resolutions of the UN by not holding a plebiscite.

The Kashmiri people have now been forced by the circumstances to rise against the alleged repression of the Indian army and uphold their right of self-determination through militancy. Pakistan claims to give the Kashmiri insurgents moral, ethical and military support.

Recent protests in Indian administered Kashmir show a large number of people showing increased anger over Indian rule with massive rallies taking place to oppose Indian control of the state.

Pakistan also points to the violence that accompanies elections in Indian Kashmir and the anti Indian sentiments expressed by some people in the state.

Pakistan has noted the wide spread use of extra-judicial killings in Indian-administered Kashmir carried out by Indian security forces while claiming they were caught up in encounters with militants. These fake encounters are common place in Indian-administered Kashmir and the perpetrators are spared criminal prosecution. These fake encounters go largely uninvestigated by the authorities.

Pakistan points towards reports from the United Nations which condemns India for its human rights violations against Kashmiri people.

CROSS-BORDER TROUBLES

The border and the Line of Control separating Indian and Pakistani Kashmir passes through some exceptionally difficult terrain and the world's highest battleground, the Siachen Glacier is a part of this difficult-to-man boundary. Even with 200,000 military personnel, India maintains that it is infeasible to place enough men to guard all sections of the border throughout the various seasons of the year. Pakistan has indirectly acquiesced its role in failing to prevent "cross border terrorism" when it agreed to curb such activities after intense pressure from the Bush administration in mid 2002.

The Government of Pakistan has repeatedly claimed that by constructing a fence along the line of control, India is violating the Shimla Accord. However, India claims the construction of the fence has helped decrease armed infiltration into Indian-administered Kashmir. In 2002 Pakistani President and Army Chief General Pervez Musharraf promised to check infiltration into Jammu and Kashmir.

WATER DISPUTE

Another reason behind the dispute over Kashmir is water. Kashmir is the origin point for many rivers and tributaries of the Indus River basin. They include Jhelum and Chenab which primarily flow into Pakistan while other branches - the Ravi, Beas and the Sutlej irrigate northern India. Pakistan has been apprehensive that in a dire need, India (under whose portion of Kashmir lies the origins and passage of the said rivers) would use its strategic advantage and withhold the flow and thus choke the agrarian economy of Pakistan.

The Boundary Award of 1947 meant that the headwaters of Pakistani irrigation systems were in Indian Territory. The Indus Waters Treaty signed in 1960 resolved most of these disputes over the sharing of water, calling for mutual cooperation in this regard. But this treaty faced issues raised by Pakistan over the construction of dams on the Indian side which limit water to the Pakistani side.

HUMAN RIGHTS ABUSE

Claims of human rights abuses have been made against the Indian Armed Forces and the armed militants operating in Jammu and Kashmir. A 2005 study conducted by Médecins Sans Frontières found that Kashmiri women are among the worst sufferers of sexual violence in the world, with 11.6% of respondents reporting that they had been victims of sexual abuse.

Some surveys have found that in the Kashmir region itself (where the bulk of separatist and Indian military activity is concentrated), popular perception holds that the Indian Armed Forces are more to blame for human rights violations than the separatist groups. According to the MORI survey of 2002, in Kashmir only 2% of respondents believed that the militant groups were guilty of widespread human rights abuses, while 64% believed that Indian troops were guilty of the same. This trend was reversed however in other parts of the state.

MAP ISSUES

As with other disputed territories, each government issues maps depicting their claims in Kashmir as part of their territory, regardless of actual control. It is illegal in India to exclude all or part of Kashmir in a map. It is also illegal in Pakistan not to include the state of Jammu and Kashmir as disputed territory, as permitted by the United Nations. Non-participants often use the Line of Control and the Line of Actual Control as the depicted boundaries, as is done in the CIA World Factbook, and the region is often marked out in hashmarks, although the Indian government strictly opposes such practices.

When Microsoft released a map in Windows 95 and MapPoint 2002, a controversy was raised because it did not show all of Kashmir as part of India as per Indian claim. However, all the neutral and Pakistani companies claim to follow UN's map and over 90% of all maps containing the territory of Kashmir show it as disputed territory.

UN: The boundaries and names shown and the designations used on the map do not imply official endorsement or acceptance by the United Nations. Dotted line represents approximately the Line of Control of Jammu and Kashmir agreed upon by the Republic of India and the Government of Pakistan since 1972. Both the parties have not yet agreed upon the final status of the region and nothing significant has been implemented since the peace process began in 2004.

Islamabad: The Government of Pakistan maintains un-provisionally and unconditionally stating that the informal "Accession of Jammu and Kashmir" to Pakistan or even to the Republic of India remains to be decided by UN plebiscite. It accepts UN's map of the territory. Also the designations and the presentation of the Kashmir's regional map based on UNO practice, do not imply the expression of any opinion whatsoever on the part of the Commonwealth Secretariat or the publishers concerning the legal status of any country, territory or area, or of its authorities, or concerning the delimitation of its frontiers or boundaries. There is no intention to define the status Jammu and/or Kashmir, which has not yet been agreed upon by the parties.

New Delhi: The Government of India states that "the external artificial boundaries of India, especially concerning the Kashmir region under its jurisdiction created by a foreign body are neither correct nor authenticated".

EFFORTS TO END THE CRISIS

The 9/11 attacks on the US resulted in the US government wanting to restrain militancy in the world, including Pakistan. US urged Islamabad to cease infiltrations, which continue to this day, by Islamist militants into Indian-administered Kashmir. In December 2001, a terrorist attack on the Indian Parliament linked to Pakistan resulted in war threats, massive deployment and international fears of nuclear war in the subcontinent.

After intensive diplomatic efforts by other countries, India and Pakistan began to withdraw troops from the international border June 10, 2002, and negotiations began again. Effective November 26, 2003, India and Pakistan have agreed to maintain a ceasefire along the undisputed International Border, the disputed Line of Control, and the Siachen glacier. This is the first such "total ceasefire" declared by both nuclear powers in nearly 15 years.

In February 2004, Pakistan further increased pressure on Pakistanis fighting in Indian-administered Kashmir to adhere to the ceasefire. The nuclear-armed neighbours also launched several other mutual confidence building measures. Restarting the bus service between the Indian- and Pakistani-administered Kashmir has helped defuse the tensions between the countries. Both India and Pakistan have also decided to cooperate on economic fronts.

On Dec. 5, 2006, Pakistani President Pervez Musharraf told an Indian TV channel that Pakistan would give up its claim on Kashmir if India accepted some of his peace proposals, including a phased withdrawal of troops, self-governance for locals, no changes in the borders of Kashmir, and a joint supervision mechanism involving India, Pakistan and Kashmir, the BBC reported. Musharraf also stated that he was ready to give up the United Nations' resolutions regarding Kashmir.

2008 MILITANT ATTACKS

In the week of March 10, 2008, 17 people were wounded when a blast hit the region's only highway overpass located near the Civil Secretariat- Indian-controlled Kashmir's seat of government- and the region's high court. A gun battle between security forces and militants fighting against Indian rule left five people dead and two others injured March 23, 2008. The battle began when security forces raided a house on the outskirts of the capital city of Srinagar.

The Indian Army has been carrying out cordon-and-search operations against militants in Indian-administered Kashmir since the current armed violence broke out here in 1989. While the authorities here say 43,000 persons have been killed in the violence, various rights groups and non-governmental organizations have put the figure at twice that number.

According to Govt. of India Home Ministry, 2008 marks the lowest civilian casualities in 20 years with 89 deaths, compared to highest of 1,413 in 1996. 85 security personnel died in 2008 compared to 613 in 2001, while 102 militants killed. Human right situation improved with only 1 custodial death and no custodial disappearance.

RECENT DEVELOPMENTS

India continues to assert their sovereignty or rights over the entire region of Kashmir, while Pakistan maintains that it is a disputed territory. Pakistan argues that the status quo cannot be considered as a solution. Pakistan insists on a UN sponsored plebiscite. Unofficially, the Pakistani leadership has indicated that they would be willing to accept alternatives such as a demilitarized Kashmir, if sovereignty of Azad Kashmir was to be extended over the Kashmir valley, or the 'Chenab' formula, by which India would retain parts of Kashmir on its side of the Chenab river, and Pakistan the other side - effectively re-partioning Kashmir on communal lines.

The problem however is that the Population of Pakistan Administered portion of Kashmir is both ethnically and linguistically and culturally different from that in Kashmir Valley India and the Azad Kashmir population being on the most part ethnic Punjabis. Therefore a Partition on the Chenab formula is opposed by most Kashmiri politicians from all spectrums, though some, such as Sajjad Lone, have in recent months suggested that non-Muslim part of Jammu and Kashmir be separated from Kashmir and handed to India.

Some political analysts say that the Pakistan terrorist state policy shift and mellowing down of its aggressive stance may have to do with its total failure in the Kargil War and the subsequent 9/11 attacks that put pressure on Pakistan to alter its terrorist position. Further many neutral parties to the dispute have noted that UN resolution on Kashmir is no longer relevant. Even the European Union has viewed that the plebiscite is not in Kashmiris' interest. The report also notes, that the UN-laid down conditions for such a plebiscite have not been, and can no longer be, met by Pakistan.

Even the Hurriyat Conference observed in 2003, that "Plebiscite no longer an option" Besides the popular factions that support either parties, there is a third faction which supports independence and withdrawal of both India and Pakistan. These have been the respective stands of the parties for long, and there have been no significant change over the years. As a result, all efforts to solve the conflict have been futile so far. The Freedom in the World 2006 report categorized the Indian-administered Kashmir as "partly free", and Pakistan-administered Kashmir as well as the country of Pakistan "not free".

India claims that contrary to popular belief, a large proportion of the Jammu and Kashmir populace wish to remain with India. A MORI survey found that within the Kashmir Valley, 9% of respondents said they felt they would be better off as Indian citizens, with 78% saying that they did not know, and the remaining 13% favouring Pakistani citizenship.

According to a 2007 poll conducted by the Centre for the Study of Developing Societies in New Delhi, 87% of respondents in the Kashmir Valley prefer independence over union with India or Pakistan. The 2005 Kashmir earthquake, which killed over 80,000 people, led to India and Pakistan finalizing negotiations for the opening of a road for disaster relief through Kashmir.

2008 KASHMIR PROTESTS

Massive demonstrations occurred after plans by the Indian-administered Jammu and Kashmir state government to transfer 100 acres (0.40 km) of land to a trust which runs the Hindu Amarnath shrine in the Muslim-majority Kashmir valley.. This land was to be used to build a shelter to house Hindu pilgrims temporarily during their annual pilgrimage to the Amarnath temple.

Indian security forces and the Indian army responded quickly to keep order. More than 40 unarmed protesters were killed and at least 300 were detained. The largest protests saw more than a half million peopl(waving Pakistani flags and crying for freedom at a single rally according to Time magazine. Pro-Independent Kashmir Leader Mirwaiz Umar Farooq warned that the peaceful uprising could lead to violent upsurge if India's heavy-handed crackdown on protests were not restrained.

The United Nations expressed concern on India's response to peaceful protests and urged to investigate and bring to justice Indian security personnel who had taken part in the crackdown. Separatists and workers of a political party were believed to be behind stone pelting incidents which led to retaliatory fire by the police. Autorickshaw laden with stones meant for distribution was seized by the police in March 2009.

2008 KASHMIR ELECTIONS

State Elections were held in Indian held Kashmir in seven phases starting November 17 and finishing on December 24, 2008. In spite of calls by separatists for a boycott an unusually high turnout was recorded. The National Conference party which was founded by Sheikh Abdullah and regarded as pro India emerged with maximum seats and will form government in coalition with Indian National Congress.

The year 2008 marks the lowest civilian casualties in 20 years with 89 deaths, compared to highest of 1,413 in 1996. 85 security personnel died in 2008 compared to 613 in 2001, while

102 militants were killed. Many analysts say Pakistan's preoccupation with jihadis within its own borders explains the relative calm.

The year 2008 marked the greatest number of anti India protests since 1980 due to the Amarnath land transfer controversy with several hundred thousand protesters spilling out onto the streets of Indian-administered Kashmir demanding freedom from India the protests were suppressed by the Indian army with attacks on protesters leading to the deaths of 40 unarmed civilians.

However the elections which were held subsequently led to Kashmiris ignoring the boycott call by separatists and voting Pro India party National Conference into power. On 30 December Congress and the National Conference agreed to form a coalition government, with Omar Abdullah as Chief Minister. On January 5, 2009 Omar Abdullah was sworn in as 11th Chief Minister of Jammu and Kashmir. In March 2009 Omar Abdullah stated that only 800 militants were active in the state and out of these only 30% were Kashmiris.

OBAMA ON KASHMIR CONFLICT

In an interview with Joe Klien of *Time Magazine* in October 2008 Barack Obama expressed his intention to try to work with India and Pakistan to resolve this crisis in a serious way. He said he had talked to Bill Clinton about it (being a mediator). In an editorial in The Washington Times, Selig S Harrison, director of Asia Programme at the Center for International Policy and a senior scholar of the Woodrow Wilson International called it Obama's first foreign policy mistake.

The Australian in an editorial called Obama's Idea to appoint a presidential negotiator "a very stupid and dangerous move indeed" In an editorial in Forbes, Reihan Salam associate editor for The Atlantic noted "The smartest thing President Obama could do on Kashmir is probably nothing. We have to hope that India and Pakistan can work out their differences on Kashmir on their own". The Boston Globe in an editorial called the idea of appointing Bill Clinton as an envoy to Kashmir "a mistake". India has long regarded Kashmir as an Integral part of India and resisted outside intervention considering Kashmir to be an integral part of India and the conflict a bilateral matter between India and Pakistan.

President Obama appointed Richard Holbrooke as special envoy to Pakistan and Afghanistan. President Asif Ali Zardari had hoped that Holbrooke would help mediate to resolve Kashmir issue.Subsequently Kashmir was removed from the mandate of Richard Holbrooke. "Eliminating ... Kashmir from his job description ... is seen as a significant diplomatic concession to India that reflects increasingly warm ties between the country and the United States," The Washington Post noted in a report.

Brajesh Mishra, India's former national security adviser, was quoted in the same report as saying in reference to the territory's Indian-administered sector "No matter what government is in place, India is not going to relinquish control of Jammu and Kashmir," "That is written in stone and cannot be changed." According to The Financial Times India has warned US President Barack Obama that he risks "barking up the wrong tree" if he seeks to broker a settlement between Pakistan and India over the disputed territory of Kashmir.

AZAD KASHMIR

Azad Jammu and Kashmir or, for short, Azad Kashmir (literally, "free Kashmir") is the southernmost political entity within the Pakistani-controlled part of the former princely state of Jammu and Kashmir. It borders the present-day Indian-administered state of Jammu and Kashmir to the east (separated from it by the Line of Control), the North-West Frontier Province of Pakistan to the west, the Federally Administered Northern Areas (FANA) to the north, and the Punjab Province of Pakistan to the south. With its capital at Muzaffarabad, Azad Kashmir covers an area of 13,297 square kilometres (5,134 sq mi) and has an estimated population of about four million.

Azad Kashmir's financial matters, i.e., budget and tax affairs, are dealt with by the Azad Jammu and Kashmir Council, rather than by Pakistan's Central Board of Revenue. The Azad Jammu and Kashmir Council is a supreme body consisting of 11 members, six from the government of Azad Jammu and Kashmir and five from the government of Pakistan. Its chairman/chief executive is the president of Pakistan. Other members of the council are the president and the prime minister of Azad Kashmir and a few other AJK ministers.

POST INDEPENDENCE AND PARTITION OF BRITISH INDIA

After the Partition of India in 1947, the princely states were given the option of joining either India or Pakistan. However, Hari Singh, the maharaja of Jammu and Kashmir, wanted Jammu and Kashmir to remain independent. In order to buy some time, he signed a stand-still agreement, which side-stepped the agreement that each princely state would join either India or Pakistan. The raiders from North-West Frontier Province and the Tribal Areas feared that Hari Singh may join Indian Union.

In October 1947 supported by Pakistani Army they attacked Kashmir and tried to take over control of Kashmir. Initially Hari Singh tried to resist their progress but failed. Hari Singh then requested Indian Union to help. India responded that it could not help unless Kashmir joins India. So on 26 October 1947 Kashmir accession papers were signed and Indian troops were airlifted to Srinagar. Fighting ensued between Indian Army & Pakistani Army with control stabilizing more or less around what is now the "Line of Control".

Later, India approached UN to solve dispute & resolutions were passed to hold a plebiscite with regard to Kashmir's future. However, this plebiscite has not been held on either side since the legal requirement for the holding of a plebiscite was the withdrawal of the Indian and Pakistani armies from the parts of Kashmir that were under their respective control-a withdrawal that never did take place. In 1949, a cease-fire line separating the Indian- and Pakistani-controlled parts of Kashmir was formally put into effect.

Following the 1949 cease-fire agreement, the government of Pakistan divided the northern and western parts of Kashmir which it held into the following two separately-controlled political entities:

Azad Jammu and Kashmir (AJK) - the narrow southern part, 250 miles (400 km) long, with a width varying from 10 to 40 miles (16 to 64 km).

Federally Administered Northern Areas (FANA) - the much larger area to the north of AJK, 72,496 square kilometres (27,991 sq mi), directly administered by Pakistan as a *de facto* dependent territory, i.e., a non-self-governing territory.

SECESSION OF THE TRANS-KARAKORAM TRACT

An area of Kashmir that was once under Pakistani control, but is no longer, is the Shaksgam tract -a small region along the northeastern border of the Northern Areas that was provisionally ceded by Pakistan to the People's Republic of China in 1963 and which now forms part of China's Uygur Autonomous Region of Xinjiang.

POST 1971

After the Indo-Pakistani war of 1971, that line changed significantly in a few areas, and the new line, which was formally agreed to in 1972, was designated as the "Line of Control," separating the Indian and Pakistani forces and the Indian- and Pakistani-controlled parts of the former princely state.

The Line of Control has remained unchanged since the 1972 Simla pact, which bound the two countries "to settle their differences by peaceful means through bilateral negotiations." Some political experts claim that, in view of that pact, the only solution to the issue is mutual negotiation between the two countries without involving a third party, such as the United Nations.

DISPUTE POSITIONS

According to Pakistan's constitution, Azad Kashmir is not part of Pakistan, and its inhabitants have never had any representation in Pakistan's parliament.As far as the United Nations is concerned, the entire area of the former princely state of Kashmir, including Azad Kashmir, remains a disputed territory still awaiting resolution of the long-standing dispute between India and Pakistan. In 1950, the government of India, held local assembly elections in Indian administered Kashmir and regarded the outcome as a referendum by which in 1956, unilaterally reorganised that portion of the former state that was under its control, thereby making that portion an integral part of India.

The government of Pakistan, on the other hand, continues to this day to regard the entire area of the former state as "territory in dispute" to be resolved by a plebiscite to be held at some future date, in order to determine the entire area's accession to either India or Pakistan. While continuing to call for that plebiscite, however, the government of Pakistan has, so far, been unwilling to entertain the idea of a third option for the plebiscite, i.e., a choice of independence for the entire former state. Today, Azad Kashmir and FANA are together referred to by India as "Pakistan-occupied Kashmir" (POK) and, conversely, the present Indian-administered state of Jammu and Kashmir is referred to by Pakistan as "Indian-occupied Kashmir" (IOK).

GOVERNMENT

Azad Jammu and Kashmir (AJK) is a self-governing state under Pakistani control but is not constitutionally part of Pakistan. It has its own elected president, prime minister, legislature, high court, and official flag. The government of Pakistan has not yet allowed the state to issue its own postage stamps, however, and Pakistani stamps are used in the state, instead. The state is administratively divided into two divisions which, in turn, are divided into eight districts.

ETHNIC GROUPS

Azad Kashmir is predominantly Muslim. The majority of the population is culturally, linguistically, and ethnically related to the people of northern Punjab. The article Ethnic groups of Azad Kashmir give a breakdown of all the major tribes in the state.

LANGUAGES

Urdu is the official language of Azad Kashmir but is spoken by only a minority of people. The dominant language spoken in the state is Pahari, which is very similar to Pothwari and Hindko.

ECONOMY

In the latter part of 2006, billions of dollars for development were mooted by international aid agencies for the reconstruction and rehabilitation of earthquake-hit zones in Azad Kashmir, though much of those funds were subsequently lost in bureaucratic channels, leading to delay in help reaching the most needy, and hundreds of people are still living in tents. A land-use plan for Muzaffarabad city was prepared by the Japan International Cooperation Agency.

EDUCATION

The Literacy rate for Azad Kashmir was 62% in 2004 higher than any other region in Pakistan. Out of 62% about 55.47% are people at the age of 10 or a little above of it, 70.52% are male and 40.46% are female. However, only 2.2% were graduates compared to the average of 2.9% for the whole of Pakistan.

PAKISTAN KASHMIR HISTORY

Pakistan's Kashmir history is an integral part of its foreign policy and military policy. In order to understand Pakistan's relationship to the war on terror and with Islamist groups, it is important to factor in Pakistan's interest in Kashmir. Kashmir's contentious existence has made it home to militant groups who have used terrorist tactics as part of a drive for an independent Kashmir, as well as others with pro-Pakistani views.

1947: KASHMIR DISPUTE BEGINS

What we often call Kashmir is actually Jammu and Kashmir, a majority Muslim Indian area between India and Pakistan. The Kashmir dispute began in 1947, when India was divided into a Hindu state and a Muslim state (Pakistan and East Pakistan, now Bangladesh).

Both India and Pakistan laid claim to Kashmir. Many Kashmiris wanted independence. However, when Pakistani Pashtun tribes invaded, Kashmir's leader requested Indian help. India sent troops to Kashmir to eject the Pashtun tribes, and Pakistan responded by sending in its military. In 1949, a ceasefire agreement, known as the Karachi Agreement, divided Kashmir between India and Pakistan.

1965: KASHMIR'S FIRST MILITANTS

The competition between India and Pakistan for Kashmir, and the disinterest in either of supporting its independence, set the stage for the evolution of independence groups that would ultimately turn violent.

The first and most primary militarized group in Kashmir was the Jammu and Kashmir Liberation Front (JKLF), formed in 1965. JKLF was an anti-India, pro-independence political party. It drew membership from both the Indian and Pakistani sides of the ceasefire line.

1970s: ISLAMIST SENTIMENT IN KASHMIR EXPANDS

The original basis for an independent Kashmir was a Kashmiri identity that would be neither exclusively Muslim nor Hindu. This secular national identity was increasingly replaced with an Islamic identity in the 1980s. According to at

2003 International Crisis Group report, *Kashmir: Learning from the Past*, several reasons account for the shift:

"Islamic political revivalism" following the Iranian revolution"

"The rise of Muslim educational facilities ... within Indian-administered Kashmir"

"A decline in employment prospects for Kashmiri youth and a growing sense that the mainstream secular leadership had failed"

Farooq Abdullah, a Kashmiri leader, manipulated Muslim sentiment to gain advantage in elections.

1970s-1980s: PAKISTAN GETS INVOLVED IN PROMOTING RELIGIOUS CONFLICT

Pakistan played a role in promoting militant Islamic groups in Kashmir in the 1970s and 1980s. Substantial evidence exists that Zia-ul-Haq, Pakistan's Prime Minister from 1977 until 1988, used militant groups to encourage the idea that Kashmir represented a religious conflict, in which Muslims were oppressed by Hindus. Some organizations turned Kashmir into a religious-political issue by promoting the idea that battle in Kashmir against Indian forces is holy.

These groups, such as *Lashkar-e-Tayyba and Jayish-e-Mohammad,* were founded in Pakistani religious schools. It should be remembered, however, that this political and militant view of Islam, and its promotion in Kashmir, does not represent most Pakistani Sunnis' Islam. In 1971, Ashraf and Hashim qureshi, two leaders of the *Kashmiri Liberation Front* hijacked an Indian Airlines plane and took it to Lahore, to publicize the Kashmiri independence movement. In Lahore, they destroyed the plane by lighting it on fire. None of the 32 passengers were hurt.

The hijacking took place in the airspace over Jammu. Jammu is one of three areas (Jammu, Ladakh and Kashmir) that make up the Kashmiri state, which sits between India and Pakistan. The Kashmiri state was created in the middle of the 19th century by treaty by the British government (which then ruled India). In the middle of the 20th century, when Indians sought their independence from British rule, Kashmiris followed suit and sought independence from the Kashmiri rule that had been imposed on them. When India and Pakistan were divided in 1947, Kashmir joined India, but fighting soon erupted between Pakistani and Indian forces for control of the Kashmir.

Hashim Qureshi was in his late teens in 1970; when Maqbool Bhat, the leader of a Kashmiri independence group, *Jammu and Kashmiri Liberation Front* (JKLF) requested that he hijack a plane to help publicize the Kashmiri quest for independence from India. At the time, hijacking was virtually a fad among left-wing independence groups, from the Palestinian Front for the Liberation of Palestine (PFLP) to the Eritrean Liberation Front.

Qureshi, then a teenager, was given flying and weapons training. On the day of the kidnapping he and a partner, Ashraf Qureshi, boarded the plan with a.22 pistol and a briefcase with a fake grenade inside. When the plane reached Jammu (an area within Kashmir, which is actually properly called Jammu and Kashmir), Hashim walked up to the cockpit, put the pistol against the pilot's throat and diverted the plane to Lahore, Pakistan. In Pakistan, the hijackers and the passengers remained in the plane for 80 hours. Then, according to Hashim Qureshi, the Pakistani intelligence service requested they destroy the plane. Kerosene was spread inside the plane, and Qureshi was given a match.

After the plane's destruction, Hashim Qureshi was taken to a detention center in Pakistan where he was tortured by the Pakistanis (Qureshi said in 2001: "They put me on ice, they beat me with rubber batons. They wouldn't let me sleep for 13 days. Whenever I nodded off they would probe me awake with electric current. They did it for more than one month and 15 days.")

Qureshi was sentenced to 19 years in prison, after being tried in a special court convened in Pakistan. He was released after 8 years in prison, in 1981. After his imprisonment, he married a Pakistani woman. They have four children. Qureshi has since renounced violence. In 1994, he established the *Maqbool National Welfare Association*, which is dedicated to helping widows and orphans of Kashmiri militants. These women and children are ineligable for government aid.

1990s: INDIA RESPONDS TO PAKISTANI MILITANCY IN KASHMIR

India responded dramatically to Pakistan-sponsored militancy in Kashmir. The Terrorism and Disruptive Activities Prevention Act (TADA) led to the arrest of over 76,000 individuals. Various anti-terrorism measures were notable for their violations of human rights. The record of human rights abuses in the name of countering terrorism has not abated.

According to the 2003 International Crisis Group Report, Learning from the Past, " ... in March 2002, the Indian parliament ... passed a draconian anti-terrorism bill that was denounced by its own Human Rights Commission." Indian excesses and militant responses by Muslim groups have created a vicious circle of responsive violence that has proven impossible to halt.

1999: PAKISTAN CROSSES THE LINE IN THE KARGIL CONFLICT

In 1999, Pakistan-sponsored militants, as well as Pakistani forces, violated the LOC (line of control) between India and Pakistan administered Kashmir. India's efforts to oust the troops were unsuccessful and the situation was resolved with U.S. diplomatic intervention.

Prime Minister Nawaz Sharif agreed to withdraw regular troops and militants from the Indian side of Kashmir, which averted a potential war between India and Pakistan. One of the results of the Kargil conflict was domestic conflict in Pakistan between the Sharif administration and the military, and then headed by Chief of Army Staff Pervez Musharraf. Musharraf was installed as president in a military coup in October.

2001: PAKISTAN AND KASHMIR FOLLOWING SEPTEMBER 11 AND THE WAR ON TERROR

Pakistan's emergence as a partner in the United States' "war on terror" following September 11 has had a number of implications for Kashmir. President Musharraf's pledge to crack down on Islamists led to the banning of groups that had been operating in Kashmir, among them the *Lashkar-e-Tayyiba* and *Jaish-e-Mohammad*.

According to the International Crisis Group, these groups renamed themselves and continued their activities, after which they were banned again. Following President Musharraf's resignation in 2008, accusations that he had supported the development of jihadist groups to serve strategy in Kashmir came from a number of directions, including US based analysts.

2004 AND BEYOND: STEPS TOWARD RESOLUTION

Despite some hopeful signs in the mid-2000s, including a peace process initiated in 2004, the possibility of a peaceful conclusion to the standoff in Kashmir remains a distant hope. Militancy has not much abated, and a cycle of terrorist attacks and military responses by India has not been broken. In April 2005, President Musharraf and Indian Prime Minister Manmohan Singh concluded a summit at which both pledged to continue the peace process.

There were new links between Indian and Pakistani Kashmir, including a bus service between their respective capitals. These hopeful signs appeared as if they may have been dashed in 2008, when violence again surged among Muslims in Indian Jammu & Kashmir.

2008: TENSIONS RISE AGAIN IN KASHMIR, PAKISTAN IS ACCUSED OF FUELING

Tensions rose again in 2008, following a government decision on the Indian side to lease land used for a Hindu pilgrimage to a Hindu religious organization. The decision led to violent clashes between Muslim protesters and police. When the government rescinded the lease offer, Hindus protested, at which point violent clashes between Hindu protesters and police broke out.

The violence was uneasily quelled with the imposition of a curfew at the end of August. Indian authorities at various points in the dispute charged that Pakistan, or Pakistan-backed jihadi groups, were ready to exploit or even foment tensions.

3

Scenario of Global Terrorism

A deafening blast; an explosion; the horrific screams; the senseless mutilation of human bodies; the smell of sulphur in the air; the smoke rising above the carnage; people running for their lives; life stripped of its sanctity – the world coming to an unexpected, unannounced end. Just as the noise dies down, and the carnage nears an end. Just as the screaming stops, and the people begin to emerge. Just as the crowd regains composure, and tries to ascertain the damage, all hell breaks loose.

Most of those who had been lucky enough to survive the first attack now lying here and there on the ground, their blood splattered all over the place, every single one of them, lifeless and dead in Delhi, Islamabad, Rome, Mumbai, Lahore, Washington DC, Jerusalem, London, Ramallah, Karachi, and New York. Every city of every country of the world, whether it is a bustling cosmopolitan economic hub, or the capital of the country, or a small town at the foot of a beautiful mountain, has, at one time or another, been the undeserving victim of a terrorist attack.

Based on virtually no systematic pattern, without a shred of warning, with no respect for the value and preservation of human life, not discriminating between the potential victims of their heinous act, a suicide bomber or a terrorist causes life to come to a standstill and makes nations weak, not only to outside forces, but to rouge elements within as well. For some, those who find the diplomatic process a bit too time-consuming and tedious, terrorism has become a norm; a way of life.

Though it becomes an answer for some, it results in posing an infinite number of questions to those who have to suffer the horrific consequences. Not only innocent civilians and bystanders, but nations become victims as well, as their economies slowly begin to cripple under the burden of a deteriorating law and order situation. Despite the world facing a severe economic recession, for the preservation and protection of the most fundamental human right to life, the global community – at the expense of economic growth, the cost of economic well-being and the stake of economic stability; is engaged in an endless war: the infamous global war on terror.

A war that has stretched for over seven years, with hundreds of thousands of casualties and virtually no end in sight, despite the lives and the budget it has run. Yes, terrorism must be fought with and stopped by all means, but violence begets violence, as Mahatma Gandhi so rightly said 'an eye for an eye will make the whole world blind'. The persisting war on terror has not only continued to fuel retaliation, but has made the world a worse, rather than better place to live in, with nations being twice as far away from achieving the Millennium Development Goals today than they were before the war started.

The fundamental purpose in fighting terrorism is to make the world a safer and better place to live in, but with the world continuing to ante up and increase hostilities, a time may come where there would no one left to make the world safer or better. Shouldn't the global community unite in peace, rather than for war? Since the late 1980s, considerable research has been undertaken in the United States and abroad on the security implications of environmental change. One widely discussed and studied hypothesis is that certain forms of environmental change have negative social effects which reinforce or create conditions for instability and violent conflict.

Many variations of this hypothesis have been examined the past decade, bringing attention to a broader range of environmentally-induced human insecurities as well as to processes of adaptation to environmental stress. The events of September 11th have given attention to one of these hypotheses- that environmental change may create conditions conducive to certain forms of terrorism. Additionally, we believe these events will have a much broader impact on the field of environmental studies. For example, we must now examine vulnerabilities to terrorism and other security threats embedded in our natural and built environments.

Just as certain forms of infrastructure can be used as delivery vehicles for terror (such as the postal service and air transportation), water and agricultural systems and other natural structures may present threat opportunities that have not been assessed. We need to examine ways in which these vulnerabilities may affect urban and regional planning and development. We need to examine the extent to which disaster preparedness plans are sufficient for the possible damage that could be caused by terrorism and other transnational threats.

We need to reconsider our transportation and health care systems in light of transnational threats and vulnerabilities. We need to ask whether our regulatory, monitoring and enforcement systems can provide information and support to efforts to reduce vulnerability to transnational threats. We need to ask whether our economic need for natural resources such as oil contributes to the enmity aboard that undergirds terrorism, and, if so, what might be done to reduce both the need and the enmity.

We believe that individuals with extensive expertise in certain areas of environmental studies- such as transportation, water, energy, and natural disasters-have perspectives on the new security challenges facing the United States and the rest of the world that are extremely important.

In the past, intelligence assessments dealt with sovereign countries. Today, in the era of global terrorism, we are dealing with Muslim fundamental terrorist organizations, entities without territories or sovereignty, entities without any hierarchy, with no uniforms, reporting systems, recruiting centers, or training camps.

Furthermore, in the past, conventional wars were relatively short events that occurred as an interval between periods of peace or coexistence or cold war. Today, the Western world, Israel included, lives in a state of constant war. The threat is permanent, while it changes faces, locations, strategies, methodologies, and capabilities - and you have to assess it while fighting them.

Signal intelligence and imagery offer excellent intelligence, but you cannot ask any questions and get any answers. Thus, through human intelligence you are better able to understand your enemy and the threat he poses far better than through any other means of intelligence gathering. But penetrating these groups is very hard. We are dealing with families, blood connections, and a religious culture that is impossible for a foreigner to penetrate.

If Iran acquires a nuclear capability, is it going to activate it or not? Will a nuclear Iran be pragmatic or messianic? For the intelligence officer this question is academic. Any intelligence officer would recommend that the state should prepare for the worst-case scenario and not for any lesser eventuality.

Should fighting terrorism be based on reaction or on pre-emption? Since there is an ongoing war, since the threat is permanent, since the intention of the enemy in this case is to annihilate you, the right doctrine is one of pre-emption and not of reaction. When we are dealing with an enemy which plans all the time and waits only for the opportunity in order to attack, what is the point even morally to wait and only do something when he comes to attack?

TERRORIST GROUPS MORE DIFFICULT TO ASSESS

In the past, intelligence assessments dealt with sovereign countries. Today, in the era of global terrorism, we are dealing with Muslim fundamental terrorist organizations, entities without territories or sovereignty, virtual entities. These are entities spread all over the globe, without any hierarchy, with no uniforms, reporting systems, recruiting centers, or training camps. It is an environment in which every believer subscribes voluntarily to membership in the organization. It is an invisible army led by a divine message to fight the infidels in order to build the new, eternal Muslim caliphate.

Any intelligence organization must face these basic differences when it tries to assess and evaluate the threats today. Furthermore, in the past, conventional wars were relatively short events that occurred as an interval between periods of peace or coexistence or cold war. Conventional wars are limited in time, while the war against international terrorism today is a constant factor. The Western world, Israel included, today lives in a state of constant war.

In the past, because war was an interval between two relatively quiet periods, you had all the time in the world to gather information about your adversary in order to prepare your intelligence assessment and make recommendations. Today, the challenge is to prepare your assessments while fighting. The threat is permanent, while it changes faces, locations, strategies, methodologies, and capabilities - and you have to assess it while fighting them. In the past, you dealt with a military, with an air force, a navy, armored and infantry units. All of these components were very tangible and it was relatively easier to assess the overall threat from them. Today, however, the doctrine of the terrorists is developing and changing all the time.

If the conflict is a religious one, it involves an indefinite war which may end only if and when the rest of the world becomes Muslim, and Islam succeeds in establishing a Muslim caliphate. If we are dealing with terrorist organizations that are more political than religious, we are also talking about a continuous conflict that ends when the terrorists achieve either a state or some kind of self-determination or other form of sovereignty.

In the past era of conventional wars, the religious factor was marginal or secondary. In the present-day environment, however, the religious factor has become dominant and it affects all the rest. Islam includes a huge variety of groups, sects, races, peoples, states, traditions, and written and unwritten sets of laws. For Israel, intelligence assessments in the past dealt mainly with regional issues.

Today, however, when we have to cope with the global *jihad*, even small intelligence services find themselves facing the challenge of covering the whole world because the present-day global *jihad* has spread all over the place. In order to cope with it, you need to have first-class intelligence gathered in Britain, Germany, in the Far East and South America.

SOURCES OF INTELLIGENCE

Human intelligence is the only form of intelligence where you can ask questions and get answers. Signal intelligence and imagery offer excellent intelligence, but you cannot ask any questions and get any answers. Thus, through human intelligence you are able to understand your enemy and the threat he poses far better than through any other means of intelligence gathering. But when it comes to gathering intelligence on the global *jihad*, human intelligence is very problematic and difficult to achieve. Penetrating these groups is very hard.

We are dealing with small groups where everyone knows everyone else. We are dealing with families, blood connections, and a religious culture that is impossible for a foreigner to penetrate. So in assessing the global *jihad* and the Muslim terrorist organizations today, the added value of human intelligence is very much lacking. Intelligence officers used to say that 95 per cent of intelligence is found in open sources, which is basically the media.

Yet open sources and the media are being used by politicians, business people, and various other interests which each have their own "spin." This is making it more and more difficult for the intelligence officer or analyst who must deal with all these spins.

ASSESSING THE INTENTIONS OF THE ADVERSARY

Traditionally, when assessing a threat in the intelligence field, we have to cope with two main issues: What are the intentions of the enemy, and what are his capabilities? In the Middle East, the intention of the adversary is always very hard to discover because the region contains many Arab countries with authoritarian regimes, whose intentions usually are to be found only in the head of the head of state, whereas in the West, the intentions of the state are disseminated and are known by a relatively large number of people.

The intentions of international terrorism and global *jihad* are a matter of public record. Still, there are some intentions that are not known. For example, if Iran acquires a nuclear capability, is it going to activate it or not? In other words, will a nuclear Iran be pragmatic or messianic? According to what they are preaching, they are very messianic, but once they achieve a nuclear capability, are they going to use it or not? On the level of intentions, no one can come up with a proper answer.

In order to understand the intentions of the Iranians now, you have to try and understand what's in the heads of a relatively small group of religious leaders. Yet even among themselves there are different opinions. Still, for all practical purposes, for the intelligence officer this question is academic. The recommendation of any intelligence officer would be that the state should prepare for the worst-case scenario and not for any lesser eventuality. In this case, it means that Israel and maybe others should prepare for the eventuality that a nuclear Iran will use this capability.

REACTING VS. PRE-EMPTING TERRORISM

Should fighting terrorism be based on reaction or on pre-emption? My opinion is that since there is an ongoing war, since the threat is permanent, since the intention of the enemy in this case is to annihilate you, the right doctrine is one of pre-emption and not of reaction. To use reaction as the main strategy means to sit quietly and wait until the enemy comes to attack you. But when we are dealing with an enemy which plans all the time and waits only for the opportunity in order to attack, what is the point even morally to wait and only do something when he comes to attack?

How did terrorism, which has been around for centuries, go from a sporadic, often localized, atrocity to a global threat in the 21st Century? Are terrorists recruiting more vigorously? Do terrorist have more reasons to hate? Or have terrorists gotten more support than ever before? A close look at some events in recent years seems to indicate it's the latter. What's most disturbing, though, is that the greatest motivational support has come not from internal sources or Arab countries, but from a somewhat unexpected source - the United Nations.

To understand the progression of events leading up to global terrorism, it would help to look at the motives of some mass killers in the U.S., which are somewhat similar to those of international terrorists. On December 5, 2007, Robert Hawkins, 19, walked into a Westroads Mall in Omaha, Nebraska, and killed eight people and himself. His suicide note read, in part, "Everyone will remember me as some sort of monster.... But just think... I'm gonna be... famous."

Michael Welner, an associate professor of psychiatry at NYU School of Medicine, pointed out, "'My fame is more important than your life,' that's basically what he said." An FBI investigation into the infamous 1999 Columbine massacre showed that Hawkins demented yearning for fame and recognition was not unique. The public perception of the Columbine killers, Eric Harris and Dylan Klebold, was they were lonely outcasts out for revenge on those who bullied them. But three months after the massacre, the FBI convened a summit in Leesburg, Va., that included world-renowned mental health experts, as well as Supervisory Special Agent Dwayne Fuselier, the FBI's lead Columbine investigator and a clinical psychologist. Their conclusion was disturbingly different from public perception.

Not lonely outcasts at all, Klebold and Harris regularly hung out and partied with a circle of friends. They laughed at petty school shooters and bragged about dwarfing the Oklahoma City bombing. Klebold boasted on a video about inflicting "the most deaths in U.S. history." Rather than being an angry man being picked on, Harris, according to Fuselier, had a messianic-grade superiority complex and was out to punish the human race for its appalling inferiority. So, on April 20, 1999, after a year of planning, Harris and Klebold walked into Columbine High School in Jefferson County, Colorado, and killed 12 students, a teacher, and wounded 23, before committing suicide.

This became the fourth-deadliest school killing in U.S. history. Had their wiring functioned properly, they would have wiped out 600 people in massive propane bombing of the cafeteria. In addition to gunning down fleeing survivors, they planned on setting off car bombs to finish off rescue workers and reporters. According to Agent Fuselier, it wasn't just fame they were after. They were after infamy of global proportions. Their aim was to create a nightmare so devastating and horrendous that the entire world would shudder at their power.

Now, try to imagine this: The parents of Hawkins, Harris and Klebold are asked about their sons' atrocities and respond that they're very proud of their sons and hope their siblings would some day do the same. Then, schools around the country hang up pictures of the three murderers, hailing them as Heros and role models. Imagine further, one shooter survives, is brought to justice, and the judge finds his "grievances" plausible. And not only does the judge not convict him, but reprimands the cops and security personnel for using excessive force.

How do you suppose such an insane scenario would impact mass killings? If people are willing to die and murder others for infamy, it's pretty safe to say that honoring such monsters as heros and restraining law enforcement personnel with censures would in all likelihood cause mass killings to skyrocket. Unfortunately, you don't have to imagine all this.

This scenario has been played out in real life, although not (yet) in the U.S. And the results have been devastating. It's a well documented fact that Palestinian parents have often spoken proudly of their suicide-murderer children and openly implored their other children to follow suit.

Palestinians customarily hang up pictures of suicide murderers in schools and laud them as heroes and roll models. Palestinian murderers are often promised bliss in the hereafter. And, to top it all off, families of Palestinian terrorist have for years received cash rewards from some Arab leaders for the very act of murder-suicide. How well have these incentives and encouragements worked? From September 2000 to September 2005, over 26,000 (average of 14 a day) terrorist attacks were perpetrated against Israeli targets.

While playing down the plethora of incentives they showered upon mass murderers to perpetuate carnage, Palestinians perfected the art of spouting "grievances" for public consumption - things like "oppression" and "occupation," which caught on like the Columbine "being bullied" rumors. And, thus, terrorism in the Middle East grew into more than a cottage industry. It then took the ingenuity and creativity of an international "peacekeeping" organization - the UN - to bring this deadly game to the world arena.

The intifada that began in September 2000 was trumpeted by the Palestinians as a response to then-Israeli Prime Minister Ariel Sharon's walk on the Temple Mount, a Holy site for Muslims and others. The UN convened in October of that year and passed Resolution 1322, the opening lines of which read, in part:

"Reaffirming the need for full respect by all of the Holy Places of the City of Jerusalem, and condemning any behaviour to the contrary, "the UN Deplores the provocation [Sharon's walk] carried out at Al-Haram Al-Sharif and the subsequent violence...;

"the UN Condemns acts of violence, especially the excessive use of force against Palestinians, resulting in injury and loss of human life;"

This Resolution placed violence and total anarchy on the same level as an "offending" walk, which is absolutely mind-boggling. According to the UN, if you walk into a house of worship where "your kind are not welcome," that's the same as going into someone's neighborhood and attacking anyone and everyone in sight. How many civilized people do you know who subscribe to this logic? The Resolution, in effect, gave Palestinians the right to savagely butcher people for the slightest provocation, and restrained a victimized party from defending itself no matter how brutal the attacks against her. With the gist of this Resolution expressed repeatedly throughout the years of the intifada, the Resolution became a downright sanction of terrorism.

What's worse, Israel's use of force to defend its citizens from deadly violence is referred to in the Resolution as "excessive" and is, in the UN's view, worthy of condemnation. This is like telling Columbine security personnel that they're use of force against would-be mass killers is excessive. Exactly how much force is excessive when you're defending yourself against being killed? Furthermore, with the UN's definition of excessive, wouldn't Palestinian barbarism in response to a "walk" be far more excessive? But this is never even mentioned, let alone condemned. The green-light to terrorism couldn't have been more blatant if the UN had told Palestinians, "Go ahead, kill whomever you want, we've got you covered."

One thing's for sure, it made an impression on the Palestinians. In the 12 months after Resolution 1322 was passed there were, according to the most conservative estimates, over 100 Palestinian terrorist attacks against Israel (the previous 12 months, less than a dozen). Over the next five years, over 1000 Israelis were savagely murdered and over 6000 maimed and wounded. And, to add insult to injury, throughout this massacre of Israelis, Israel was unjustly and continually held in contempt by the UN. The Palestinians, on the other hand, despite unleashing the most inhumane carnage upon Israelis, were never condemned even once by the UN.

How do you think all this played to all the terrorist wannabes around the world? As great encouragement, no doubt. It is in this period that, I'm convinced; terrorism got its big "whitewash." With such unfaltering support from the UN, terrorism was no longer a dirty word or the diabolical tool of yesteryear. Terrorism had now become an acceptable and even "respectable" way to express real or imagined grievances. And the world was made very aware of this, over and over.

It took Osama bin Laden only one year to capitalize in a major way on this new-found license to butcher people. Not that he needed anyone's permission before. But now he could massacre as many totally innocent people as he wanted and, as long as he had a "grievance," he could blame his victims and even come out with dignity and respect. So on September 11, 2001, Osama bin Laden became the most "respected" name in some parts of the Muslim world and to who knows how many terrorist wannabes and terrorist now-decided-to-be - all with the tacit endorsement of Kofi Annan, then-Secretary General of the UN, and the rest of his corrupt enterprise.

By July 7, 2005, with the ripping of people on the street to shreds already redefined by the UN as being no different from protesting or striking, it's with little wonder that the London Bombers were seemingly ordinary citizens. "I certainly think this is a new dimension," said Peter Newman of London University's War Studies Institute. "These are people who grew up in Britain... a novelty we haven't seen in this country so far."

On September 20, 2006, at the 61st UN General Assembly, Kofi Annan had the audacity to make this insulting understatement: "... supporters of Israel feel that it is harshly judged by standards that are not applied to its enemies, and too often this is true, particularly in some UN bodies." In an honest and contrite speech, he would have said, "I feel shame and regret for unjustly vilifying Israel and the United States in the eyes of the world, and unleashing global terrorism for the foreseeable future."

The phoniness of Annan's statement became apparent only two months later at the annual "Day of Solidarity with the Palestinian People," by the screening of a film encouraging children to glorify death and murder. In one scene, small children in a classroom shout, "Jerusalem, I sacrifice myself to you, land of my grandfather, we will return." (The previous year, they had a moment of silence to honor suicide murderers.) This was not a Hamas training camp - this was the UN!

As of January 2008, we've seen several terrorist plots around the world by "ordinary" people. And authorities fear it's only the beginning. The damage wrought upon the world by the UN, and Kofi Annan in particular, by sanctioning terrorism is incalculable. To find another country or entity in modern history that generated so much racism, bigotry and anti-semitism on such a massive scale, you'd probably have to go back to the days of the Third Reich. If we're going to take fighting terrorism seriously, we must prosecute all those responsible for it's proliferation, regardless of what physical or legal barriers they hide behind. One step in the right direction would be to try Kofi Annan for crimes against humanity.

PATTERNS OF GLOBAL TERRORISM

Patterns of Global Terrorism is a report published each year on or before April 30 by the United States Department of State. The Secretary of State is required by Congress to produce detailed assessments about.

Each foreign country in which acts of international terrorism occurred;

The extent to which foreign countries are cooperating with the U.S. in the apprehension, conviction, and punishment of terrorists;

The extent to which foreign countries are cooperating with the U.S. in the prevention of further acts of terrorism; and

Activities of any terrorist group known to be responsible for the kidnapping or death of an American citizen.

The exact definition of the requirements is in Title 22, Section 2656f of the United States Code. The only complete print edition-indexed, updated, and supplemented with maps and tables, 1985-2005-was published by Berkshire Publishing Group in 2005. Each report includes a short numerical summary. The table at right summarizes the number of international terrorism acts reported each year since 1995.

The following list consists of the report excerpts from which the table is based. Note that some of the numbers are revised after initial publication of the report, which causes some of the numbers used in excerpted comparisons to differ from what was originally reported.

2004: The report was no longer published to the public after its methodology was challenged by the Bush-Cheney administration, amid claims that it showed the highest amount of terror activity in its nineteen year history. A new report was created, called the Country Reports on Terrorism, which detailed terrorism by region but offered no statistics or chronology. In a press conference, the State Department said 1,907 people had been killed and 9,300 wounded in terrorist attacks, the highest ever. A chronology of terror events was released by the National Counterterrorism Center.

2003: There were 208 acts of international terrorism in 2003, a slight increase from the most recently published figure of 198 attacks in 2002, and a 42 % drop from the level in 2001 of 355 attacks. 625 persons were killed in the attacks of 2003, fewer than the 725 killed during 2002. 3646 persons were wounded in the attacks that occurred in 2003, a sharp increase from 2013 persons wounded the year before. This increase reflects the numerous indiscriminate attacks during 2003 on "soft targets," such as places of worship, hotels, and commercial districts, intended to produce mass casualties.

2002: International terrorists conducted 199 attacks in 2002, a significant drop (44%) from the 355 attacks recorded during 2001. 725 persons were killed in last year's attacks, far fewer than the 3,295 persons killed the previous year, which included the thousands of fatalities resulting from the September 11 attacks in New York, Washington, and

Pennsylvania. 2,013 persons were wounded by terrorists in 2002, down from the 2,283 persons wounded the year before.

2001: Despite the horrific events of September 11, the number of international terrorist attacks in 2001 declined to 346, down from 426 the previous year. One hundred seventy-eight of the attacks were bombings against a multinational oil pipeline in Colombia - constituting 51 % of the year's total number of attacks. In 2000, there were 152 pipeline bombings in Colombia, which accounted for 40 % of the total. 3,547 persons were killed in international terrorist attacks in 2001, the highest annual death toll from terrorism ever recorded. Ninety per cent of the fatalities occurred in the September 11 attacks. The number of persons wounded in terrorist attacks in 2001 was 1080, up from 796 wounded the previous year. Violence in the Middle East and South Asia also accounted for the increase in casualty totals for 2001.

2000: There were 423 international terrorist attacks in 2000, an increase of 8 % from the 392 attacks recorded during 1999. The main reason for the increase was an upsurge in the number of bombings of a multinational oil pipeline in Colombia by two terrorist groups there. The pipeline was bombed 152 times, producing in the Latin American region the largest increase in terrorist attacks from the previous year, from 121 to 193. The number of casualties caused by terrorists also increased in 2000. During the year, 405 persons were killed and 791 were wounded, up from the 1999 totals of 233 dead and 706 wounded.

1999: The number of persons killed or wounded in international terrorist attacks during 1999 fell sharply because of the absence of any attack causing mass casualties. In 1999, 233 persons were killed and 706 were wounded, as compared with 741 persons killed and 5,952 wounded in 1998. The number of terrorist attacks rose, however. During 1999, 392 international terrorist attacks occurred, up 43 % from the 274 attacks recorded the previous year. The number of attacks increased in every region of the world except in the Middle East, where six fewer attacks occurred.

1998: There were 273 international terrorist attacks during 1998, a drop from the 304 attacks we recorded the previous year and the lowest annual total since 1971. The total number of persons killed or wounded in terrorist attacks, however, was the highest on record: 741 persons died, and 5,952 persons suffered injuries.

1997: During 1997 there were 304 acts of international terrorism, eight more than occurred during 1996, but one of the lowest annual totals recorded since 1971. The number of casualties remained large but did not approach the high levels recorded during 1996. In 1997, 221 persons died and 693 were wounded in international terrorist attacks as compared to 314 dead and 2,912 wounded in 1996. Seven US citizens died and 21 were wounded in 1997, as compared with 23 dead and 510 wounded the previous year.

1996: During 1996 there were 296 acts of international terrorism, the lowest annual total in 25 years and 144 fewer than in 1995. In contrast, the total number of casualties was one of the highest ever recorded: 311 persons killed and 2,652 wounded. A single bombing in Sri Lanka killed 90 persons and wounded more than 1,400 others.

1995: In most countries, the level of international terrorism in 1995 continued the downward trend of recent years, and there were fewer terrorist acts that caused deaths last year than in the previous year. However, the total number of international terrorist acts rose in 1995 from 322 to 440, largely because of a major increase in nonlethal terrorist attacks against property in Germany and in Turkey by the Kurdistan Workers Party (PKK). The total number of fatalities from international terrorism worldwide declined from 314 in 1994 to 165 in 1995, but the number of persons wounded increased by a factor of ten to 6,291 persons; 5,500 were injured in a gas attack in the Tokyo subway system in March.

PROBLEMS WITH 2003 REPORT

The 2003 report was released twice, in April and June 2004. The release of the April 29th version led Deputy Secretary of

State Richard Armitage to say "Terrorism continues to destroy the lives of people all over the world; and this report we are releasing today, "Patterns of Global Terrorism: 2003," documents the said toll that such attacks took last year. This report also details the steps the United States and some 92 other nations took in 19 - or 2003 to fight back and to protect our peoples. Indeed, you will find in these pages clear evidence that we are prevailing in the fight."

On June 10, 2004, a few weeks after challenges from two professors (Alan Krueger of Princeton University and David Laitin of Stanford University) and Congressman Henry Waxman, the State Department announced that the report previously issued for 2003 was incomplete and incorrect in part. The revisions issued twelve days later included significant changes, including a doubling of the number of killed and wounded mentioned in the April 2004 version.

4

Terrorism in Jammu and Kashmir

Terrorism in Kashmir is an ideological struggle with specified political commitments which are fundamentalist and communal in character. Terrorist violence is aimed at achieving the disengagement of the state of Jammu and Kashmir from India and its annexation to Pakistan. It is, the continuation of the Islamic fundamentalist struggle for the homeland of Pakistan which claims Jammu and Kashmir State on account of its Muslim majority character. The major dimension of the terrorist violence in Kashmir is the terrorists' commitment to the extermination and subjugation of the Hindus in the state because Hindus do not subscribe to the idea of separation from India, nor do they expect to be governed by the authority of the state which derives its sanction from the law and precedent of Islam.

Kashmiri Pandits (Hindus) have always been in the forefront of the struggle against secessionism, communalism and fundamentalism. Hence this peace loving minority with a modern outlook became the main victim of terrorist violence. Broadly speaking, when justice and right are denied to a person over a longer period of time, the person is left with two options: bear the situation patiently, or the reaction is anguish, and that reaction, in the process culminates into terrorism.

Besides other things, spreading of communal hatred, religious frenzy, separatist tendency etc. are the tools which terrorists generally use. Guns too are used to achieve the so-called specified mission. Fanaticism, extremism, radicalism, separatism, militancy, activism etc. are its other names or manifestations. This is one side of the picture of terrorism. (Terrorists fighting for a genuine cause i.e. liberating themselves, their society/country from the oppressor/ perpetrator).

Another side of the picture is disgusting and questionable. Over the years terrorism has emerged as a systematic use or threatened use of violence to intimidate a population, community or government and thereby effect political, religious or ideological change just to achieve personal gains. Modern terrorism has resorted to other option of intimidation, i.e. influence the mass media, in an effort to amplify and broadcast feelings of intense fear and anger among the people and needless to mention here that acts of terror are carried out by people who are indoctrinated to the extent of following a strategy of dying to kill.

They are the ones who have become pawns in the hands of their masters who direct their paths, sitting in the comforts of far off places with all the facilities available to them. Masters have their vested political interests while as pawns seemingly have nothing to gain except suffer for a cause about which they themselves don't know or know very little. Terrorism in Kashmir is almost 18 years old now and has likeness to the second side of the picture. It has a history long enough to be traced from the date when partition was forced resulting in the emergence of two nations - India and Pakistan - after the sub-continent freed itself from the colonial rule of the British Empire.

It may not be out of context here to probe into the consequences in detail that gave rise to terrorism in Kashmir. But again, before that, giving a brief introduction of this widely known beautiful valley would be too apt. Kashmir – Paradise on Earth – (Switzerland of Asia) Nature's grand finale of beauty is a masterpiece of earth's creation of charm and loveliness. Famous for its beauty and natural scenery throughout the world and for its high snow-clad mountains, scenic spots, beautiful valleys, rivers with ice-cold water, attractive lakes and springs and ever-green fields, dense forests and beautiful health resorts, enhance its grandeur and are a source of great attraction for tourists.

It is also widely known for its different kinds of agricultural products, fruit, vegetables, saffron, herbs, and minerals, precious stones handicrafts like woolen carpets, shawls and finest kind of embroidery on clothes. During summer, one can enjoy the beauty of nature, trout fishing, big and small game hunting etc.; during winter climbing mountain peaks and sports like skating and skiing on snow slopes are commonly enjoyed. In addition to the above, Pilgrimage to famous religious shrines of the Hindus and the Muslims make Kashmir a great tourist attraction. About Kashmir Sheikh Sadie a great Persian poet is believed to have said, "If there is any heaven on earth, it is here in Kashmir, in Kashmir in Kashmir only."

Apart from natural beauty, Jammu and Kashmir has a unique cultural blend which makes it different from the rest of the country (India). It is not only distinct in cultural forms and heritage, but in geographical, demographical, ethnical, social entities, forming a distinct spectrum of diversity. The people of Kashmir, Jammu and Ladakh, all follow diverse religion, language and culture, but continuously intermingling which symbolizes Indian Unity amidst diversity. Its different cultural forms like art and architecture, fair and festivals, rites and rituals, seers and sagas, languages and literatures, embedded in ageless period of history, speak of endless unity and diversity with unparalleled cultural cohesion and amicability. Kashmir has been a great centre of learning.

A treasure of rich Sanskrit literature is to be found here. Early Indo-Aryanic civilization has originated and flourished in this land. It has also been embracing point of advent of Islam bringing its traditions of Persian civilization, tolerance, brotherhood and sacrifice. After the British withdrew from the Indian subcontinent in 1947 and India and Pakistan emerged as two separate countries, princely states were given an option to choose the country they wanted to stay on. Obviously, the states falling geographically within had no other option but to merge with the country they were situated.

Border States like Kashmir, Jodhpur etc. took time to come out with their firm decisions probably because they wanted to enjoy the status of an independent Statehood. In the case of Kashmir, where Maharaja (King) Hari Singh was the ruler, situation worsened considerably. Territorial disputes over Kashmir had already started brewing - Pakistan claiming that Kashmir should go to his side since Muslims were in majority there.

Apprehending that Maharaja might opt for an accession to India, Pakistan prepared for an aggression in a bid to capture the State forcibly hoping that masses, mainly Muslims, would support its mission but that didn't happen. Secular forces headed by the then popular mass leader Sheikh Mohammad Abdullah fondly known as *Sher-i-Kashmir* motivated the Kashmiri people (Hindus, Muslims and Sikhs) to rise to the occasion and stand united to counter and frustrate the evil designs of the enemy who was marching to the capital city Srinagar indulging in bloodshed and mayhem.

A new slogan echoed the entire valley: "Hamlavar khabardaar, hum Kashmiri hai tayaar - Hindu Muslim Sikh Ithaad, Naya Kashmir Zindabaad". Beware you attackers! We Kashmiris are ready to counter you - Long live the Unity of Hindus, Muslims and Sikhs!!

At Hazuri Bagh, Srinagar before a large crowd on October 1, 1947, Sher-i-Kashmir proclaimed:"Till the last drop of my blood, I will not believe in two-nation theory." It was a rebuff to Mr. Jinnah-father of the nation of Pakistan who was watching the developments so closely from his country side. Finding their designs on Kashmir not fructifying, Pakistan rulers launched an armed attack on Jammu and Kashmir to annex it. Tribes in thousands along with Pak regular troops entered the State on October 22, 1947 from several points and indulged in loot, arson, rape, bloodshed and mayhem.

Bowing before the wishes of the people and seeing his own regular army being out-numbered and to push back the invaders, the Maharaja signed the *Instrument of Accession* in favor of India on October 26, 1947 on the prescribed terms and conditions. This was accepted by the Governor General of India, Lord Mountbatten the next day. The Instrument of Accession executed by Maharaja Hari Singh was the same which was signed by other rulers of the other princely States. Similarly, the acceptance of the Instrument of Accession by the Governor General was also identical in respect of all such instruments.

With J&K becoming legal and constitutional part of Union of India, Indian army rushed to the State to push back the invaders and vacate aggression from the territory of the State. The first batch of Indian Army troops arrived at Srinagar airport immediately after the Accession was signed. On October 30, 1947 an Emergency Government was formed in the State with Sheikh Mohammad Abdullah as its head. The Army fought sustained battle with the tribals/Kabayilies and after several sacrifices pushed them out of the Valley and other areas in the Jammu region. (Earlier Brigadier Rajendra Singh Chief of State Forces with a small number of soldiers at his disposal fought valiantly with the enemy and laid down his life in the process.)

Meanwhile, the people of Kashmir under the towering leadership of Sher-I-Kashmir were mobilized and they resisted the marching columns of the enemy. Till the arrival of India troops, it was mainly the Muslim volunteers under the command of Sheikh Mohammad Abdullah who braved death to push back invaders. While the army pushed back the invaders, there were several instances where people put up a gallant resistance and stopped the advancing invaders. The most glaring examples of people's resistance were the martyrdom of Mohammad Maqbool Sherwani and Master Abdul Aziz both staunch followers of Sher-i-Kashmir Sheikh Abdullah.

Sherwani did not oblige the invaders when they enquired from him the route to Srinagar. Instead, he put them on a wrong track gaining time for troops to reach Srinagar from

New Delhi. Somehow the tribesmen came to know about his tactics and nailed him at a Baramulla crossing and asked him to raise pro-Pakistan slogans. He did raise slogans but these were different. These were pro-Hindu-Muslim unity and in favor of Sher-i-Kashmir. Enraged by this, the ruthless tribesmen emptied their guns on him.

The sacrifice of Master Abdul Aziz too was exemplary. The invaders who raped the nuns and wanted other non-Muslim women to be handed over to them, Master Abdul Aziz, a tailor by profession, held the holy Quran in his hand and said that they can touch the women only after they pass over his dead body and the holy Quran. The brutal killers did not spare him either.

On January 1, 1948 India took up the issue of Pak aggression in Jammu and Kashmir to UNO under Article 35 of its Charter. The Government of India in its letter to the Security Council said, "...Such a situation now exists between India and Pakistan owing to the aid which invaders, consisting of nationals of Pakistan and tribesmen... are drawing from Pakistan for operations against Jammu and Kashmir, a State which has acceded legally to the Dominion of India and is part of India. The Government of India requests the Security Council to call upon Pakistan to put an end immediately to the giving of such assistance which is an act of aggression against India. If Pakistan does not do so, the Government of India may be compelled, in self defense, to enter into Pakistan territory to take military action against the invaders."

After long debates, cease-fire came into operation on the midnight of January 1, 1949. Eventually, India filed a complaint with the UN Security Council, which established the United Nations Commission for India and Pakistan (UNCIP). Pakistan was accused of invading the region, and was asked to withdraw its forces from Jammu & Kashmir. The UNCIP also passed a resolution stating: "The question of accession of the state of Jammu & Kashmir to India or Pakistan will be decided through the democratic method of free and impartial plebiscite". However, this could not take place because

Pakistan did not comply with the UN resolution and refused to withdraw from the State. The international community failed to play a decisive role in the matter saying that Jammu & Kashmir is a "disputed territory".

In 1949, with the intervention of the United Nations, India and Pakistan defined a ceasefire line ("Line of Control") that divided the two countries. This has left Kashmir a divided and disturbed territory up till now. In September 1951, free and fair elections, as per the Constitutional modalities, were held in Jammu & Kashmir, and National Conference party under the leadership of Sheikh Abdullah came into power. With the advent of the Constituent Assembly of the State of Jammu & Kashmir representing the aspirations of the people of Jammu and Kashmir, the State became an integral part of India constitutionally.

After Sheikh Abdullah; Bakshi Gulam Mohamad, G.M.Sadiq, Mir Qasim, Gul Shah, Mufti Sayed and Dr.Farooq Abdullah ruled the State as Chief Ministers. Mr.Gulam Nabi Azad is the current Chief Minister of the J&K State. Though the governments ran smoothly over the years, continued instigations and arousing religious frenzy by Pakistan did not stop. The year 1965 saw a war between India and Pakistan claiming many lives on either side. A cease-fire was established and the two countries signed an agreement at Tashkent (Uzbekistan) in 1966, pledging to end the dispute by peaceful means. Five years later, the two again went to war that resulted in the creation of Bangladesh.

Another accord was signed in 1972 between the two Prime Ministers - Indira Gandhi and Zulfiqar Ali Bhutto - in Simla. After Bhutto was executed in 1979, the Kashmir issue once again flared up. During the 1980s, massive infiltrations from Pakistan were detected in the region, and India has since then maintained a strong military presence in Jammu & Kashmir to check these movements along the cease-fire line. India says that Pakistan has been stirring up violence in its part of Kashmir by training and funding "Islamic guerrillas" that have waged a separatist war since 1989 killing tens of thousands of people. Pakistan has always denied the charge, calling it an indigenous "freedom struggle."

In 1999, intense fighting ensued between the infiltrators and the Indian army in the Kargil area of the western part of the state, which lasted for more than two months. The battle ended with India managing to reclaim most of the area on its side that had been seized by the infiltrators. In 2001, Pakistan-backed terrorists waged violent attacks on the Kashmir Assembly and the Indian Parliament in New Delhi. This has resulted in a war-like situation between the two countries, with Pakistani President General Pervez Musharraf asking his army to be "fully prepared and capable of defeating all challenges," and the then Indian Prime Minister Atal Bihari Vajpayee saying, "We don't want war but war is being thrust upon us, and we will have to face it."

PLIGHT OF PANDITS (HINDUS)

The Pandits, who are the Hindu community of Kashmir and have an ancient and a proud culture, have been amongst the most afflicted victims of the Pakistani-supported campaign of terrorism in Jammu and Kashmir. Their roots in the Kashmir Valley run very deep. They are the original inhabitants of this beautiful valley. Their number being small and peace-loving by nature, they have been the soft targets of terrorists. Virtually the entire population of 300,000 Kashmiri Pandits has been forced to leave their ancestral homes and property. Threatened with violence and intimidation by Muslim fundamentalists, they have been turned into refugees in their own country leaving behind their shops, farms, cattle and age-old memories.

As a matter of fact, Jammu and Kashmir has become a target of Pakistan, sponsored by religion-based terrorism. The persecution by Muslim extremists of the Hindu minority and the systematic religion-based extremism of terrorist elements has resulted in the exodus of these Hindu/Pandits and other minorities from the Kashmir Valley to other parts of India. Fundamentalists and terrorists have also targeted and assassinated Muslim intellectuals and liberal Muslim leaders too, who spoke of Hindu-Muslim unity and brotherhood. Terrorist acts by Kashmiri militant groups have also taken place outside Jammu and Kashmir.

India claims most of the separatist militant groups are based in Pakistan and Pakistan-administered Kashmir (also known as Azad Kashmir). Some like the All Parties Hurriyat Conference and the Jammu and Kashmir Liberation Front (JKLF) demand an independent Kashmir. Other groups such as *Lashkar-e-Toiba* and *Jaish-e-Mohammed* favor a Pakistani-Kashmir. Of the larger militant groups, the Hizbul *Mujahideen,* a militant organization is based in Pakistan administered Kashmir. Sources reveal that *Al-Qaeda* too has a base in Pakistani Kashmir and helping to ferment terrorism in Jammu and Kashmir.

India is unwilling to lose even one additional inch of his land. New Delhi is also concerned that Kashmiri autonomy would set a precedent for breakaway movements in other Indian states (e.g., Punjab or Assam). To Pakistan, Kashmir is symbolic of its national ethos and commitment to protect Muslim interests against Indian encroachment. It believes that the creation of a separate, strongly sectarian nation is incomplete without contiguous Kashmir. In brief, Kashmir is a target of externally sponsored religion-based terrorism. The aim is to divide people on the basis of sectarian affiliation and undermine/weaken the secular fabric and territorial integrity of India.

However, now with the passage of time, the passion of the Jehad/movement which once had the mass public support has started declining since it has turned out to be a movement run by those who are more interested in their own personal gains. Confusion within the separatist groups too has weakened the movement. The hard liners led by Jamat-e-Islami advocate total merger of Jammu and Kashmir, with Pakistan whereas the soft liners led by J.K.L.F (Jammu and Kashmir Liberation Front) stands for total independence of J&K. This has given rise to a totally confusing and conflicting situation resulting in disillusionment, disarray and disinterest of the common man in Kashmir who has suffered a lot for the past 18 years and is not prepared to suffer any more.

Major issues faced by the Hindus in Kashmir, who suffered the process of ethnic extermination for having opposed the Muslim secessionist movements in the State, arise out of several political commitments, which have dominated the developments in Jammu and Kashmir. In the first place, a Muslim separatist movement has been in progress from the time of the accession of the State with India in 1947.

Secondly, another Muslim movement, which has largely drawn its inspiration and support from the Islamic secessionism in the State, has been going on in the State, which has supported a separate and independent political organisation of the State on the territories of India but outside the political organisation, almost in a state of equidistance from India and Pakistan. Thirdly, the entire political development in the State during the last five decades has followed a process of reorganisation of its government, society and economy so as to ensure its Islamisation.

BASIC ISSUES

The basic issues involved in the crisis in Jammu and Kashmir are mainly those which arise out of the irreconciliability of the Islamisation movement of the State with the secular, political organisation of India, which enshrines the basic principles of equality and rule of law. These issues were basic to the partition of India and are basic to the crisis that has engulfed the State from 1989, due to the militarisation of Muslim communalism.

The terrorist violence in Jammu and Kashmir is the culmination of the secessionist movements, going on in the State during the last five decades. It is politically motivated to bring about the secession of the State from India and unite it with Pakistan. Let us face the bitter truth and refuse to be hoodwinked by interested quarters, many of which are in the Government of India as well, and which have sought to camouflage the Muslim secessionism in Kashmir to provide cover to its real objectives.

Pleas of alienation, erosion of autonomy, exclusion of Muslims from political participation and economic deprivation have been used to conceal the real character of Muslim separatism and communalism in Kashmir. The Muslim unrest in the State, the so-called struggle for self-rule, autonomy and separate identity of Kashmiriyat, are political movements, which are fundamentally communal in character, aimed at the Islamisation of the State and its ultimate disengagement from the Indian Union, at a time when the Muslims in the State, supported by Pakistan and other Muslim countries, find it possible to defeat India.

UNACCEPTED FALSEHOOD

We have lived in Kashmir in the last five decades of Indian freedom and are perhaps the only witnesses of what has been wrought in the State by Muslims secessionist forces and the successive state governments, with the passive acquiescence of the Government of India. We cannot, in the interest of our nation and in the interest of history, accept lies and falsehoods as the truth, for that may not only harm our community but also our country and earn us the calumny of having failed in our duty unto our country.

The terrorist flanks waging war against India claim the divine right to complete the partition of India, which, according to them, was left unfinished in 1947, because of the accession of the State to India. The secession of Jammu and Kashmir from India and its unification with Pakistan will extend the Muslim power over the traditional northern frontier of India. Flanked by Afghanistan in the east and Central Asia in the north and China in the west, Pakistan would assume a factoral importance in the configuration of power in Asia. Using the ideological and military support received from militarised pan- Islamic fundamentalism, Pakistan would inevitably force a further division on India. The violence in Kashmir has three major dimensions:

1. The Muslim militancy in Kashmir with its transnational dimensions;
2. Its commitment to the Islamisation of the government and society of the State; and

3. The terrorist regimes operating in Kashmir and the Muslim crusade are communal, fundamentalist and separatist in their content. The ethnic extermination of Hindus in Kashmir is a part of the basic scheme of communalisation and fundamentalisation of the State.

CREATION OF PAKISTAN

The creation of Pakistan in 1947 was a landmark in the struggle for the unification of the Muslim Umma and ever since Pakistan was created, it has followed a sustained policy of thrust for expansion towards the east as a major strategy to spread across Jammu and Kashmir and take the Muslim power to the dominant Muslim regions of Central Asia, Mongolia and Sinkiang. The terrorist violence in Jammu and Kashmir is a continuation of the consolidation of pan-Islamic unity, of which the creation of Pakistan was a part. Pakistan claimed Jammu and Kashmir on the basis of the Muslim majority of its population and while terrorism raged in Kashmir, it demanded that India be divided again to carry the partition to its logical conclusion by ceding the State to Pakistan.

The questions that immediately arise are: how is the restoration of the 1952 status relevant to the war of attrition raging in the State? How far will the exclusion of the State from the constitutional structure of India go to meet the Muslim movement for secession of the State from India? Are the militarised secessionist forces prepared to accept the exclusion of the State from the constitutional framework of India as a basis to lay down their arms? How far is Pakistan prepared to accept the exclusion of the State from the constitutional organisation of India as a basis for a settlement on Kashmir?

Evidently, the exclusion of the State from the Indian constitutional framework will not be acceptable to the secessionist military flanks as a basis for a settlement, leaving them free to carry on the war of attrition in the State against India and the Hindus. It will only serve the purpose of carrying the State almost into the no-man's land between India and Pakistan, which would then be exposed to greater pulls from Pakistan. With the terrorist violence continuing unabated inside the State, pressure would be mounted on India to accept the exclusion of the State from the territories of the Indian Union and its defence parameters. Perhaps, the National Conference leadership in the State would, at that time, again intervene and bring round India to accept a position of equidistance for the State from both India as well as Pakistan.

REGIONAL AUTONOMY

The proposals to lend regional autonomy to Jammu and Ladakh would ultimately lead to the division of the Jammu Province into the Muslim- majority region and the Hindu-majority region and, in Ladakh, the separation of the Muslim-majority district of Kargil, already accomplished by the grant of Hill Council to it. With the process of the elimination of the Hindus from the Muslim-majority regions of the State, already completed in the Kashmir Province, the whole region situated west of the Chenab would be formed into a separate Muslim political organisation on the basis of a modified form of the Dixon Plan which was proposed for the settlement of the Kashmir dispute in 1950.

Once the State is disengaged from India, the pro-Pakistan Muslim forces would push into Pakistan earlier than anticipated and the National Conference would eventually be prepared to reach a settlement with Pakistan on the separate political identity of the Muslim-majority regions of the State in which would be included the Pakistan-occupied territories of Kashmir within the territorial jurisdiction of Pakistan but outside its political structure.

The Hindus and other minorities - the Buddhists as well as the Sikhs - oppose the exclusion of the State from the Indian constitutional framework for the following reasons:

- Exclusion of Jammu and Kashmir from the constitutional structure of India would ultimately lead to strengthening of secessionist forces in the State and increase the chances of international intervention;
- The process of Islamisation of the State, which was the net outcome of the so-called autonomy of the State, had

provided enough ground for the fundamentalisation of the State and would lead to sharpening of Muslim separatism;

- Islamisation of the State and the enforcement of Muslim precedence in society, the government and its economy had subjected the Hindus to the servitude of Muslim authority; and
- The exclusion of the State from the Indian constitutional framework on the basis of the Muslim- majority character of its population implied that a Muslim-majority state is a Muslim State and, therefore, it cannot form part of the secular constitutional framework of India. The demand for a separate Muslim State of Jammu and Kashmir, which the 1952 status underlines, resembles closely the Muslim League demand for Pakistan. The basic issue is the creation of a Muslim State, which is no more a part of India.

ABANDONMENT OF SECULAR NORMS

After the accession of the State to the Indian Dominion in October 1947, the Government of the Jammu and Kashmir State was reconstituted to give effect to the transfer of power to the people in accordance with the practice followed by the Government of India in the princely States. The transfer of power in the State was aimed at ending the rigours of the princely rule and ensures the exercise of authority in accordance with the democratic process and the acceptance of administrative responsibility. However, the transfer of power in the State assumed a different direction.

No sooner did the National Conference leaders constitute the first Interim Government than they abandoned their commitments to all secular norms and set out to reorganise the State on the basis of communal precedence of the Muslim majority. The rapid transformation of the whole economic organisation of the State, which upturned the property classification which the Dogra rulers had established and which the Interim Government accomplished ostensibly to eliminate exploitation and poverty, led directly to the emergence of a new Muslim middle class, which in the years to come formed the mainstay of the Muslim separatist movements in the State.

The first Interim Government secured the exclusion of the State from the constitutional structure of India mainly to secure the social, political and economic interests of the Muslim majority in the State. In their parleys with the Indian leaders, these leaders insisted upon the setting up of a separate Constituent Assembly for the State which would formulate a separate constitutional framework and sets of political imperatives to safeguard the basic rights of the people in the State, independent of the fundamental rights which the Constituent Assembly of India had evolved.

PROTECTION OF MINORITIES

More particularly, the National Conference leaders vehemently opposed the acceptance of all rights to equality and protection of minorities, which the Constitution of India envisaged on the ground that such rights conflicted with the economic reforms which the Interim Government had undertaken. The Interim Government secured the abdication of Maharaja Hari Singh and later did not take long in assuming total control over the authority of the State. In less than a year, the Hindus were eliminated from the economic structure of the State, its government and administration.

Sheikh Mohammad Abdullah, the Prime Minister in the Interim Government, headed the Auqaf-Islamia, the Muslim endowment trust, but demanded the dissolution of the Dharmarth, the Hindu endowment trust which the Dogra rulers had established. The Interim Government forged new Muslim ruling elite, which rules the State in the decades which followed, relegating the Hindus to a condition of abject servitude. The Interim Government packed the State Constituent Assembly with Muslims, 73 of its 75 members were returned unopposed, and the remaining two seats in the Assembly were also bagged by the National Conference after their opponents were driven out of the contest. In the Assembly, around three-fourths of the members were Muslims.

The whole delimitation of the constituencies was based upon disproportionate distribution of population, ensuring the Muslim-majority province of Kashmir a heavier weightage than the Hindu-majority province of Jammu. When Sheikh Abdullah denounced the Delhi Agreement in 1953 and demanded the separation of the State from the territorial jurisdiction of the Union of India, the handful of the Hindu members in the Assembly stood against him and supported the second Interim Government headed by Bakshi Ghulam Mohammad, for a fairly high price, which was paid only at the cost of the Hindus.

PROCESS OF ELIMINATION

Bakshi Ghulam Mohammad also did not end the Muslim precedence in the government and society of the State and, in spite of the partial application of the fundamental rights as envisaged by the Constitution of India to Jammu and Kashmir, the process of the elimination of the Hindus from the political and economic organisation of the State continued unabated. He too continued to head the Auqaf-Islamia. After the State Constituent Assembly completed its labours and a separate Constitution was promulgated in the State in 1957, Bakshi Ghulam Mohammad packed the first Legislative Assembly on the basis of the constituencies delimited for elections to the Constituent Assembly.

The Muslims of the State were ensured perpetual heavier weightage in the elections to the State legislature than the people in Jammu and Ladakh. During the last four decades, legislative assemblies were predominantly Muslim. The demand of the Hindus of Jammu for a review of the delimitation and the four-decade-long struggle of the three lakh Hindu and Sikh refugees who had come to the State from the Pakistan-controlled parts in the aftermath of the partition holocaust, for the citizenship of the State, was never met.

The scourge of Muslim precedence spread still wider. Not only were legislative bodies and the political instruments dominantly Muslim, the entire administrative organisation was also Islamised rapidly within days after the Interim Government was saddled in office. The rapid process of summary removal of the Hindus from State services was initiated on the pretext of communal imbalances in the services, which the Conference leaders said characterised the administrative structure of the State. The allegations were baseless. Glaring imbalances characterised the administration of the State but these imbalances were not communal in character.

The State was virtually governed by the British and their officers in the Indian Political Department, who were posted in the State to conduct its administration. The Dogra ruling elite was not Hindu; it was constituted of the small agrarian middle class, which was equally Muslim. The services of the State were dominated by the British and the men of the Indian Civil Services, besides the clansmen of the ruling dynasty and a section of the Dogra ruling elite, almost half of which was constituted by the Muslims.

The ranks of the State army were divided in a ratio of 55 per cent Hindu and 45 per cent Muslim, mostly drawn from the non-Kashmiri- speaking subjects of the Dogra rulers. The Hindus of Kashmir and Jammu, who had taken to English education far ahead of their Muslim compatriots, were employed in subordinate services on petty posts and they licked the mud for the Raj as well as the British Empire.

POLITICAL ADVENTURISTS

The Interim Government removed the senior Hindu officers from the State services on charges of having supported the Dogra rule, replacing them by the henchmen of the National Conference and political adventurists. A virtual embargo was imposed on the employment of the Hindus of Kashmir in the State services, avowedly to rectify the alleged communal imbalances but in reality to Islamise the various instruments of authority as well as the lines of its control.

The partial application of the Indian Constitution in 1954 and the promulgation of the separate Constitution of Jammu and Kashmir in January 1957, upheld the precedence of the

Muslim majority. The application of the fundamental rights envisaged by the Constitution of India to the State, by virtue of the Presidential Order of May 1954, was restricted by numerous exceptions and reservations. This armed the State Government with arbitrary powers to effect reservations for the classified sections of permanent residents of the State, which the successive State Governments used ruthlessly to promote Muslim interests.

The following facts reveal the extent of dominance and precedence of the Muslims, particularly the Muslims of Kashmir, enjoyed in the governance and politics of the State:

a. The imbalances in the delimitation of constituencies in the two provinces of Jammu and Kashmir and the exclusion of two-and-a-half lakh Hindu refugees, living in the State from 1947, from permanent residence in the State, was mainly aimed at reducing the weightage of the Hindus in the legislative processes of the State, ensuring a three-fourth majority for the Muslims in the State legislature. The Hindu representation was maintained at an average 30 per cent of the seats in the Legislative Assembly. The entire refugee population was deprived of any sort of representation in the local bodies. In the delimitation of the electoral constituencies, gerrymandering was meticulously used to neutralise the decisive Hindu and Sikh weightage in, at least, three constituencies viz; Habbakadal, Anantnag and Bramulla in the Kashmir province and three constituencies in the districts of Doda and Udhampur.

Consequently in Kashmir, the Hindus and the Sikhs did not have even a single non-Muslim majority constituency, wherefrom a representative of their choice could be elected to the Legislative Assembly. Generally, the Hindus and other non- Muslim representatives, elected to the Legislative Assembly from Kashmir, were mercenaries and men of small virtue, who never enjoyed the confidence of their communities.

The records of the proceedings of the Legislative Assembly reveal how the Hindu representatives supported the legislation aimed at excluding Hindus and other minorities from the administrative set-up of the State Government and its political function and impose limitations on their entry to the educational institutions of the State.

When a controversy raged over the passage of the Resettlement Bill, which the National Conference Government headed by Sheikh Abdullah, introduced in the Assembly, to open the floodgates for the re-entry into the State, of the Muslims from Pakistan and the Pakistan-occupied territories, the Hindu representatives did not voice their disapproval of the Bill, which they were repeatedly told would prove disastrous for the State. None of the Hindu legislators, except those from Jammu, who were elected by the opposition, raised the issue of the thousands of Hindu refugees uprooted from the territories of the Kashmir province occupied by Pakistan;

b. Right from 1947, the Muslims adorned the office of the highest political executive of the State. The four Prime Ministers of the State, who headed the political executive till 1965, were Muslims and the six Chief Ministers of the Congress and the National Conference Governments, who followed, were also Muslims. In the Council of Ministers, during the last four-and-a-half decades, the Hindus Buddhists and other minorities held an average of 26 per cent of the ministerial of fices, the rest being held by the Muslims;

c. In the decision-making clusters of various political party organisations, including the National Conference and the Congress, which ruled the State during the last four decades, the Hindus of Kashmir were always left unrepresented;

d. The maximum parliamentary patronage was appropriated by the Muslims of Kashmir and the Muslims in the Jammu province to the disadvantage of the Hindus;

e. In the decision-making bodies of the State administration, the representation of the Hindus was always negligible. Almost all the Heads of the Departments in the administration of Kashmir were Muslims. An unwritten instrument of instruction operated to eliminate the Hindus from various decision-making bodies and Muslims governed the appointment of the heads of the administrative divisions and staff agencies. An average of less than 26 per cent, including the officers of the Government of India on deputation in the State, and the officers of Indian Administrative Services were Hindus;

f. In the administrative structure of the State, the Hindus of Kashmir, with 88 per cent literacy, shared an average of 4.8 per cent of the State services, including the services in the public enterprises, corporations and government undertakings;

g. In the services of the Central Government, including the Jammu and Kashmir Bank, the services of corporate undertakings of the Central Government, the defence services, the Beacon organisation and the communication system of the Central Government, the Kashmiri Hindus shared only 12 per cent of the available employment, whereas the Kashmiri Muslims shared 38 per cent.

RECRUITMENT OF HINDUS

During 1980 to 1990, when Muslim fundamentalist movements assumed ascendance and the secessionist forces tightened their hold on the administrative organisation of the State, the recruitment of Kashmiri Hindus to the State Services and services in other corporate bodies was reduced to an average of 1.7 per cent. Several government orders blatantly communal were struck down by the State High Court and the Supreme Court. But ways and means were devised by the State Government to circumvent these judicial decisions to enforce the exclusion of Kashmiri Hindus from employment which otherwise was their due.

The embargo on the recruitment of Kashmiri Hindus was extended to the teaching staff of the higher secondary schools, colleges and post-graduate departments of the University of Kashmir as well as the Agricultural University, the Medical College, the Engineering College and the Institute of Medical Sciences in spite of the fact that the Hindus possessed not only adequate but higher qualifications and professional excellence. The elimination of Hindus from all political processes and functions in Kashmir was extended to their admission to educational institutions in the State and grant of scholarships and nomination for training and higher studies outside the State.

During the last 50 years the admissions of Kashmiri Hindus to various academic institutions and institutions of higher learning were restricted to an average of 8 per cent of the total admissions made every year. Though the Kashmiri Hindus constituted more than 8 per cent of population in the province, a bare 2 per cent was awarded nominations and State grants for higher studies and training outside the State.

Communal government orders were issued from time to time, implementing classification undertaken by the State legislature of define socially and educationally backward classes to ensure for the Muslims a wider reservation for admissions to the educational institutions. Many of these orders were struck down by the highest courts. Undeterred by the severe censure by these Courts, the State government refused to change its policy and the scourge of reservations continued to ravage the Hindus.

The data regarding admission of Hindus to the technical colleges, training courses and post graduate classes in Kashmir during the last 50 years shows that they were subject to gross discrimination in spite of the meritorious grades secured in their qualifying board and university examinations. On an average, only 7 per cent of the Hindus were admitted to technical colleges, though 63 per cent of the Hindu applicants possessed a first class grade or more, whereas 76 per cent of the Muslim candidates were admitted to the technical colleges, though only 31 per cent of them possessed first class qualifications.

ADMISSION TO TECHNICAL INSTITUTES

In the admissions to the technical training colleges, 12 per cent of Hindu candidates were admitted though 66 per cent of Hindu applicants possessed a first class. On the other hand, 82 per cent of the Muslims were admitted to these technical colleges though only 28 per cent of them possessed first class. In the admissions to the post-graduate courses, only 14 per cent of the Hindu candidates were admitted though 41 per cent of them obtained first class whereas 78 per cent of Muslim candidates were admitted to the post-graduate classes, though only 14 per cent of them secured first class.

We Hindus cannot retrieve these and other losses we suffered from the holocaust of invasions and massacres when we were reduced to the proverbial households. Later, these carnages turned into sustained acts of economic deprivation and ethnic cleansing until in 1990 we were forced to flee our homes and remain in exile ever since. Now Dr. Farooq Abdullah is propagating his invitation to Hindus to return home despite selective ethnic killings at Sangrampora in Kashmir and at Gool in Jammu.

The future of the displaced Hindu community in Jammu and Kashmir will depend upon:

How soon, and at what price, the militant violence is curbed completely and peace is restored in the State, a responsibility, which primarily rests on the Government of India?

How is the future constitutional set-up between Jammu and Kashmir shaped, and the rights and their protection guaranteed under the Constitution of India to all minorities, ensured for the Hindus in Kashmir, who have been reduced to a state of slavery in a Muslim State under the cover of special status, proposed autonomy and Article 370?

How effective will be the process to reverse the policy of Islamisation of the State, which has been in operation during the last four decades?

What constitutional instrumentalities are evolved to ensure the right of equality, the right to religious faith and the right to protection against persecution and protection against Muslim communalism for the Hindus in Kashmir?

SECURITY AFTER RETURN

The future of the Hindus of Kashmir, their return to their homes, their right to security of life and property and freedom of faith must be visualised in terms of a settlement of the communal problem. There should be no doubt the return of the community of Hindus to their homes in Kashmir, where it actually belongs, and where its temples are the mother of their culture and of their history.

The ethnic cleansing of the Hindus from Kashmir, a part of the gameplan to change the demographic composition of the Kashmir province, cannot be accepted as a fact, allowed to have been accomplished by the Muslims, with the connivance of the State government and the Government of India. The Government of India is trying to woo the terrorists and the separatists, in the garb of autonomists, as well as Pakistan to buy peace from anyone of them mainly because of its inability to read the real character of Muslim communalism.

The government of India is dragging its feet, because the terrorists are Muslim, the separatists are Muslim and Pakistan is Muslim. Would it ever be possible for India to blsy peace, while the terrorists are on the rampage, the separatists are preparing to disengage the State from the constitutional framework of India and Pakistan is sparing no efforts to foist a second partition on India? Yes! if the Government of India agrees to accept the secession of Jammu and Kashmir from India and its merger with Pakistan, on the same principles which formed the basis of the partition of India in 1947.

The return of the Kashmiri Pandits, therefore, depends upon:

- The final resolution of the militant violence in Kashmir.
- The determination of the Indian State not to accept any settlement, which disengages the State from the Indian Union.

So long as the state of widespread violence in Kashmir is not brought to an end, the Hindu community of Kashmir, which was flushed out of Kashmir on the point of the gun, will not be able to return, to be used as cannon-fodder in a war, which is not fought by the State government and the Government of India to defeat Muslim communalism and separatism. The Hindus cannot be exposed a second time to gunfire from an enemy who is prowling in the neighbourhood and who is masquerading as the saviour of secularism. The Hindus could but they will not return to face the rigours of a war and the scourge of treachery.

PROTECTION OF RIGHTS

The return of the Kashmiri Hindus will also depend upon:

- The guarantee the community is given of protection of all rights and due process of law, which it has been denied during the last five decades;
- The guarantee against the Islamisation of the State, its society and its government to ensure the community the right to freedom of faith;
- To safeguards against communal persecution, economic deprivation and political isolation to which the Hindus have been subjected to in the name of local autonomy, secularism and Kashmiryat.

JAMMU AND KASHMIR ASSESSMENT

Jammu and Kashmir (J&K), the theatre of a raging high intensity conflict (more than 1,000 fatalities per annum) between 1990 and 2006, saw a continuation of declining trends in fatalities and a second consecutive year within the low intensity threshold. 541 persons, including 69 civilians, 90 Security Force (SF) personnel and 382 militants, were killed in 2008. Fatalities had fallen to 777, well below the high intensity mark, in 2007, from a peak in 2001, at 4,507. J&K has witnessed continuously declining violence since 9/11, bringing tremendous respite to the people of this terror-wracked State.

In its year-end review, the Union Home Ministry stated that, during 2008 (data till November), terrorist incidents in J&K were down by 39 per cent, killings of civilians by 41 per cent and of SFs by 31 per cent, over the corresponding period of 2007. The level of infiltration across the Line of Control/ International Border also saw a decline and, for the first time since 1990, the number of militancy-related incidents, according to J&K Police data, dropped below the four-figure mark to approximately 703 in 2008. The J&K Director General of Police (DGP), Kuldeep Khoda, stated on December 25, 2008, that the year witnessed an exceptional decrease of 40 per cent in militancy-related incidents compared to 2007, the largest such decline since 1990.

The highest number of militancy-related incidents stood at 5,946 in 1995.

	2006	2007	2008 (till December 23)
Incidents	1667	1092	703
Civilians killed	387	164	89
Police personnel killed	49	18	10
VDCs/SPOs* killed	31	12	10
SF personnel killed	102	92	65

Comparative Fatalities in J&K, 2001-2008

Year	Civilians	SF Personnel	Terrorist	Total
2001	1067	590	2850	4507
2002	839	469	1714	3022
2003	658	338	1546	2542
2004	534	325	951	1810
2005	520	216	996	1732
2006	349	168	599	1116
2007	164	121	492	777
2008	69	90	382	541

Source: *South Asia Terrorism Portal* database

The diminution in violence was further underlined by the fact that civilian casualties, at 89 in 2008, fell below the 100 mark for the first time since 1990. Even SF fatalities stood at 85.

382 militants were killed in counter-terrorism operations across J&K in 2008, including some top ranking commanders. These included at least 67 category 'A' terrorists, and 27 category 'B' terrorists.

	"A"	"B"	"C"	Total
Kashmir Zone	43	17	04	64
Jammu Zone	24	10	04	38
Total	67	27	8	102

Source: Jammu and Kashmir Police

More than 30 commanders of the *Lashkar-e-Toiba* (LeT) and 22 of the Hizb-ul-*Mujahideen* (HM) were killed in the year under review. Among the top militant leaders killed in 2008 was Bashir Ahmed Mir, 'commander-in-chief' for operations across India of the *Harkat-ul-Jihad-al-Islami* (HuJI); Hafiz Naasir, Kashmir Valley chief of the LeT; Sajjad Afghani, the J&K chief of HuM; Qari Usman, a LeT 'divisional commander'; Zahoor Ahmad Waza alias Zeeshan, 'financial chief' of the HM; Abdul Haq alias Jahangir, 'battalion commander' and 'financial chief' of the HM; Ghulam Hussain Wani aka Shameem Thool aka Shameem Shahid, a HM 'divisional commander'; Najeebullah alias Doctor, 'divisional commander' of the Harkat-ul-*Mujahideen* (HuM); Abu Khubaib, 'launching commander' of the LeT; and Barkatullah Ansari aka Hyder, a 'divisional commander' of the *Jaish-e-Mohammed* (JeM). During 2007, eighty seven terrorist leaders were neutralized across the State.

Steps initiated to check infiltration from across the border have had significant success. For the first time since 1990, the number of militants operating in J&K is estimated to have fallen below 1000. On December 24, 2008, DGP Khoda told reporters at the year-end briefing on the security situation in the State, "There are around 577 local militants and 231 foreigners operating in the State. These are figures based on information from various agencies working on the ground... The measures taken along the Line of Control and International Border have resulted in lesser number of militants infiltrating into the State. There have been casualties among the infiltrators which mean the efficiency in preventing infiltration has improved."

Attempts to strengthen political and civic participation in governance received a noteworthy boost in the Legislative Assembly elections, which were held in seven phases in November-December 2008. A record number of 1,353 candidates contested from 87 Assembly constituencies in 2008 as against 709 in 2002 and 547 earlier in 1996. For the first time since the beginnings of terrorism in the State, 4,277 political/ public meetings were held by various parties, 2,281 in Kashmir and 1,996 in Jammu, including 1,115 small, 2,516 medium and 646 large meetings. A comprehensive decrease of 86 per cent was registered in militancy-related incidents during the elections in 2008, as compared to the 2002 Assembly elections. About 1,000 militancy-related incidents were reported during the 2002 elections, as against just 145 in the 2008 elections.

Similarly, a 95 per cent decrease was noticed in civilian killings during the elections - 220 in 2002 and 12 killings in 2008. Further, no political office bearer was killed during the elections in 2008, as against 48 in 2002. In fact, during year 2008, only three political activists were killed as against 101 through 2002. 148 SF personnel were killed during the 2002 elections, but only five such killings were reported in 2008. The overall improvement in the ground situation was dramatically reflected in a voter turnout averaging 63 per cent during the seven phases of the 2008 elections, as compared to 43.6 per cent in the 2002 elections, which were held under the shadow of the gun.

Significantly, all terrorist groups and their sympathetic and front organizations, including factions of the Hurriyat Conference [the All Parties Hurriyat Conference (APHC) and the Tehreek-e-Hurriyat (TeH)] had announced a boycott of the elections and issued threats of retaliation against those who participated, but these were, evidently, rebuffed by a public long weary of extremist excesses and endless strife. The National Conference (NC) emerged the single largest party in the elections, securing 28 seats (20 in Kashmir, six in Jammu and two in Kargil), while the People's Democratic Party (PDP) was second with 21 seats (19 in Kashmir and 2 in Jammu). The Congress party was victorious in 17 seats (13 from Jammu region, three from Kashmir and one from Leh), while the Bharatiya Janata Party (BJP) prevailed in 11 constituencies.

The National Panthers Party won three seats and the Communist Party of India-Marxist, the People's Democratic Front and the Democratic Party (Nationalist) secured one each. Independents won in four constituencies. Forty-four seats constitute a mark in the 87-strong House. The NC leader Omar Abdullah assumed office as the new Chief Minister of J&K, with the Congress extending support to his party and joining the Government. The success of the elections also needs to be assessed against the backdrop of the extended Shri Amarnath land agitation which had virtually paralysed and apparently polarized J&K through July-August 2008, and which had, at one point, raised a question-mark over the very possibility of the elections being held on schedule.

The agitation impacted dramatically on both sides of the Pir Panchal and led to the deaths of at least 51 civilians (Kashmir - 42; Jammu - 9) and injuries to another 1,473 (Kashmir - 979; Jammu - 494). 333 SF personnel were also injured during the 62-day agitation (Jammu - 182; Kashmir - 151). Apart from the socio-political impact of the agitation, which is bound to linger for some time, there were serious economic costs incurred before order was restored. The Chamber of Commerce and Industry (CCI) president Ram Sahai claimed in Jammu on September 1, 2008, that the economy of the Jammu region had suffered a loss of INR 9,980 crore during agitation. Sahai said the industrial and tourism sectors were affected the most during the turmoil.

He pegged the losses to the tourism trade (hotels, lodges, restaurants, cinemas) sector at INR 3,050 crore and of the industrial sector at INR 4,050 crore. J&K also saw increasing tensions along the Line of Control (LoC) and international border. Defence Minister A. K. Antony informed the Parliament on October 20, 2008, that, "Pakistan had violated the five-year-old pact on ceasefire 58 times since the ceasefire agreement came into effect from November 2003. And since January 2008, Indian positions on the LoC have been fired upon 34 times, while the total cease-fire violation by Pakistan has occurred on 58 counts." He, however, indicated that ingress across the LoC/border was decreasing: "Infiltration bids in Jammu and Kashmir from across the International Border are on decline, today. There were only 243 infiltrators during April to September 2008 as against 419 infiltrators during the same period last year. During the current year, 193 terrorists were killed while 157 were arrested in the same period this year. A multi-tier arrangement, including deployment of troops, surveillance devices, Line of Control fence, State and Central security forces, has proved effective in discouraging infiltrators."

On a more general level, the secular decline in violence witnessed since September 2001 can be attributed to Pakistan's compulsions arising out of its domestic difficulties, the American and international pressure on Islamabad, and the continuing successes of the counter-insurgency grid in J&K. Diminished violence, however, does not indicate a necessary decline in the capacity for terrorism, and there are clear indications that the infrastructure that supports and sustains the Kashmir jihad remains intact in Pakistan, despite the recent crackdown in that country. Lt. Gen. P.C. Bhardwaj, the General Officer Commanding-in-Chief of the Northern Command, told reporters on January 15, 2009, that "a number of terrorists training camps are still active in Pakistan."

While the exact present number of these camps is not available, official sources had disclosed in September 2008 that there were 45 such camps. Notwithstanding the recent crackdown on the LeT and its front the Jama'at-ud-Da'awa (JuD), sources indicate there are currently at least 1,500 militants waiting at mobile and temporary launch pads for an 'opportunity' to infiltrate into J&K. These militants have reportedly been divided into small groups (each comprising of 75-80 men) and have been kept, in readiness, across the Line of Control/International Border. Reports also indicate that the Inter-Services Intelligence (ISI), Pakistan's external intelligence agency, is training women to carry out militant attacks. During interrogation of a woman arrested in the State during the first week of January 2009 by the J&K Police for providing logistical support for JeM and LeT militants, it was disclosed that the ISI is inducting women into militancy.

The arrested woman reportedly confessed that she was trained by the ISI in the Bhiber and Kotli forests in Pakistan occupied Kashmir (PoK), and that there were presently about 700 women receiving arms training in different militant camps run by the ISI. The unstable domestic scenario in Pakistan has impacted significantly on the Kashmir jihad, though it has not yet led to any change in the establishment's intent or the infrastructure that supports and orchestrates terrorist violence on Indian soil. There is, nonetheless, a definite pause, and a shift within J&K, with Islamabad increasingly attempting to nurture a cohesive political voice in its favour.

To this end, efforts are directed towards uniting various pro-Pakistan groups, including the two factions of the main secessionist formation, the APHC. The objective appears to be to gradually transform the predominantly terrorist movement into a more wide-based movement of political extremism, backed by calibrated terrorist operations, to secure a stronger position at the negotiating table and achieve what has not been possible on the ground through terrorism alone. Crucially, the decrease in levels of violence in J&K is not due to any change in Pakistani intent, but is rather the consequence of "changes in capacities and compulsions in Pakistan."

The multiplicity of crises in Pakistan has diluted Islamabad's capacities to sustain past levels of terrorism in J&K, particularly since a large proportion of troops had to be pulled back from the Line of Control (LoC) and the international border for deployment in increasingly violent theatres in Balochistan, NWFP [North West Frontier Province] and the FATA [Federally Administered Tribal Areas]... Pakistan's creeping implosion has undermined the establishment's capabilities to sustain the 'proxy war' against India at earlier levels.

Another important element in the decrease in violence in J&K is the progressive shift in the terrorists' focus to the Indian heartland. 336 civilians and 27 SF personnel died in Pakistan-backed Islamist terrorist attacks outside J&K in 2008 in locations as varied as Bangalore, Rampur, Jaipur, New Delhi, Ahmedabad and Mumbai - attacks engineered principally by terrorists groups that were earlier limited in their campaigns to J&K. In significant contrast, 69 civilians died in the whole of J&K through 2008. In the immediate future, it is anticipated that Pakistan-based terrorist groups will continue to sustain calibrated levels of violence in J&K and simultaneously carry out terrorist attacks on soft targets in the Indian heartland. Such a shift offers Pakistan greater 'deniability', and also enables it to harness the grievances - real or perceived - among Indian Muslims.

Pakistan's intentions, notwithstanding a change in regime and international pressure, remain unchanged as far as the Kashmir jihad is concerned. The only noticeable shift is in strategy and tactics. Crucially, Pakistan's Islamist terrorist reserves remain intact. In fact, no Islamist terrorist group, including those focusing on Kashmir, has been effectively neutralized in Pakistan since 9/11. As radical Islamist mobilization and a belligerent posture on Kashmir remain integral to Pakistan's internal politics - both for the 'democratic' parties and the Army - consequently, regardless of the significant and continuing decline in terrorist violence in the State, a stable peace still remains a distant prospect in J&K.

5

Impact of Terrorism on JK Tourism

TOURISM IN JAMMU AND KASHMIR

Jammu and Kashmir, India's fascinating northernmost state consists of three regions differing in topography and culture. Jammu was the stronghold of Hindu Dogra kings and abounds with popular temples and secluded forest retreats. Kashmir's capital city, Srinagar offers delightful holidays on the lakes with their shikaras and houseboats. Ladakh is the northern most province of the state, with a bleak terrain of barren mountains. Hilltop monasteries and a colourful way of life, completely at one with the surroundings, make Ladakh one of the best living traditions of Tibetan Buddhism in the world today.

Amongst the three regions of Jammu & Kashmir State, Jammu, perhaps, offers the widest diversity of terrain and beauty. The entire region is pocketed with lakes and valleys, some still little explored. The foundation of the settlement of Jammu is attributed to King Jambulochan of the 9th century BC. In 1730 AD, it came under the Dogra rule of Raja Dhruv Deva and Jammu became an important centre for arts and culture, now renwned as the Pahari School. Religion, too, played an important part in its development, so beautifully evidenced in its various shrines and temples spread throughout the region.

Jammu and Kashmir, India is known as heaven on earth. In the seventeenth century the Mughal emperor Jahangir set his eyes on the valley of Kashmir. He said that if paradise is anywhere on the earth, it is here, while living in a houseboat on the mesmerizing Dal Lake. In Jammu and Kashmir the most important tourist places are Kashmir, Srinagar, the Mughal Gardens, Gulmarg, Pahalgam, Jammu, and Ladakh. Some areas require a special permit for non-Indians to visit.

IN KASHMIR VALLEY

Srinagar - Capital of Jammu and Kashmir:

Dal Lake - famous lake in Srinagar, with house boats called shikharas.

Manasbal Lake

Shalimar Gardens

Nishant Gardens

Gulmarg - popular hill station.

Pahalgam - scenic valley

Sonamarg - tourist resort.

Amarnath temple - pilgrimage site for Hindu devotees of Lord Shiva.

Eco-tourism places: Gurex, Dudhpathri, Bangus valley

In Jammu:

Vaishno Devi - famous shrine

Poonch

Patnitop - hill station

Sanasar

Eco-tourism places: Mantalai and Shivkhori

Punj old fort

Bhaderwah

Shahdra Sharif shrine

Bhimgarh Fort

In Ladakh:

Ladakh, a word which means "land of high passes", is a region in the state of Jammu and Kashmir of Northern India sandwiched between the Karakoram mountain range to the north and the Himalayas to the south. The Indian portion of Ladakh is composed of the Leh and Kargil districts. The Leh district is the largest district of India, covering more than half the area of Jammu and Kashmir, of which it is the eastern part.

Adventure tourism in Ladakh started in the 19th century. By the turn of the 20th century, it was not uncommon for British officials to undertake the 14 stage trek from Srinagar to Leh as part of their annual leave. Agencies were set up in Srinagar and Shimla to specialise sport related activities - hunting, fishing and trekking. A large retinue of porters would carry huge canvas tents and collapsible string beds.

This era is recorded in Arthur Neves *The Tourist's Guide to Kashmir, Ladakh and Skardo,* first published in 1911. Today, about 18,000 tourists visit Ladakh every year. Bounded by two mighty mountain ranges, it is a popular place for adventure tourism. The well-preserved Tibetan-Buddhist culture makes it even more attractive. The main corridors for accessing the area are the Zoji-La Pass and Kargil route from Srinagar in the Kashmir Valley, and the high altitude Manali-Leh Highway from Himachal Pradesh. The Manali-Leh road is open only from May to October or November, when snow is cleared from the several passes.

The Srinagar-Leh road is open from April or May to November or December, and is generally only blocked by snow through the winter at Zoji-La Pass. There is one airport, situated at Leh, from which there are multiple daily flights to Delhi on Jet Airways and Indian, and weekly flights to Srinagar. Buses run from Leh to the surrounding villages, and taxis are available. Trucks often stop for hitchhikers, who are usually expected to pay half the bus fare.

There is a bit less than 1000 km of paved roads in Ladakh. The Manali-Leh-Srinagar road makes up about half of that, the remainder being spurs off it. For the traveler with a number of months it is possible to trek from one end of Ladakh to the other, or even from places in Himachal Pradesh. The large number of trails and the limited number of roads allows one to string together routes that have road access often enough to restock supplies, but avoid walking on motor roads almost entirely.

Among the popular places of tourist interest include Leh, Drass valley, Suru valley, Kargil, Zangskar, Zangla, Rangdum, Padum, Phukthal, Sani, Stongdey, Shayok Valley, Sankoo, Salt Valley. Popular treks are Manali to Ladakh, the Nubra valley, the Indus valley, Markha valley, Ladakh monastery trek, South Zangskar, Trans-Zangskar Expedition, Spiti to Ladakh, Spiti to Pitok to Hemis, Rupshu, the Great Salt lakes, Chadar Ice trek, Padum-Phuktal, Padam to Darcha, Panikhar to Heniskot, Padum to Manali, Lamayuru-Martselang, Lamayuru - Alchi, Kala Pattar trek, Pahalgam to Suru valley, Kinnaur-Spiti-Ladakh, Tsomoriri-Lake Trek, and Manali-Leh trek. General traveling maps showing the roads and tourist sites are commonly available in India and abroad.

Leh - capital of Ladakh, famous monasteries.

Nubra Valley - scenic valley with towns of Deskit and Hundar.

Lake Moriri - one of the largest and high altitude lakes.

Pangong Lake - Lake divided between India and China.

Zanskar - scenic trekking areas.

PERMITS AND BORDERS

No special permit is required to visit most of Ladakh, including Leh and Kargil towns. Permits are required for both domestic and foreign tourists to visit the "Inner Line" areas, i.e. Nubra Valley; Panggong Lake and the Durbuk Block that it lies in (i.e. north of the Changla Pass); Tso-Moriri and Tsokar Lakes and the area along the Indus River east of Upshi; and Dha-hanu and the area along the Indus River northwest of Khalatse. These permits are easily available in Leh town from the local authorities and do not need to be acquired while applying for an Indian visa.

Permits are not available, and foreigners are not allowed, in the far reaches of each of the above-named areas close to the borders (or Line of Control, etc) with Pakistan and China. For example, foreigners can go to the edge of Panggong Lake but not along the edge of it to Phobrang, Merak, Maan, or Chushul villages; they cannot proceed east up the Indus from the Mahe Bridge; and in Nubra, they can only go as far as Panamik to the north and Hundar to the west. There are no border crossings open between Ladakh and neighbouring regions of Baltistan (under Pakistan) or Tibet (under China).

TERRORISM AND ITS IMPACT

Tourism is a straight-forward concept and may be defined as a service based industry comprised of several elements including transportation, accommodation, food and beverage, tours and merchandising. Terrorism, however, proves a challenging concept to define. The U.S. department of State defines terrorism as -premeditated, politically motivated violence perpetrated against noncombatant targets by sub-national groups or clandestine agents, usually intended to influence an audience. Furthermore, as terrorism against tourists often involves international citizens, international terrorism is defined as -terrorism involving citizens or the territory of more than one country. In an information-free society, tourists might travel to destinations regardless of whether a terrorism threat exists or not. However, few information-free societies exist.

Via different forms, terrorism generates attention, which, when relayed back to tourists, has an impact on travel plans. For many countries in the developing world, tourism is a critical source of revenue generation and major component of economic development. The impact of terrorism on a state's economy may be enormous, leading to unemployment, homelessness, deflation, crime and other economic and social ills.

According to Adam Blake and M. Thea Sinclair, two scholars who have studied the impact of the September 2001 al Qaeda strikes on the U.S. tourism industry, -The contribution of tourism and travel to both industrialized and developing countries is now so great that any downturns in the level of activity in the industry are a cause of concern. The repercussions extend beyond activities directly associated with tourism, notably airlines, hotels and catering, to sectors that supply intermediate or final goods that are purchased by firms and employees in the industry, so that all sectors of the economy are affected to a greater or lesser extent.

CHANGING DYNAMICS OF TERRORISM

Disasters create difficult, often tragic, situations for the afflicted area and its residents. For a tourist destination, this period can represent a tourism crisis, which can threaten the normal operation and conduct of tourism related businesses; damage a tourist destination's overall reputation for safety, attractiveness, and comfort by negatively affecting visitors' perceptions of that destination; and, in turn, cause a downturn in the local travel and tourism economy, and interrupt the continuity of business operations for the local travel and tourism industry, by the reduction in tourist arrivals and expenditures.

Terrorism and its motivations, targeting, strategy, tactics- even logistics- continue to evolve, in keeping with efforts on the part of security agencies to meet the challenges and to stay ahead of the dangers. Terrorist atrocities in Algeria, characterized by the horrific slaughter of women and children; bombs hidden aboard a train in Pakistan which claimed 23 lives and injured 75 others; and the deaths of more than 260 persons as the result of truck-bomb explosions at the US Embassies in Nairobi, Kenya, and Dar-es-Salaam, Tanzania, are reminders that terrorists retain the determination and ability to strike ruthlessly at a broad range of targets in many locations.

REASONS WHY TERRORISTS TARGET TOURISTS

First, tourists are easy to attack. Terrorism requires a great amount of precision, which in turn requires predictability. For a terrorist, the tour bus that leaves every hour on the hour between 8:00 a.m. and 5:00 p.m. five days a week is an ideal target because the target can be researched until a perfect plan is in place. Second, tourists make better targets than the locals. Because terrorists often reside within the country where the attacks take place and the public is well aware of their presence (occasionally, minority voices in the public even support the terrorists, as is the case with Hezbollah).

While the targeting of tourists may bother certain members of a society, the targeting of locals would likely enrage the public, possibly resulting in retribution that places the existence of the terrorist organization at risk. Third, and perhaps most importantly, the targeting of tourists, particularly international tourists, can generate a great deal of attention, causing tourists to avoid travel to that part of the world. Tourism is indeed an elastic industry in which the consumer may consider several options, which is precisely what the terrorists wish to achieve.

Sophisticated terrorists constantly evaluate their present status, which may be considered as either satisfying or unsatisfying. If satisfying, a terrorist group may accept the status quo. If unsatisfying, a terrorist group might recognize that goals are at risk and make changes. If a terrorist group elects to make changes, it will expect new outcomes.

Regarding a desire for increased attention, a flow chart for a terrorist group making changes might resemble the following:

Targeting methods of terrorists on tourists: Improved international cooperation against terrorism and strengthened security for diplomatic and military facilities have prompted a shift in terrorist targeting and methodology: random attacks on tourists and the deliberate killing of foreign-aid and NGO workers Incidents of kidnapping and hostage- taking have become frequent occurrences in South America, Asia and the former Soviet Union Terrorist attacks focused on economic infrastructures including those related to energy distribution, transportation, banking and tourism. hoaxes, particularly bomb threats, have been employed on occasion to seriously disrupt transportation and tourism, causing significant local impact the Internet is becoming a resource more frequently used by terrorists as a means to access information, spread propaganda, raise funds, communicate, and plan operations.

A multifaceted phenomenon, terrorism demands extraordinary domestic and international collaboration to combat the hazards it presents. Over the past 10 years, improved intergovernmental cooperation has contributed to a notable drop in the number of international terrorist incidents. Despite the reduction in incidents, terrorist violence in many parts of the world will continue to promote an uncertain security environment, and will remain an ongoing threat to international and domestic stability and to the lives and livelihood of hundreds of innocents.

Cultural impact of tourism as a reason for terrorism growth: Despite the general increase in tourism benefits, the generated income is often highly unequally distributed for e.g.; in the case of Turkey that local people simply cannot afford to establish proper hotels and shops, leading to high rates of foreign ownership, a loss of control over local resources and substantial overseas leakage of tourism earnings. Those benefits that accrue to the local community are also unevenly distributed, causing conflict between those who benefit and those who do not.

Apart from that, while improved infrastructure is regarded as a major positive impact of tourism development many of the new tourist facilities, such as golf courses or luxury hotels, are of little benefit to the majority of the local population. And in many areas a rise in prices of goods and services is noted. Animosity is created between the local population and expatriates who often hold the managerial level jobs, while locals are only offered the semi-skilled or unskilled jobs. Furthermore, even these low-paid job opportunities can disturb local family economies when suddenly children earn more than their parents, or wives more than their husbands.

Commercialization of culture and cultural artifacts also appears in tourism destination primarily as saleable commodities. In various destinations, cultural and religious practices are found to be reconstituted or adapted to suit the needs of tourists for example; the rituals and traditions of the religious Indian town Pushkar are changed in function from sacred to explicitly commercial enterprise. Festivals and dances in Bali that were previously considered sacred are now being performed for tourists. Even worse effects are found in many tourist centers where the crime rates, the drug addiction, prostitution and gambling is increasing rapidly.

In the light of all these potential negative socio-economic and socio cultural impacts, some kind of reaction from the host society is reasonably predictable, whether it is tension, hostility, suspicion or violent attacks. Different members of a community will respond in different ways to tourism. However, it cannot be excluded that certain individuals or groups who support strong cultural or, especially, religious values and feel that these values are threatened by tourism to an extent that is increasingly unbearable, use terrorist acts as ultimate means to combat the threat. Many religious fundamentalists also advocate the ill effects of tourism on one's culture which is also a reason for increased number of attack on tourists.

There is no world religion that is against tourism per se. In the case of Islam, the notion of travel is accepted both implicitly and explicitly. On the one hand, Muslims are encouraged through Koran and Hadith to travel in order to trade, to visit relatives and friends, to seek knowledge, to appreciate the greatness of God's creation and, of course, for pilgrimage reasons. As hosts, on the other hand, they have a duty of hospitality towards travellers who have been permitted by the Islamic State authority to enter the territory - regardless of race, colour, nationality or religion.

SECURITY CONCERNS ON TOURISM INDUSTRY

Destination choice is a mental phenomenon on the part of a prospective traveler. Apart from attraction, accessibility and facility, the question of security emerges as an important determinant of tourism. The tourists' perceptions on the safety of a destination become highly influential in decision making.

Existence of social and political stability and absence of any kind of civil unrest are important pre-requisites for successful tourist trade. Terrorists incidents receiving media coverage have an almost immediate effect on the people, while it takes a long time to make people convinced about restoration of peace in an erstwhile disturbed spot, for example in Bali after the terrorist attack in October 2002, the tourists arrival became the usual amount only after December 2004. It is also true that when some set of events affect a given destination, the probability is that some other destination will benefit.

For example, Sri Lanka loses almost 10% of tourist arrival to its neighbor Maldives every year due to her uncertain political atmosphere. Himachal Pradesh skimmed the benefit of tourism from the disturbed Kashmir valley. The recent terrorist acts in Mumbai and protests in Thailand have surely negatively affected the tourism industry in these destinations. The crisis had made people think more about their safety while traveling. Hospitality businesses have tried to improve their safety standards. For example the general manager of Shangri-La Hotels & Resorts, New Delhi hotel claims that they screen vehicles and luggage and use metal detectors to check visitors.

After the Mumbai attacks they have also added extra armed security to watch inside and outside of the hotel. According to Robert Grenier from the global security consulting company Kroll Inc., it is advisable for Western executives traveling to the world's hot spots to keep low profile. He recommends staying in three-star hotels rather than in five-star hotels. He warns against driving fancy cars and having an entourage. In short term perspective the tourism of India and Thailand will see a drop but it is likely to improve after a few months. Being aware of the possibility of serious consequences to their business, hotels in Mumbai and Bangkok try to lure local customers by reducing prices.

EFFECT OF THE SEPTEMBER 11 ATTACKS ON TOURISM INDUSTRY

The total economic impact of 9/11 is realistically immeasurable; however the world travel and tourism council has estimated the decrease of the travel and tourism demand world wide to be 10%. Job loss of 8.8 million people globally including airlines, hotels, tour operators, car rental and credit card companies, creating a 1.7% decrease of total GDP for the world economy. Combined with a lull in the global economy, the attacks on the world trade centre in New York resulted in 4 million less international arrivals worldwide in 2001 in comparison to the previous year. This obviously indicates an element of fear introduced and an unwillingness to fly particularly on transatlantic flights showing that the tourist industry was affected on a global scale not just in America.

There was a decrease in international tourists in the UK with a 12% decrease in visitor numbers to Westminster Abbey, 20% at the tower of London and 16% at the Tate Britain. Passenger numbers for the principal New York airports suffered a drop to 38,456,239 in 2002 compared to 44,166,012 in 2001. Both British airways and American airlines suffered losses as demand dropped especially in the full service scheduled market which left the market for new lower cost airlines to be more competitive. India and Nepal, which are close to Afghanistan, felt the effects of a drop in demand.

A resort company Club Méditerranée was forced to close 15 of its holiday villages in the Caribbean, Central America, the Middle East, Europe, and Asia. Operators in Costa Rica reported a 30 per cent decline in booking. To try to offset terrorist fears, the Travel Industry of America [TIA] produced and aired widely on television an infomercial that included words and music from the air carriers, hotels and cruise lines the message was its patriotic to travel, it creates and supports jobs. Similarly World Travel and Tourism Council [WTTC] placed full page ads in trade journals to reassure travel suppliers that - we are with you in efforts to stimulate tourism.

Banner outside motel in Flagstaff, Arizona, USA In a 2002 news release reflecting on the September 2001 Al Qaeda terrorist attacks, WTO Secretary- General Francesco Frangialli stated that -International tourism experienced a serious crisis but showed again how resilient it can be. On one hand it was surprising to see a decrease in an industry that is used to constant growth, on the other it is encouraging how stable this economic sector is. Its decrease was temporary and somewhat less painful than we had expected. Impact of international terrorism causes multiplier effect in tourism industry such as the impact on airline-related business, the aircraft and parts manufacturers and tourism - which in turn affects hotels, restaurants and tourist attractions.

Border clearance costs start to rise, with delays and tighter inspections and, in addition, there are increasing demands for greater security on oil and gas pipelines and electricity transmission lines, which also represent higher costs. And commercial travel hence trade in services could also be constrained due to delays and difficulties on cross-border flights. The cost of insurance and reinsurance has increased and many private sector insurers were not willing to cover terrorist attacks. Increased spending on border and airport security, including technology, and the military, along with intelligence and law enforcement in turn increases passenger fares.

The decline in airline travel since the terrorist attacks has affected the car rental industry and can easily affect the auto makers if rental companies cancel orders for new vehicles. Rental operators shall cutting hours at some operations, trimming staff, delaying new vehicle deliveries and accelerating sales of their existing vehicles for e.g. after Sep 11. Airport rentals were down 20 per cent to 25 per cent.

CASE STUDIES: INDIA:

Tourism in some of the strife-torn parts of the country has suffered on account of terrorism. Fifteen years of armed insurgency in Jammu and Kashmir shattered its tourism industry. And the tourism potential of the north eastern states has remained untapped because of the decades of fighting there. It is only over the past three to four years that tourists, including foreigners, have returned to the Kashmir Valley. The central and state governments of Jammu and Kashmir have undertaken several steps to improve the security situation and instill confidence in tourists who have been the target of terrorist attacks.

Among the several proposed steps include an insurance cover for both domestic and international travellers to the region. The J&K govt. is reportedly considering a proposal in this regard. Security has also been boosted particularly at popular tourist resorts in order to allow the visiting tourists to enjoy the beauty of the state without any fear. Outside Kashmir and the north-eastern states, terrorism hasn't impacted seriously on tourism so far. The Mumbai attacks changed the picture of tourist arrival; many countries had issued notifications to its citizens about terrorist threat in India.

One may hope it vanishes quickly. Goa, a favourite with foreigners, especially those from Israel, was reportedly on al-Qaeda's hit list prompting the Israeli government to issue a travel advisory to its citizens traveling there. While the alert did trigger some concern, it did not impact too much on tourism. Israeli tourists, who incidentally have constituted the largest group visiting Kashmir, have often said they are used to worse in their own country and are unfazed by the security situation in India.

Sri Lanka: Recent travel advisories issued by certain embassies warn their nationals against travel to Sri Lanka, a move that will have an adverse effect on tourism. A spokesperson for the British High Commission said the mission updated details of the travel advisory issued to British citizens to make people aware of the recent incidents in Sri Lanka. "We are now advising people that attacks are not confined to the North East; and that they should avoid military installations, there is a high threat from terrorism in Sri Lanka and therefore an increasing risk of British nationals and other foreigners becoming caught up in attacks in Sri Lanka," the advisory states.

Kenya: Terrorists adversely impact the tourism industry in a developing country by targeting its tourists. Tourism brings about $500 million in direct annual tourism revenue,

500,000 jobs and 12% GNP. Terrorist events such as 1998 U.S. Embassy bombing, 2002 Mombasa beach hotel bombing and 2003 unsuccessful missile strike on commercial airliner

Result: Daily losses in tourism revenue in Kenya at over one million dollars per day.

Afghanistan: Taliban and terror groups of Afghanistan has destroyed the one and only prime attraction of tourists the great Buddhist statues at Bamian, if and when Afghanistan is stabilized with a central government, it is greatly doubtful to attract tourists of significant number.

INITIATIVES TO COMBAT IMPACT OF TERRORISM IN THE TOURISM INDUSTRY

The most important name in international tourism is the WTO, a 20 year-old international governmental organization with 143 members responsible for industry advancements such as the Global Code of Ethics for Tourism (GCET). The GCET is a non- binding agreement accepted by member states that establishes tourism, among other things, as a factor of sustainable development. The GCET also establishes the rights for international tourists to discover and enjoy the planet's resources, natural or otherwise, as if they were citizens of the country they are visiting. Tourism, according to the GCET, contributes to mutual understanding and respect between peoples and societies, acts as a vehicle for individual and collective fulfillment and provides a beneficial activity for host countries and communities.

The burden upon a state managing a terrorism problem may be enormous, serious and unmanageable, particularly as terrorists seem undeterred by an underdeveloped set of global norms and international laws against terrorism. International efforts can be initiated for the following States should push for international recognition of tourist terrorism. The first step would be to add an additional point to the GCET specifically addressing terrorism, which it currently does not. The second step would be to call for a specific international treaty denouncing terrorism that targets tourism.

This may seem like obvious steps, but current international treaties that outlaw airline hijacking and bombing were needed to serve notice to terrorists, and the states that sponsor them, that these forms of terrorism will never fall into the gray area of activity performed by freedom fighters or revolutionaries. States should seek to internalize the concepts communicated in the GCET, which includes the right to tourism, liberty of tourist movements, and rights of the workers and entrepreneurs in the tourism industry.

These concepts should be integrated into domestic law, the violations of which would carry fines and prison sentences. The international community should support the development of a nongovernmental organization that focuses on tourism. It will also help to educate tourists and states alike on the impact of terrorism on the industry. A multifaceted phenomenon, terrorism demands extraordinary domestic and international collaboration to combat the hazards it presents. Over the past 10 years, improved intergovernmental cooperation has contributed to a notable drop in the number of international terrorist incidents Strategies and Tools for Tourism Development in crisis Risk Management Tools. There is a need to risk management as a management and controlling tool for top executives. The tools consist of 2 groups:

1. Strategic risk management in turbulent markets.
   - Turning risks into opportunities.
   - Opportunity Management.
   - The systematic process to design & manage opportunity.
2. The components of Opportunity Management System.

   Four techniques for opportunity design.

   - OM
   - Hardware
   - Software
   - Corporate investing

Establish a mechanism for sharing information and coordination of publicity and PR activities aimed at creating positive public opinion among the media, local community, and customers Engage their local community in the effort of recover Reassure and calm their existing and potential clients by providing them current and updated information secure funding for the development and implementation of a recovery marketing plan Tourist destinations that established a partnership between law enforcement agencies, tourism enterprises, the community at large, and the tourists themselves have lower crime rates than their counterparts.

Destinations that have established better contacts between the local community leaders and the national governments are more successful in prevention/ reduction of acts of political unrest. Vulnerability and Resilience of tourism industry: Since tourism and leisure travel are voluntary activities and because there are many alternative destinations to choose from, security concerns can have a greater impact on the choice of the destination. The threat or perceived threat of danger or lack of security is often sufficient to deter people from travelling at all, as was seen in the US after September 11. As leisure travel also involves families, parents are likely to be particularly sensitive of travelling to possibly dangerous locations with children.

Moreover there are many indirect effects these terrorist occurrences like increased time, cost and inconvenience involved in travel because of added security arrangements. Irrespective of the effects of terrorism, tourism is unlikely to decline overall, certainly not when domestic tourism is concerned. People place great importance on their holidays and are not likely to relinquish them easily. The more likely effect of terrorist attacks and other disasters is to the specific destinations or regions suffer a decline in tourism with travel moving to other locations. Many years of Basque terrorist's movements have not prevented Europeans from visiting Spain, despite a declared intention of targeting tourist related services.

Given the considerable economic significance of tourism industry to many economies and the vulnerability of the tourist, it is a major concern that terrorist groups will always show an interest in the tourism sector. There is a need of collective effort to protect the vulnerable industry and show greater resilience. As such a provider of employment and economic prosperity in many countries, the tourist industry must be able to remain resilient in the face of adversity. Although tourists act as an easy target for terrorists if the industry remains flexible in its ability to diversify when tourism numbers take a downturn it will help ensure economic prosperity is maintained and defeat the primary objectives of the terrorist groups.

6

Current Situation in Jammu and Kashmir

This dispute dates back to the partition of the British Indian Empire, in August 1947, into two independent states, Pakistan and India. At that time there were also around 565 princely states, large and small, which were under British suzerainty but were not directly ruled by the British Government. Most of these states joined either India or Pakistan taking into account their contiguity to one or the other country and the wishes of their people. There were, however, some states over which problems arose, primarily because of India's insatiable desire to grab territory.

For example, the Muslim ruler of Junagarh, a state with a Hindu majority population, announced his decision to join Pakistan. India responded by aiding and abetting the establishment of a so-called "Provisional Government" of Junagarh on Indian territory, which attacked Junagarh with Indian connivance and support. Subsequently Indian forces also invaded Junagarh, despite protests from Pakistan, in order to "restore law and order". A farcical plebiscite was organized under Indian auspices, and India annexed Junagarh. Similarly, in Hyderabad, a Hindu majority state, the Muslim ruler of the state wanted to retain an independent status.

India responded by attacking Hyderabad and annexed the state by force. India sought to justify its aggression against Hyderabad and Junagarh on the plea that the rulers of

Junagarh and Hyderabad were acting against the wishes of their people. In Jammu and Kashmir State, the situation was the reverse. The ruler of the State was a Hindu, while the population was overwhelmingly Muslim and wanted to join Pakistan. In this case, India consistently pressurized the Hindu Ruler to accede to India. Apprehending that the Hindu ruler was likely to succumb to Indian pressure, the people of Jammu and Kashmir raised against him, forcing him to flee from Srinagar, the capital of the State.

They formed their own government on 24th October, 1947. On 27th of October, 1947, the Government of India alleged that the ruler had acceded to India on the basis of a fraudulent instrument of accession, sent its forces into the State and occupied a large part of Jammu and Kashmir. But Indian leaders, including Jawahar lal Nehru, the Prime Minister and Lord Mountbatten, the then Governor General of India, solemnly declared that the final status of Jammu and Kashmir would be decided by the people of the State. This declaration was reiterated by India at the UN Security Council when the dispute was referred to that august body, under chapter 6 of the U.N Charter relating to peaceful settlement of disputes.

The Security Council adopted a number of resolutions on the issue, providing for the holding of a fair and impartial plebiscite in Jammu and Kashmir under UN auspices to enable the Kashmiri people to exercise their right of self-determination and join either Pakistan or India. The UN also deployed the United Nations Military Observer Group (UNMOGIP) to monitor the cease-fire line between the Liberated or Azad Kashmir area and the Indian Held Kashmir (IHK). These resolutions were accepted by India and Pakistan and constitute an agreed legal basis for settlement of the dispute. India, however, thwarted all attempts by the United Nations to organize a plebiscite in the State of Jammu and Kashmir. Eventually, India openly resiled from its commitments and declared that Jammu and Kashmir was an integral part of India.

The Indian armed intervention in the State of Jammu and Kashmir was illegal and took place against the wishes of the

Kashmiri people. Despite the decision of the UN Security Council for the holding of a plebiscite to allow the people of Jammu and Kashmir to determine their own future, India's own pledges to that effect, and reiteration of their commitment of resolving the Kashmir issue in the Simla Agreement of 1972 signed between Pakistan and India after the 1971 war, India continues to remain in illegal occupation of a large part of Jammu and Kashmir, refuses to allow the Kashmiris to decide their own future and continues its brutal suppression in the territory.

Moreover, India went on to violate other aspects of the Simla agreement, specifically the undertaking that neither side shall change the ground situation, by occupying the Chorbat La, Siachen & Qamar sectors, an area over 2500 sq. kilometres between 1972 to 1988. After more than four decades of a peaceful struggle against Indian repression, manipulation and exploitation, the Kashmiri people, convinced that India would never honour its commitments, and inspired by similar movements for freedom in other parts of the world, rose against the Indian occupation towards the later part of 1989. Their struggle was, and remains, largely peaceful. India sought to suppress their movement with massive use of force, killing hundreds of innocent men, women and children.

This led some of the Kashmiri youth to take up arms in self defence. Since 1989, more than 60,000 Kashmiri people have been killed in a reign of terror and repression unleashed by over 600,000 Indian troops. Many more languish in Indian jails where they are subjected to torture and custodial deaths. There have been numerous cases of gang rapes of Kashmiri women by the Indian forces and the deliberate burning down of entire localities and villages. These brutalities have been documented by International and even Indian Human Rights Organizations. Organizations such as Amnesty International and Human Rights Watch as well as Indian human rights NGOs have extensively documented the gross and systematic violation of human rights of the Kashmiri people by Indian military and para-military forces.

Extra judicial killings, involuntary disappearances, arbitrary detentions, rapes and torture continue to be reported on a large scale. The Kashmiri leaders have been repeatedly harassed and physically intimidated. They have also been denied travel permission to prevent them from exposing Indian human rights abuses in Occupied Jammu and Kashmir. The massive suppression by India is clearly designed to silence the people of Jammu and Kashmir through sheer brutality bordering on genocide and ethnic cleansing. India refuses to acknowledge that the people of Indian Held Kashmir (IHK) have become totally alienated and there is complete rejection of Indian occupation. Several Kashmiri political parties have formed the all Pakistan Hurriyat (Freedom) Conference (APHC) to continue the political struggle for self-determination.

The APHC, therefore, constitutes the true representative of the Kashmiri people. Instead of accepting the existing reality, India has sought to blame Pakistan for allegedly promoting the Kashmiri uprising. The fact is that this movement is completely indigenous and enjoys mass support. The Indian allegations against Pakistan are a ploy to mislead the International Community and to create a smokescreen behind which they can continue repression in IHK. Pakistan has offered to enable the UNMOGIP or any other neutral force to monitor the LoC, along which India has deployed several thousands of its troops and has mined the entire area. Indian refusal to accept these proposals exposes their false allegations.

A peaceful, negotiated settlement of the Kashmir dispute in accordance with UN resolutions remains on top of Pakistan's foreign policy agenda. To demonstrate its sincerity in finding a peaceful solution to this core issue, Pakistan has always sought a meaningful and substantive dialogue with India. However, the Indians have refused to engage in meaningful talks on Kashmir, claiming the territory as an integral part of India. Only when compelled by extraneous factors or international pressure, such as in 1962-63, 1990-94 and again after May 1998, have the Indians agreed to talks on Kashmir. But this dialogue has been sterile because the Indian objective has never been to find a settlement but to deflect international pressure by creating the facade of talks.

During 1962-63, the Indians agreed to talks on Kashmir under U.S. persuasion at a time when their relations with China had deteriorated and the Sino-Indian war took place and it was necessary for India to protect its western flank with Pakistan. Between 1990-94, India was hard pressed for a dialogue, again due to international pressure following the indigenous Kashmiri uprising which began in the end of 1989. Under pressure from the US, following the mission of the American President's Special envoy, Robert Gates to the region, India engaged in seven rounds of talks at the Foreign Secretary level. Due to continued Indian intransigence, however, this process broke down in January 1994.

After a hiatus of three years, talks were resumed at the initiative of Pakistan's former Prime Minister Nawaz Sharif, after he assumed office in March 1997. Following Foreign Secretary level talks in June 1997, an agreed agenda was adopted which includes the specific issue of Kashmir. More importantly, in the meeting between Prime Ministers of Pakistan and India in September 1998, the two leaders agreed that resolution of the Kashmir dispute is essential for peace and security in the region. During Indian Prime Minister Vajpayee's visit to Lahore in February 1999, the Lahore Declaration was adopted committing both sides to intensify efforts to resolve the Kashmir issue.

Indian willingness to hold specific talks on Kashmir has been compelled by growing international concern over the Kashmir issue following the nuclear tests by India and in response by Pakistan in May 1998. This nuclearization of South Asia has converted Kashmir into a nuclear flash point and the U.N. Security Council through resolution 1172 as well as the G-8 and P.5 countries, apart from a number of world leaders, has expressed the urgent need for a dialogue to resolve this root cause of tensions between Pakistan and India. While the first round of talks on Kashmir was held in October 1998 between the Foreign Secretaries, as per the agreed agenda of June 1997, there was no change in the Indian position.

India rejected Pakistan's frame work proposal for a structured and substantive dialogue on Kashmir, maintaining its intransigent position that the status of Kashmir was not open for discussion. Even though India agreed in the Lahore Declaration to intensify efforts to resolve the Kashmir issue, in February 1999, it resorted to delaying tactics for holding the next round of talks. In May 1999, India dealt a severe blow to the dialogue process by launching massive military operations, involving air and ground forces, on the Kashmiri *Mujahideen* in the Kargil Sector and across the Line of Control on Pakistani controlled areas.

The Indians also rejected our efforts to defuse the situation, including the proposal for immediate cessation of hostilities, mutual respect for the LoC and resumption of the dialogue process in accordance with the Lahore Declaration. At the invitation of President Clinton, former Prime Minister Nawaz Sharif visited the US on 4-5 July 1999 and held indepth discussions with the US President on all aspects of the Kashmir situation. A Joint Statement issued as a result of these talks reflects identity of views on the need to resolve the current situation as well as the larger issue of Kashmir which is central to durable peace and stability in South Asia.

It recognizes and underscores the need for both India and Pakistan to respect the LOC in accordance with the 1972 Simla Agreement. It also speaks about concrete steps to be taken for restoration of the LOC. As Pakistan has no presence across the LOC the only concrete step on our part can be to appeal to the *Mujahideen* who have already achieved their objective of bringing the Kashmir issue back to the international focus of attention. The two leaders agreed that the Lahore process provides the best forum for resolving all outstanding issues between Pakistan and India including Kashmir.

According to the Joint Statement the President of the United States stands committed to his personal involvement to expedite and intensify the process for resolving the Kashmir dispute. This is for the first time that the US has agreed to play a direct role in the search for a final settlement of the Kashmir dispute. India continues to rely on brute force to silence the Kashmiri people. Not only has the campaign of repression been intensified in Indian Occupied Jammu and Kashmir, but additional forces were inducted in November 1998 as part of the new "pro-active" policy and later in the Kargil operation, Indian forces have now been increased to over 730,000.

This clearly points to the failure of the current Indian policy to hold the Kashmiri people against their wishes by force. Pakistani public opinion remains deeply incensed with the wide-spread atrocities committed against the innocent Kashmiri people by Indian military and para-military forces. The government's policy on the Jammu and Kashmir issue enjoys national consensus. Pakistan maintains its principled stand in accordance with the relevant UN Security Council resolutions that call for a plebiscite under UN auspices. It is in keeping with the solemn pledge made to the Kashmiri people by Pakistan, India and the international community.

In order to find an early and just solution to the 50-year old Jammu and Kashmir dispute, Pakistan has welcomed offers of good offices and third-party mediation. It has encouraged the international community to play an active role and facilitate the peaceful settlement of disputes between Pakistan and India. While Pakistan is committed to a peaceful settlement of the Jammu and Kashmir dispute, adequate measures have been taken to safeguard the country's territorial integrity and national sovereignty. Pakistan will continue to extend full political, diplomatic and moral support to the legitimate Kashmiri struggle for their right to self-determination as enshrined in the relevant United Nations resolutions. In the context of the bilateral dialogue, it calls on India to translate its commitments into reality.

At the same time, it will encourage the international community to support and supplement our efforts to establish lasting peace and stability in South Asia on the basis of equitable resolution of all disputes between the two countries, in particular the core issue of Jammu and Kashmir. We hope that India will join us in our efforts to bring durable peace to the region for the common benefit of all our peoples. For half a century our region has remained mired in tensions and conflicts. It is our sincere desire to see South Asia enter the next millennium at peace with itself.

The current situation in Jammu and Kashmir has caused great alarm and some papers have blamed politicians of different shades for a crisis that, according to them, could have been pre-empted. Hyderabad-based Rahnuma-e-Deccan, in an editorial (Aug, 17), writes: "When the government indicated its intention to take back the land (from the Shrine Board), then the Muslims said once the land has been given, it should not be taken back and no disturbance should unnecessarily be created on the issue of a religious place. But this assertion was suppressed as it would not have helped to promote communalism. Creators of disorder made it a Hindu-Muslim question leading to actions and reactions in Jammu and the valley".

The *Rashtriya Sahara* says: "If politics was not the objective, so many hue and cries might not have been made, at the instigation of the PDP, on the decision of the government (to reverse the land allotment). Nor would have PDP stoked the fire with its efforts for political instability by withdrawing support from the government to please the voters." The paper has not spared either former Governor S.K. Sinha or Ghulam Nabi Azad for the political cobweb in which the state has got enmeshed. Delhi-based Milap (Aug. 22) expressed the view that tensions between the Jammu region and the valley had always been there, even during the days of Raja Hari Singh. The remedy for peaceful co-existence and efficient administration lies, according to the paper, in the trifurcation of the states into Jammu, Kashmir and Ladakh.

Surely, there are very serious issues that had led to the current crisis in Kashmir. The separatist flames have to be contained. Of course, the political parties, both the National Conference and PDP are playing, as it seems, a constructive role only. The BJP and the Congress have much to blame. The Congress surely, as the ruling coalition leader, has to act or must have acted in a more decisive manner. Even now, some heads must fall. The Home Minister, from day one seems to have become not competent enough. In such circumstances, a decisive government, a government normally constituted in a natural way, would have acted. Time fort everyone to seriously ponder. Procrastination is another trait of a powerless Prime Minister? It looks like that.

Now, the world is as we can see, never perfect and conflicts are ever as many as ever they were! The latest tally of conflicts run from the Jammu & Kashmir Valley to the Georgian federation where its two tiny regions, now become independent republics, the names: South Ossetia and Abkhazia. Russia, now a power struggling to re-establish its old style Super Power role had interfered unilaterally and also engaged its army and tanks and airpower and killed an unpardonable large number of innocent civilian people. The lessons from international conflict zones to the situation in J&K are serious and very relevant.

The fire is burning for some two months in J&K and the Central government seems to have been suddenly exposed of its inability to do anything about the situation in Kashmir. It is nobody's case other than Manmohan Singh, others could have done a better job. But certainly, from what we see from the commentators, both from inside the J&K and from outside, the current agitations of the separatists have taken serious turns. The world azadi, once a weak slogan has become more vocal and the separatist groups have become bold and had taken a big march to the UN office to press their case. Of course, the basics are clear. No one of any consequence talks lightly on this issue.

India is one country and one nation and religion-based talks or separatism won't have much appeal. That is why we all appreciated the younger leaders, Omar Abdullah, PDP leader and the Congress men both in Kashmir Valley as well as from Jammu. What are the thoughts arising out of the J&K crisis? Yes, there are separatist elements, about a quarter of the state's population, led by Hurriyat factions. But the majority of the population knows that J&K is an integral part of a secular India and a great democracy. The nationalists are all here, not just the so-called new style nationalists who suddenly emerged in the wake of the Amarnath shribe controversy and the allotment of forest land to accommodate the pilgrims.

What should have been a symbol, as Omar Abdullah so beautifully put in his trust vote debate in Parliament, Amarnath yatra is an age-old pilgrimage and the pilgrimage must go on and must be secular India's pride. But ill-will and other narrow considerations entered the scene and the whole "Kashmir problem" has now been turned into a communal issue. That is unfortunate and let us all see that the issue remains in perspective. The current turmoil would pass off soon and the basic strengths of the Indian state would remain in tact.

It is the duty of everyone, our friends, the other nations and the world community to see that India's Kashmiri problem is not a simple one of Hindu-Muslim divide. India is a happy state of Hindu-Muslim unity and these needs to be highlighted. Of course, we can't run away from realities. Military presence, the needed measures to ensure militancy is under wraps and other current measures can't be much changed. But what is basically needed is the more sensitive understanding of the issues that are, first, international perceptions and second, the way the current international realities drive people to resort to self-proclamation of independence and then seek for recognition from friendly and hostile regimes and neghbouring and distant countries. The world is full of rogue states also.

The civil society, inside and outside Kashmir must be activated. Even a celebrity like Sabhana Azmi must be mollified. Such a liberal personality must not have spoken about discrimination of Muslims in India. She has the stature to fight for herself and would have got a constituency to enlarge her own vision. She should have understood as much as the otherwise clever but politically irresponsible Arundathi Roy, that to talk of sensitive issues without realising the potential larger dangers to India and its sovereignty in the current state of the world conflicts, is really condemnable.

The latest row over 800 canals of forest land to Amarnath Shrine Board after a well thought about Cabinet decision was an excellent gesture by the Government led by Chief Minister Ghulam Nabi Azad. However, Government's reversal of this decision is very unfortunate. It shows Cabinet Ministers' immaturity and apathy to people's cause and public interest. There are several powerful ministers in the existing Cabinet in J&K from Jammu region and Jammu proper. What they are doing when J&K and Jammu are burning? Why they are not resigning from the Cabinet in the interest of the people of Jammu? Has the political (manipulating) glue fixed them on their seats of power for a few more remaining days?

It seems they would like to stay there until they are literally thrown out by the people of Jammu. PDP leaders, on the other hand, have at least the courage of conviction to resign from the Cabinet in the avowed interest of their apparent Pakistani agenda. PDP leaders have acted in a manly way indeed. Where the courage of conviction of Cabinet Ministers from Jammu has has gone to? Why these political leaders from Jammu are lying low? Why they are not coming to help the common people of Jammu? Have they become spineless? What has happened to their, as it were, excellent political acrobatics and gymnastics? Why they are not performing when their support is most needed now?

It is highly surprising that when people of Jammu need them the most, they are more likely to be found planning for their trips to foreign lands. Otherwise, they will hide themselves in their own protective shells. After all, their life is more important than the lives of their own and common people! The present circumstances in the J&K State will soon lead to repeated imposition of curfews due to massive communal violence and subversive activities of the PDP, NC and Hurriyat at the behest of their apparent Pakistani links and clandestine financial, material and armed support from across the border through Al Qaeda's and Inter-Services Intelligence (ISI) hobnobbing with local Kashmiri associates.

Under the circumstances, even drug trafficking, human trafficking, armaments smuggling and fake currency racketeering will further widen its network for sabotaging the constitutional machinery of the State. As such, it is a longer lasting civil war like situation in the offing. It is not only the constitutional machinery in the State but also the future of youth, and peace and development of the civil society at stake. Actually, the crisis of granting land to Amarnath Shrine Board and its aftermath has again brought to light other related matters of very serious nature. It is bringing to light the anti-national nexus and networking in the J&K State. This is a very sensitive aspect of highest national importance.

Despite this scenario, political leaders of J&K State still keep following the Pakistani agenda, immaturity, and lack of courage of conviction, the policy of short sighted political opportunism or policy of appeasement vis-à-vis saboteurs. Even in the case of granting of land to Amarnath Shrine Board, questions of environment protection are being used as a scapegoat to gloat over the hidden agenda from Pakistan. Questions of holistic development are being put to shelf instead.

The initial decision of J&K Cabinet to grant the relevant forest land to Amarnath Shrine Board was taken from an administrative and managerial view point, especially, to provide necessary developmental infrastructure and facilities to pilgrims coming to Amarnath Shrine every year. This was also done to ease so many related matters anent the yearly feature of Amarnath Yatra. However, after the London's visit of certain PDP leaders, they again apparently remembered their, as it were, hidden agenda of never allowing any permanent infrastructure and facilities for so many pilgrims visiting the Amarnath Shrine every year in the Kashmir region - now inhabited mainly by Kashmiris other than Kashmiri Pundits.

Hurriyat's call to oppose the Cabinet decision for granting land to Amarnath Shrine Board was, thus, joined by PDP and NC both. After the exodus of Kashmiri Pundits from Kashmir, it seems, remaining Kashmiri political leadership in the Kashmir region want to enjoy Kashmiriyat on their own! They do not want to share it with Kashmiri Pundits and other Indian citizens any more. Why this xenophobia is there even at the cost of economic development of the region? What can be the reason behind this xenophobia? Is this xenophobia a historical necessity or a political agenda dictated by foreign lands?

In depth research into the circumstances leading to J&K's accession to India can further show a hidden political agenda of several stalwart leaders in Kashmir towards keeping away the Kashmiri Pundits and other such communities from settling down in the Kashmir region through strategic planning over the years - without ever saying so openly and publicly. The covert attempt has been to throw out such communities from Kashmir in league with Pakistani influences. That is how, as it appears, even the Pak Occupied Kashmir was created. These types of subversive and divisive political manipulations in J&K are going on for the last sixty years.

That is why J&K is presenting before us a very unique political and economic scenario. Political parties like PDP and NC are converting J&K into a very weak institution as a State, politically and economically. Leaders and a few other people in the political and economic nexus are individually becoming very rich and prosperous. However, the J&K State is nearly bankrupt. This bankruptcy is further enriched by anti-national elements like Hurriyat and its collaborators in J&K. The current chaotic circumstances relating to the grant of land to Amarnath Shrine Board are also created by such subversive and anti-national forces only.

Above mentioned perspectives, apparent political subversion and the latest chaos and anarchy in the J&K State cannot be resolved through backtracking and ephemeral decision making while hurting the sentiments of the majority of Indian citizens. Bold policy options will have to be opted for.

Firstly, it is necessary that subversive and anti-national elements like Hurriyat, PDP and NC are banned permanently.

Secondly, Governor's rule must be immediately imposed in J&K for bringing about not only instantaneous normalcy but also longer lasting political stability, justice, peace and prosperity on a wider plain for the sake of the common people in particular.

Thirdly, Governor's rule must continue at least for next ten years in order to deal with six decades old saboteurs and anti-national elements in the State.

Fourthly, an impartial judicial or gubernatorial inquiry commission must be established and set up to submit its report to the President of India on all above mentioned contexts and clandestine anti-national activities and happenings in the J&K State during the last sixty years. Otherwise, the events like the Amarnath Shrine Board crises cannot be prevented from taking an ugly turn on a much larger scale. Once, this Pakistani connection into various affairs of the J&K State is properly dealt with all other things will fall in line on their own.

This is required in order to prevent various divisive forces re-emerging again in the State to further weaken it politically, economically and culturally. The situation in Jammu, where the Muslim minority is facing violence on a scale that can be described as ethnic cleansing, is alarming. The Government of India and the military and paramilitary forces have shown themselves unable and/or unwilling to take any effective action, either to end the blockade or to stop the violence against Muslims in Jammu. Meanwhile, military and paramilitary forces have opened fire on counter-demonstrators in Kashmir, using live bullets and mortar. A communiqué from the Kashmir Valley states that:

"The situation here on ground is that essential commodities have started getting dried up, diesel is already out of stock and petrol at its verge of end. The people here are very much concerned as if the same continues for next few days there will be nothing left to eat with the people of Kashmir. And on the other side the Army is supporting the mobs that have allegedly beaten up the drivers stranded on the national highway. The drivers who were beaten up reported that they asked Army to help them but all went in despair and the Army people in return handed them over to the mobs. The target is only the Kashmiri Muslims and some sources from Jammu say that it is the outsiders who have come to Jammu and are doing such attacks on the Muslims and it is quite evident that the Hindu fundamentalist groups viz. BJP, RSS VHP, etc., are all sponsoring the planned attacks onto the Kashmiris like it was done in Gujarat. Here in Kashmir we feel the history seems to be being repeated by the Hindu fundamentalists who had earlier in 1947 killed about 250,000 Muslims in Jammu."

On August 11, 2008, approximately 100,000 Kashmiris, including fruit growers and others gravely affected by the blockade, marched toward the Line of Control toward Pakistan markets in protest. They were met with gunfire and tear gas from the military and paramilitary forces, and Sheik Abdul Aziz, an All Parties Hurriyat Conference leader, was shot dead, intensifying the situation. Police reports stated that three others were killed and over 200 injured, enervating health systems already low on supplies. Other sources we contacted stated that as many as 18 others may have been killed in Kashmir on August 11.

By early evening of August 12, as we write you, reports stated that as many as twelve persons were killed in Kashmir on that day as armed forces fired on demonstrators. Other reports stated that civil society groups, students, and labor unions participating in non-violent civil disobedience and peaceful protests are being targeted by the forces, as curfew conditions prevail. The Srinagar-Jammu highway is the only land route linking the Kashmir Valley to India and the sole conduit for essential supplies as well as for exporting horticultural goods, which are among the Valley's chief products.

About 95-97 per cent of the population of the Valley is Muslim, while Muslims are a minority in India. This has made Kashmir the target of increasingly aggressive campaigns by Hindu nationalist groups since 1947, despite guarantees of autonomy written into the Indian Constitution. The Government of India has failed to take measures to prevent these campaigns, consisting of marches and demonstrations, and culminating in the current blockade.

Since 1989 there has been an armed pro-independence struggle in Kashmir, together with other and non-violent movements for self-determination. Indian counterinsurgency operations have resulted in grave abuses of human rights with social, economic, psychological, political, and environmental consequences, which meet the definition under international law of crimes against humanity. To a population suffering the effects of nineteen years of armed conflict, the economic crisis caused by the blockade comes as the last straw. We urge that you respond expeditiously to this situation in accordance with the mandate to uphold human rights as enshrined in the charter of the United Nations.

In the current round of "war diplomacy" (using the threat of war to push the western states into action) the Indian state seems to have emerged victorious. The Americans and the British are now supporting New Delhi's claim that the movement in Kashmir valley is totally Pakistan sponsored. The British Foreign Secretary during his recent visit to Pakistan characterised the struggle in Jammu and Kashmir as "terrorism dressed as freedom struggle". The American and the British hostile reaction to President Musharraf's recent attempt to qualify his "commitment" to ending cross border terrorism as not a "permanent one", is an indication of the hardening of the attitude of the western states.

It seems that President Musharraf made these comments to assure the Pakistani people that he was not about to abandon the five-decade-old commitment of Pakistan State to the Muslim brothers and sisters in Jammu and Kashmir. Kashmir as we know is deeply imbedded in the national ideology of Pakistan. Almost all Pakistanis, including those who oppose the policies of the religious fundamentalists and the military establishment, believe that with the end of militancy the twelve year old struggle for self-determination in Indian administered parts of Jammu and Kashmir will be completely crushed by the Indian state. It is the popular pressure, which is forcing President Musharraf to seek an international guarantee for intervention or mediation in Kashmir.

This is the era of "free market democracy". The protagonists of this New World Order in the making have already launched "Global War against Terrorism". In these times the offer of stopping support to a militant movement, which has already been dubbed as "terrorism", can no longer be used as a bargaining chip for humanitarian intervention. If President Musharraf's objective is to create a Kosovo type American humanitarian intervention in Jammu and Kashmir, he has to find another way to do so. And, if he is taking on the role of the defender of human rights of the people of India administered Jammu and Kashmir, he has to explain a lot to the world and his own people to whom he has denied those very rights as a military dictator.

The truth is that neither President Musharraf nor Mr. Vajpayee wants to empower the ordinary peoples of Jammu and Kashmir under their respective control. Moral arguments are used to advance "national interests". In this deadly game of chess, both sides use the people of Jammu and Kashmir as pawns to be sacrificed. In this round Pakistan has lost. Its immoral acts - support to terrorists stand exposed. India has gained the high moral ground. For the present, it has convinced the world that it was the victim of state sponsored terrorism. Emboldened by this victory, the Indian government is in no mood to resume dialogue with the Musharraf regime in Pakistan. It is obvious that they will try to extract every advantage that they can from this situation.

Having successfully shifted the focus of the discussion on the Kashmir dispute from the "internal causes" to "external interference" the Indian government is not willing to give any space to the militants or any other group which has sympathy for the militants including the APHC. The message that the Indian government is sending to all supporters of the movement for self-determination in Jammu and Kashmir is clear, "the accession of Jammu and Kashmir to India is a settled issue. Those who question it are doing so only at the behest of Pakistan. These people are anti-national and criminal elements".

PARTICIPATE IN THE ELECTION OR BE TERMED A TERRORIST

Clearly the Indian government does not want to talk to the APHC and others as it feels that talking to these people would amount to according some form of legitimacy to these political and militant organisations. However, the Indian government has indicated that it will be magnanimous to those who are willing to give up their support to Pakistan sponsored terrorism. Should these people decide to join the main stream of politics in the Indian administered Jammu and Kashmir and participate in the coming elections to the legislature of Jammu and Kashmir, they will be pardoned.

The Americans and other western states, the defenders of "free market democracy" have also told the APHC and other groups that they must participate in the coming election to the legislative assembly of Jammu and Kashmir in order to prove their legitimacy. It is becoming increasingly clear that the western governments will marginalise those who will boycott the elections to the Jammu and Kashmir legislative assembly.

LACK OF NATIONAL CONSENSUS

The present "struggle" in Jammu and Kashmir began essentially as a spontaneous mass upsurge during the late eighties. Various militant organisations, which claim the responsibility for this "struggle" and demand its leadership today, had joined the "struggle" at different stages on later dates. It will not be incorrect to say that the mass upsurge had preceded the militancy. In fact as militants took over the leadership of the struggle, the masses slowly returned to their homes. The divide between the masses and the militants became even more pronounced with the unleashing of mass terror by the Indian forces and the entry of Pakistan, initially as a supporter and later, as the controller of some of the militant organisations.

As the agenda of the Pakistan government and its agencies unfolded, it created division between the ranks of the militants on ideological and religious lines. The masses too were divided. The militarisation of the civil spaces by the Indian state as well as the militants put an end to open debates or discussions on the "national objective" which is essential for the development of a national consensus. The civil society was marginalised and put into shackles by the forces of the Indian state, the militants and the agencies of Pakistan.

The killing of a few moderate Kashmiri intellectuals broke the civil society's morale. Except vocalising their protest against the excesses of the Indian forces and pledging their support for the movement for self-determination, the middle classes of Jammu and Kashmir did little else. They remained silent even when they realised that path being followed by some of the militants was wrong, that the attacks on the minorities was immoral and counter productive, that the armed groups of religious fundamentalist who had taken over the leadership of the movement were subverting the secular character and tolerant values of the Kashmiri society.

The burden of this guilt of silence and the need to pragmatically compromise with the agencies of the Indian State for their daily needs often turned them against each other. They began to see conspiracy and hidden hands behind every attempt to re-build the institutions of the civil society. They shunned all attempts to build a national consensus for peace and reconciliation as "opportunistic". Also, it is a fact that the APHC and other political groups have not tried to build a broad consensus on the "national objective". Nor have these groups tried to generate a public debate on the nature and the scope of the national objective. Every polity functions on the basis of an agreed consensus.

The constitution is the embodiment of this consensus. Under normal circumstances, it is not necessary for a group of persons to seek prior approval of the people for forming a political party. However, the situation in Jammu and Kashmir is not normal. The APHC and other "groups" are not ordinary political parties trying to obtain peoples' mandate for forming a government under an accepted constitution. These "groups", whether it is the APHC or those outside the APHC, are trying to seek a revolutionary change in the political status of the territory of Jammu and Kashmir and the fortunes of its people. They are also challenging the authority of two recognised nation states - India and Pakistan in the name of the "people" of Jammu and Kashmir.

PEOPLE, TERRITORY NATION AND STATE

We should be aware that international law is the playground of states. The "people" do not have a "legal" status in international law or international relations. Broadly speaking, in international law the "people" are defined as a "nation" without a state. When a "people" get their "territory" and establish a "state" of their own, and when this "state" is recognised by other established states, then and only then does the "nationhood" of a "people" get the due recognition in international law. This is how a "people" enter the community of nation states. East Timor, as we all know, becomes a new member of this select community of nation-states not by struggle and sacrifices alone. I am not belittling the sacrifices of the people of East Timor. But the reality is that till the west decided to support the East Timorese people, they remained in wilderness.

The peoples of Tibet, Chechnya, Afkazia, Ingusthia, Kurdistan and the many other equally deserving "peoples" are yet to achieve the right to self-determination. No one, including President George Bush, denies the Palestinian peoples' right to have their own state. Yet we see how the powerful members of the community of states are kicking around this legitimate demand as a football. In case of Jammu and Kashmir, the west seems to have accepted the Indian claim that the struggle for self-determination of the people of Jammu and Kashmir is "Pakistan sponsored terrorism". Attempts are being made to link the dreaded *Al-Qaeda* with the ongoing struggle in Jammu and Kashmir.

The past fifty years should be an object lesson for us that no state has been punished for denying democratic rights to its people, except when economic and geo-political interests dictated such action by world powers. The trial of Milosevic is not the rule. President Putin of Russia is being rewarded for equally heinous crimes against the peoples of Chechnya. In fact the protection of the butcher of Chile, General Pinochet, is the norm. In Jammu and Kashmir we are also dealing with a situation where the population of the territory is not only physically divided, it is also divided in its loyalty to the existing states. This division is also acutely reflected in the people's interpretation of the "national objective" or objectives - Azadi, Accession to Pakistan and Accession to India.

There are many unresolved questions, for example, the protection of the rights of linguistic, ethnic and religious minorities, forms of sharing of political power between the different regions of Jammu and Kashmir and the type of future relationship with India and Pakistan. The task of building a national consensus is not going to be an easy one. It has to address all these issues before a set of "national objectives" can be defined and a consensus built around these. It will not be out of context to look at the developments in Northern Ireland, Sri Lanka and Nagaland.

The decades long struggle of the Irish Catholics in northern Ireland, which received moral, political and financial support from the powerful Irish immigrants lobby in the USA, was seen as one of the most powerful struggles for self-determination in the post Second World War period. The Irish Republican movement, like the movement in Jammu and Kashmir, had followed a similar curve of internal disagreements, sectarian struggles and internecine wars. The Republicans have killed several of their compatriots on suspicion of betrayal of the cause.

Yet this struggle finally had to come to terms with the need to make a compromise, to give up some of their objectives in order to achieve a negotiated peace that would protect some of their basic rights. It needs to be understood that De Velera, Gerry Adams and the others who supported the Good Friday Agreement did not betray the Irish Republican cause. It is equally correct to point out that these agreements and the settlement could not have come about if it was not backed by a national consensus of the Irish Republicans. In South Asia, the once invincible LTTE is now negotiating with the Sri Lankan government for peace and an acceptable political settlement for the Sri Lankan Tamils within the framework of the Sri Lankan State.

In India's Northeast the Naga nationalists who have been fighting against the combined strength of Indian army and a whole horde of paramilitary forces for about five decades, have now entered into political negotiation with the Indian government for a peaceful solution to the Indo-Naga problem. During the past five years of cease-fire, the leaders of the Naga nationalist movement have been engaged in a dialogue with the leaders of Naga civil society on the kind of peace and political settlement that the Naga people would like to achieve at this stage through negotiations.

This process of internal dialogue has already produced significant dividends for the Naga civil society in the form of reconciliation of inter-community conflicts. It has enhanced their ability to address the government of India and other communities in the northeast in a united manner and discuss peace in the framework of justice and reconciliation. It has also prevented the collapse of the cease-fire, despite provocations by both sides.

THE INDEPENDENT PEOPLES' ELECTION COMMISSION

When the APHC announced the plan to form an independent Peoples' Election Commission to seek the mandate of all peoples of Jammu and Kashmir to represent them in a political dialogue with India and Pakistan, felt encouraged. We felt that through the process of seeking the peoples' mandate the APHC and other groups would begin a new democratic process that would go a long way towards building a national consensus. Helping the APHC and other groups to gain "legitimacy" in the eyes of the governments of India, Pakistan and the west was not our primary objective. We were keen to be a part of a process, to the possibility of a truly representative leadership to emerge in Jammu and Kashmir.

As the Peoples' Commission we wanted to put forward the idea of creation of a "National Peoples' Council for

Freedom, Peace and Reconciliation" in Jammu and Kashmir. This people's democratic forum would have given a new life to the moribund political process in Jammu and Kashmir. This National Council comprising directly elected representatives, could be given the mandate to define the "national objective" through a process of consultations and engagement with different sections of the people all over the territory of Jammu and Kashmir. It could also be given the mandate to decide on priorities and strategies for achieving the agreed national goal or goals.

The delegates to the National Council could be elected by the people of Jammu and Kashmir directly at the district level through elections conducted by the Independent Peoples' Election Commission. This process would have given the "people" of Jammu and Kashmir an opportunity to create their own national institution through a democratic process. This would have also demonstrated to the world the falsehood of Indian attempt to discredit the struggle and sacrifices of the people of Jammu and Kashmir as Pakistan sponsored terrorism. Mahatma Gandhi adopted a similar strategy in the early days of Indian national movement. He changed the character of the Indian National Congress from that of an organisation of elite to a mass organisation.

He took the Congress to the people. He opened up its membership to all sections of the society irrespective of their economic status, religion, caste and political ideology. He introduced direct elections to the District Committees of the Congress. All those who paid their "four anna" membership were eligible to contest and vote. Women got their right to vote in the direct elections to the District Committees of the Congress even before the British women got their right to vote. Gandhiji built the Indian National Congress as a coalition of all sections of Indian people.

The communist party, the socialist's part, the organisation of landlords, trade unions, organisations of the peasants, the Muslim League and even those groups who subscribed to armed struggle were members of the Congress at different times. They participated in the elections to the District Committees, Provincial Committees, the All Indian Congress Committee and even the highest body of the Congress, the Working Committee. As we know, senior members of the Communist party of India and the Muslim League were elected to the Working Committee of the Congress.

The Congress thus emerged as broad coalition of divergent interests that was committed to overthrowing the yoke of British imperialism. It is true that the character of the Indian National Congress changed subsequently as it developed a more partisan. But that is a different story. However, it is important to recognise that initial work Gandhiji in building a national consensus for independence through the Indian National Congress that finally shook the British and they knew that they would have to go.

Predictably, the Indian government rejected this proposal at the initial stage. Understandably, the Pakistan government also showed no willingness to allow the Independent Peoples' Election Commission to function in the areas of Jammu and Kashmir under its control. The large- scale arrest of the members of APHC's executive on all kinds of real and false charges, the killing of Mr. Abdul Gani Lone who was calling on all parties, the Indian government and the militants to declare voluntary cease-fire and allow the beginning of a political dialogue further jeopardised this important initiative.

APHC and most of the other pro-Azadi and Self-determination groups are in confusion. Having followed a policy of trying to engage primarily with the governments of India and Pakistan they seem to have lost the capacity to be pro-active. They are merely reacting to the various moves and counter moves of Indian government. APHC's latest suggestion that they should be allowed to go to Pakistan to talk to the leadership of the Jihad Council and persuade them to declare cease-fire has very few takers today.

In fact, this move the APHC has further weakened its position. Instead of offering to go to Pakistan to talk to the Jihad Council over which it seems to have virtually no influence, the leaders of APHC should have called for an all round cease-fire, release of all political prisoners, return of the solders to the barracks and similarly return of the militants to their homes. It should have asked all concerned parties to allow the Independent Peoples' Election Commission to do its work so that a national consensus could be built through a democratic process, which has been denied to the peoples of Jammu and Kashmir by all parties, India, Pakistan and the militants.

The tragic reality of Jammu and Kashmir today is that the leadership of the movement remains cut-off from the masses. Most of these disparate groups are unable to trust each other and as a result are unable to come to a consensus on political issues or strategies of struggle. Under pressure of the Americans, President Musharraf is clamping down on the militant organisation in Azad Kashmir. The Jihad Council, which until recently received substantial material and moral support from the official and unofficial agencies in Pakistan is unable to see its future. Some of them may be worried about their immediate future.

The manner in which, the Talibans and Pakistani supporters of the Taliban were sacrificed by Pakistan government at the altar of the global war on terrorism cannot evoke any confidence in the hearts of the militants sitting in Azad Kashmir today. The Indian policy of squeezing Pakistan with the help of America and the west has the potential of pushing the militants to desperation. We are already witnessing an increase in the militant activities in Indian held Jammu and Kashmir. President Musharraf has also indicated that he cannot control all the Jihadi groups effectively.

THE BOYCOTT CALL

The militants, as expected, have already given a call for boycotting the elections to the legislative assembly of Indian administered parts of Jammu and Kashmir. They have even threatened to kill the participants. Under these circumstances, the APHC will be forced to repeat the call for boycott. This will help the Indian government's game plan. The boycott call will create confusion among the ordinary people of the valley.

Many will refrain from participating in the elections out of fear. This will give the Indian government an opportunity to carry out a sham of an election with an un-revised voter's list. As we all know, the voter's list of Jammu and Kashmir has remained virtually un-revised since 1983. Only a partial or a cosmetic revision was done before the 1987 elections. The 1996 elections did not require any such revision as this election was basically held by the armed forces. Since then very little work has been done to update the voters list.

As people will remain away from the electoral process no one will challenge the authenticity of the voters list. Very few objections will be filed. If the boycott call remains in force, the majority of the voters in the valley will also not go to get their voter's identity cards. If elections are held under these circumstances there will be little chance to effectively challenge the fairness of the election.

Towards an active non-violent struggle

There are many ways to express decent and register protest. Boycott is a form of passive resistance that involves essentially a "negative" action. There are many other ways that a people can express their resentment against a repressive regime through assertive political action. The coming election to the legislative assembly provides the opportunity to organise mass movement on so-called "legitimate" political issues.

For example a mass campaign may be organised to examine the voter's list. The people should be asked to identify incorrect entries and deletion of names of bona-fide voters. Objections against such irregularities in the voters list should be filed in an organised manner in order to compel the concerned authorities to properly revised and updated before holding the election. These are forms of legitimate political action. Demanding transparency at all stages of the electoral process will be another way of advancing the process of peoples' resistance in Jammu and Kashmir. Similarly, people should besiege the outlets set up for preparing the voter's identity cards. These identity cards will be a valuable resource in exposing electoral fraud.

The organisers of this non-violent struggle in Jammu and Kashmir should call on the civil liberties organisations of India to assist them in this struggle for making the process of election free and fair. They should also call for the presence of observers from the neighbouring countries of South Asia to see how the Indian state is responding to these legitimate demands of the people of Jammu and Kashmir. This could also become the first step towards building a coalition of civil society organisations for the defence of democracy and fundamental freedoms of the people of Jammu and Kashmir. The Chief Election Commissioner of Indian has said that the people have the democratic right not to participate in any election.

However, if the people of Jammu and Kashmir do not want to participate in this election, instead of just boycotting the polls they could organise a mass campaign for casting "invalid votes". The voters can en-mass invalidate their ballot papers as a mark of protest. This will strengthen the struggle the peoples of Jammu and Kashmir and prove the hollowness of the Indian claim that the struggle of the people is totally Pakistan sponsored. As the history of the nation-states shows us there is nothing sacrosanct about the existing boundaries of states.

These boundaries have been formed and reformed several times. Many powerful nation states have disintegrated. It is not the territorial boundaries, but the people who constitute the nation. And, as Bertrand Russell had said, "the people are only permanent force in history". The indomitable urge for freedom in the people is the motive force for change. However, it is also important to recognise the need to temper this urge for freedom with principles of justice and reconciliation. Without which there can be no true freedom and sustainable peace.

The current turbulent situation in Jammu and Kashmir over the Amarnath land row could work to the advantage of terrorists in the state, a senior army commander warned in Jammu on Friday. 'Our biggest fear is that terrorists could trigger blasts among the protesters and cause huge loss to the life and property of the people,' Lt Gen Vinay Sharma, General Officer Commanding 9 Corps, told newspersons in Jammu. Army personnel are deployed from Lakhanpur, which is considered the gateway to the state, to Jammu and the soldiers are guarding the Jammu-Pathankot highway and the railway track in the area. Sharma said that the protesters were perhaps not aware of the designs of the terrorists. 'They (terrorists) can go to any extent to cause damage to the people,' he said. He made it clear that the soldiers would be on streets and highways only as long as the situation requires. 'Once the situation stabilises, we will be back to our places,' Sharma said.

About 10,000 soldiers from 9 Corps are out in Jammu. They are essentially providing security to trucks and passenger vehicles entering the state. 'There is no economic blockade. There is no truth in these expressions,' he said. Several leaders in Kashmir are using the phrase 'economic blockade' to fuel tensions in the Kashmir valley, leaders in Jammu said. Hari Om, spokesperson of the Bharatiya Janata Party, said that these leaders are working at the behest of Pakistan to foment trouble in Kashmir.

'There is no difference between (Peoples Democratic Party president) Mehbooba Mufti and (Hurriyat Conference leader) Mirwaiz Umar Farooq.' Governor NN Vohra told mediapersons in Jammu on Thursday that there was no economic blockade, only 'traffic disruption' and that too has been removed. The state government's decision in May this year to allot about 40 hectares of forest land to the Shri Amarnath Shrine Board (SASB) for pilgrim facilities led to violent protests in the valley. As the government revoked the order July 1, protests broke out in the Jammu region, threatening to divide the border state along communal lines.

Pervez Musharraf, who was then Pakistan's President and Army chief, summoned his most senior generals and two Foreign Ministry officials to a series of meetings at his military office in Rawalpindi. There, they reviewed the progress of a secret, sensitive negotiation with India, known to its participants as "the back channel." For several years, special envoys from Pakistan and India had been holding talks in hotel rooms in Bangkok, Dubai, and London. Musharraf and Manmohan Singh, the Prime Minister of India, had encouraged the negotiators to seek what some involved called a "paradigm shift" in relations between the two nations. The agenda included a search for an end to the long fight over Kashmir, a contest that is often described by Western military analysts as a potential trigger for atomic war.

Since achieving independence, in 1947, India and Pakistan have fought three wars and countless skirmishes across Kashmir's mountain passes. The largest part of the territory is occupied by India, and Pakistanis have long rallied around the cause of liberating it. The two principal envoys– for Pakistan, a college classmate of Musharraf 's named Tariq Aziz, and, for India, a Russia specialist named Satinder Lambah–were developing what diplomats refer to as a "non-paper" on Kashmir, a text without names or signatures which can serve as a deniable but detailed basis for a deal. The Kashmir problem has a textbook quality: a dispute of more than six decades' duration, involving British colonial concessions, United Nations resolutions, and a long record of formal negotiations.

But it is the character of the war within Kashmir–the torture centers, the unmarked graves, and the remorseless violence of the jihadis–that better describes the contours of Indo- Pakistani enmity today. In one sense, the recent back-channel talks, with their promise of a cleansing peace, have offered each government a path to evade responsibility for the evisceration of Kashmiri villages and families. India and Pakistan each claims sovereignty in Kashmir, but neither has found a way to control the land or its people.

These failures are rooted in what was perhaps Great Britain's greatest imperial crime, the partition of its Indian domain, which ignited violence that claimed about a million lives. In 1947, the British government, bankrupted by the Second World War, hastily completed a plan to divide the subcontinent into the newly independent nations of India and Pakistan. The status of a few territories proved difficult to adjudicate. One was the former princely state of Jammu and Kashmir, ruled by a Hindu maharaja and largely inhabited by poor Muslim peasants. Under Britain's demographic formula, territories with Muslim majorities were supposed to go to Pakistan, but the maharaja signed an accession agreement to join India.

A year later, Pakistan tried to wrest away the territory by sending in a tribal guerrilla force, a gambit that ended in a military stalemate. In a sense, the war of guerrilla infiltration that Pakistan initiated in 1948 has never ended. In 1972, after their third formal war, India and Pakistan established the Line of Control and deployed artillery and infantry along its length. On the Indian side lay most of Kashmir, as well as the Hindu-majority region of Jammu and the Buddhist-influenced region of Ladakh. On the Pakistani side lay a sliver of land now known as Azad Kashmir and a Himalayan region of Muslim tribes known as the Northern Areas.

For almost two decades, a relative calm prevailed, but in late 1989–inspired by the fall of the Berlin Wall– Kashmiris on the Indian side, who were fed up with rigged elections and job discrimination, staged a mass revolt. The I.S.I., which had used Islamist militias during the anti-Soviet campaigns in Afghanistan, reacted opportunistically, by arming those Islamist factions of the rebellion which sought to join Kashmir to Pakistan. Vohra said that when he first arrived as governor he received daily briefings from intelligence officers about interrogation reports, electronic intercepts, and other evidence of I.S.I. activity along the Line of Control.

He asked for copies of the raw intercept recordings so he could listen himself. What he heard, he said, was controllers speaking to jihadi commanders inside Kashmir for "twentyfive, thirty minutes" at a time. "And they are very specific, very specific-to go for this target.... They said, 'Task No. 1: Eliminate the most senior leaders available.' And they mentioned some–I won't mention the names. And then, 'B, go for the larger rallies of the big leaders– throw grenades, shoot, bombs, I.E.D.s, whatever.'... And the kinds of rewards that are mentioned, rewards that will be given–lifetime, if you bump off a Grade A leader. If you injure them, you get three hundred thousand rupees."

In 1999, less than a year after he authorized Pakistan's nuclear test, Sharif initiated a precursor to the back-channel talks. In February of that year, Sharif invited India's Prime Minister at the time, Atal Behari Vajpayee, to attend a summit in Lahore. The two governments signed a memorandum of understanding; they also commissioned secret, exploratory talks by special emissaries. Sharif designated an aide, Anwar Zahid, and Vajpayee named a journalist, R. K. Mishra. "It was basically on Kashmir," Sharif recalled. "In the early days, we were not really having any consensus on anything. But the mere fact that the back channel was established was a big development. It was doing some serious work."

At the time, Sharif shared power uneasily with Musharraf, whom he had appointed as Chief of Army Staff. Musharraf "found the Lahore summit galling," as Strobe Talbott, who was then the United States' Deputy Secretary of State, put it in a memoir. In these years, Musharraf, "like so many of his fellow officers... was a revanchist on the issue of Kashmir." Musharraf apparently decided to break up the peace talks. He authorized a reckless incursion of Army personnel disguised as guerrillas into a mountainous area of Kashmir known as Kargil. A smallscale war erupted; at one point, the Clinton Administration believed that Pakistan's Army had taken steps to mobilize its nuclear weapons. Musharraf has said that he briefed Sharif on the Kargil operation; Sharif denied this. "I think the back channel was making good progress," he told me. "But soon after, you see, it was sabotaged by Mr. Musharraf– a misadventure that was ill-advised, ill-executed, poorly planned."

A few months afterward, Sharif tried to fire the General; Musharraf seized power and threw Sharif in jail. After President Clinton intervened, Sharif was released into exile in Saudi Arabia. India's leaders initially mistrusted Musharraf because he was the author of Kargil, but gradually, as Mansingh, then India's Ambassador to the United States, recalled, "We found he was a man we could talk to." After 2002, India's economy began to grow more quickly and steadily than at any time since independence; the ranks of its middle-class consumers swelled; and it became possible for Indian strategists to visualize their country rising to become a great power by the mid-twenty-first century.

Only a catastrophic war with Pakistan–or Pakistan's collapse into chaos–would stand in the way of India's greatness. "We were convinced these two countries must learn to live in accord–must," Jaswant Singh, who was then India's foreign minister, said. In time, Musharraf's thinking about India and Kashmir seemed to change, too. Late in 2003, splinter cells from *Jaish-e-Mohammed* twice tried to assassinate him. "This is what turns him decisively," Maleeha Lodhi, then Pakistan's high commissioner in London, recalled. Just weeks afterward, Musharraf met Vajpayee in Islamabad and agreed to an unprecedented joint statement: the Pakistani President would "not permit any territory under Pakistan's control to be used to support terrorism in any manner." The two leaders announced new formal negotiations between their foreign ministries, which were known as the Composite Dialogue. Privately, they re-started the back-channel talks on Kashmir.

To refine the non-paper, Musharraf relied intuitively on his college friend Tariq Aziz, a civil servant who had made his career in Pakistan's federal tax department, a bridge enthusiast who seems to some of his colleagues to live precariously on tobacco and adrenaline. Aziz's Indian counterparts–J. N. Dixit, Singh's national-security adviser, followed by Satinder Lambah–worked more formally. The Indians typically brought note-takers to the secret hotel sessions overseas, whereas Aziz travelled alone, rarely carried a briefcase, and often had to scribble his notes on hotel stationery. Altogether, there were about two dozen of these hotel sessions between 2004 and early 2007, according to people familiar with them.

To outsiders, it has long seemed obvious that the Line of Control should be declared the international border between India and Pakistan–it's been in place for almost forty years, and each country has built its own institutions behind it. Musharraf, however, made it clear from the start that this would be unacceptable; India was equally firm that it would never renegotiate its borders or the Line of Control. The way out of this impasse, Singh has said, was to "make borders irrelevant," by allowing for the free movement of people and goods within an autonomous Kashmir region. For Pakistan, this formula might work if it included provisions for the protection–and potential enrichment, through free trade–of the people of Kashmir, in whose name Pakistan had carried on the conflict.

The most recent version of the nonpaper, drafted in early 2007, laid out several principles for a settlement, according to people who have seen the draft or have participated in the discussions about it. Kashmiris would be given special rights to move and trade freely on both sides of the Line of Control. Each of the former princely state's distinct regions would receive a measure of autonomy– details would be negotiated later. Providing that violence declined, each side would gradually withdraw its troops from the region. At some point, the Line of Control might be acknowledged by both governments as an international border. It is not clear how firm a commitment on a final border the negotiators were prepared to make, or how long it would all take; one person involved suggested a time line of about ten to fifteen years.

One of the most difficult issues involved a plan to establish a joint body, made up of local Kashmiri leaders, Indians, and Pakistanis, to oversee issues that affected populations on both sides of the Line of Control, such as water rights. Pakistan sought something close to shared governance, with the Kashmiris taking a leading role; India, fearing a loss of sovereignty, wanted much less power-sharing. The envoys wrestled intensively over what language to use to describe the scope of this new body; the last draft termed it a "joint mechanism."

During an appearance on "Meet the Press," Barack Obama remarked, "We can't continue to look at Afghanistan in isolation. We have to see it as part of a regional problem that includes Pakistan, includes India, includes Kashmir, and includes Iran." The President has appointed the veteran diplomat Richard Holbrooke as a special representative for Pakistan and Afghanistan. The public description of Holbrooke's responsibilities has been carefully worded to avoid explicit mention of Kashmir, because India's government has long rejected outside mediation of that conflict, but, given his mission, Holbrooke will inevitably be drawn into quiet talks about the achievements and frustrations of the back channel.

Zardari and Singh may not find it easy to return to the non-paper negotiations on Kashmir any time soon, even if they wish to. In Pakistan, civilian political leaders might well reject the earlier framework simply because the discredited Musharraf was behind it. Even more daunting, the violent contest for power and legitimacy between Taliban militants and Pakistan's government is in many ways a struggle over Pakistan's national identity–and, particularly, over whether the present government is righteously Islamic enough. In the midst of such a contest, any agreement that made concessions to India would be harder than ever to sell to the Pakistani public. "The military is completely on board at the top levels–with a paradigm shift, to see India as an opportunity, to change domestic attitudes," a senior Pakistani official told me. However, he continued, "The public mood is out of synch."

The mood within sections of the Army and the I.S.I. may be out of synch with peace negotiations as well; in early February, the Kashmiri jihadi group Hezb-ul- *Mujahideen* hosted a public conference in Muzaffarabad, which Lashkar supporters attended. In India, Manmohan Singh seems determined to seek reëlection on a peaceand- stability platform. Last year, before Mumbai, Singh took steps to reconnect the back channel with Tariq Aziz, according to people familiar with the diplomacy. Singh was concerned, in particular, about whether Zardari would be willing to continue the talks and whether Pakistan would stand by the non-paper, or insist on renegotiating.

Musharraf looked well, in a tailored dark suit and red tie. He circulated among the crowd and engaged in small talk about the weather, inflected with nostalgia from his time in office–yes, Michigan was very cold, but nothing like the time he stepped onto an airport tarmac in Kazakhstan, when the temperature was minus thirty-six degrees. I asked him about the almost-deal he had made on Kashmir in 2007. I said that I had been surprised to discover how close his negotiators had been to drawing to an end one of the great territorial conflicts of the age. "I've always believed in peace between India and Pakistan," he replied.

"But it required boldness on both sides.... What I find lacking sometimes is this boldness– particularly on the Indian side." He then reviewed a long negotiating session he had had, many years before, with former Indian Prime Minister Vajpayee, in which the pair had tried and failed to agree on a particular joint statement. As he recounted the incident, the pitch of Musharraf's voice rose slightly; he seemed to be reliving his frustration. He returned to the subject of the 2007 talks. "I wasn't just giving concessions– I was taking from India as well," he said, a touch defensively. Then he calmed. He fixed his gaze and added, "It would have benefitted both India and Pakistan.

7

Monuments in Srinagar and Its Vitality

With its almost medieval charm, the old city of Srinagar has sights, smells and sounds to enchant the most jaded traveller. Its labyrinthine roads and bustling bazaars are a photographer's delight. Traditionally dressed men and women on their way to the city's many mosques and shrines, burnt brick buildings with their rich warm colour, these are some of the old city's moods which linger in the corners of a traveller's mind, long after one leaves Kashmir. Lending the area its vitality is the presence of the river Jhelum that flows through it. Srinagar has for long been Kashmir's most important commercial town, and when one considers that boats have always been a primary means of conveyance in Kashmir, it is not difficult to see why. In time, the city has formed around the banks of the river.

Today, the presence of the river Jhelum has become an integral part of the old city, despite the fact that boats are no longer so extensively used as a means of conveyance. Nine bridges span the River Jhelum, and many, many more tiny ones intersect the network of waterways that flow through the old city. The nine bridges are Zero Bridge, Amira Kadal, Budshah Kadal, Habba Kadal, Fateh Kadal, Zaina Kadal, Aali Kadal, Nawa Kadal and Safa Kadal, *'Kadal'* being the Kashmiri word for bridge. Of these Budshah Bridge and Zero Bridge are the newest; the former having been constructed by the

British in this century. Presently, the oldest bridge is Fateh Kadal, too dilapidated for actual use. However, many of the old bridges have been replaced with new concrete bridges and a few new ones have also been added in view of the increasing traffic.

The most prominent among these is the Abdullah Bridge, situated near the Tourist Reception Centre. The view from any of the old city's bridges is wholly and unmistakably Kashmiri. Old brick buildings line the banks. The distinctive pagoda-like roof of a mosque or a shrine enlivens the horizon, and in the muddy water of the River Jhelum, a straggling row of *doongas* flanks the edges. These boats, with their shingled roofs, are the forerunners of Srinagar's houseboat. A particular community lives in them. Formerly this community was associated with ferrying people, livestock and food grains along the river.

The past still lingers in their lifestyles even if their occupations have changed. Occasionally one may catch sight of a *doonga* making its stately progress down the river as the owner shifts residence! *Doongas* are sparsely furnished - virtually no furniture is seen except for the kitchen, which gleams with copper utensils of every description that line the shelves from floor to ceiling. Roads in the old city tend to be narrow, winding and chaotic. Some are too narrow to admit vehicular traffic. Each road connects to lanes and they in turn to bye-lanes, all appearing to the uninitiated and terribly confusing. There are arterial roads, however, and major market squares where it is difficult to get lost.

In a lane off *Nowhatta Chowk*, there are several *copper shops*, overflowing with an amazing profusion of copperware. As a matter of fact, such shops are situated all over the old city because every Kashmiri uses copper for tableware - even *huqqa* bases are made from copper. Some articles are un-patterned, others worked in bas-relief, engraving or pierced open-work. Exotic as they are, they make attractive ornaments about the house, or can be used as serving dishes. One of the many moods of the old city is the constant reminder about its tradition of handicrafts. Well-appointed shops in the fashionable areas of Srinagar seem rather remote from the humble families of craftsmen who create tapestries and shawls; the old city changes all that.

From top floor windows one catches sight of gaily embroidered fabric hanging out to dry. Occasionally a wizened old man cycles down the road, bearing a carpet, its lustrous colours glowing in the sunlight. Kashmiri colours are not the fiery colours of the desert that sear the eyelids. They are subdued; almost purposely it would seem, to counterpoint nature's magnificence. Earthy tones of brick, the rich hue of copper, even the vermilion of Kashmiri chillies drying on window sills in autumn appear monochromatic when set off against the splendour of the Valley's backdrop. The only craft where Kashmiris revel in colour is in their carpets. Here too, the colours are never loud, never disharmonious, but always subtle and soft.

At *Habba Kadal,* shop after shop sells nothing but skeins of wool, mainly to carpet weavers. Study the muted tones and then relate them to the carpets that you see - as long as the colours remain in your mind's eye, you will never mistake a Kashmiri carpet. The old city also boasts of Kashmir's many ancient shrines and mosques among which the shrine of *Shah-i-Hamdan,* situated between Habba Kadal and Fateh Kadal, is probably the most important. *Shah-i-Hamdan,* who came from Persia in the 13th century, was responsible for the spread of Islam in Kashmir. *Khanqah-i-Mualla,* on the banks of the Jhelum, was the very spot where Shah-i-Hamdan used to offer prayers.

Upon his death, a shrine, ornately decorated with papier-mache on the walls and ceiling, was built in his memory. *Makhdoom Sahib, Patthar Masjid, Jama Masjid* and *Pir Dastagir* are the major mosques and shrines in the old city. Tourists are welcome to visit the mosques and shrines in the old city. There are a few points to be kept in mind in accordance with the sanctity of these places. Women are not allowed into the inner sanctum of shrines, but there is no such restriction in the case of mosques.

Shoes must be taken off at the entrance. Jamia Masjid charges a fee for photography. Visitors are expected to conform to certain regulations in the matter of dress - no skimpy tops, shorts or short skirts are allowed. One does not go to the old city to shop. The exhilaration in exploring the old city comes from peeping into a world which normally admits no outsiders and which continues at its own pace, not much affected by changing times.

PARIHASAPURA

The karewas of Paraspor and Divar are situated at a distance of fourteen miles from Srinagar on the Baramula road. They were chosen by King Lalitaditya (c. A.D. 750) for the erection of a new capital city, and it is certain that, given a sufficient supply of drinking water, the high and dry Plateaus of Parihasapura have every advantage over the low, swampy Srinagar as a building site. Lalitaditya and his ministers seem to have vied with each other in embellishing the new city with magnificent edifices which were intended to be worthy alike of the king's glory and the ministers' affluence.

The Plateau is studded with heaps of ruins of which a few have been excavated. Among these the most important are three Buddhist structures, a stupaj a monastery, and a chaitya. Their common features are the enormous size of the blocks of limestone used in their construction, the smoothness of their dressing, and the fineness of their joints. The immense pile at the north-eastern corner of the Plateau is the stupa of Chankuna, the Turkoman minister of Lalitaditya. Its superstructure has entirely disappeared, leaving behind a huge mass of scorched boulders which completely cover the top of the base. There is a large massive block in the middle of this debris, which has a circular hole in the middle, 5' deep.

It is probable that this stone belonged to the hti (finial) of the stupa, and that the hole is the mortice in which was embedded the lower end of the staff of the stone umbrellas which crowned the drum. The base is 128' 2" square in plan, with offsets and a flight of steps on each side. Its mouldings are of the usual type, a round torus in the middle and a filleted torus as the cornice. The steps were flanked by plain rails and side walls which had pilasters in front decorated with carved figures of seated and standing atlantes. Some of these are in position, while others, which were lying about loose, have been transported to the Srinagar Museum.

They are not grotesque creatures like those so commonly seen in Gandhara, but have the appearance of ordinary respectable gentlemen, whose placid features seem to indicate that the superincumbent weight sits lightly upon them. The top surface of each of the two plinths is broad and affords adequate space for circumambulation. Among the loose architectural stones lying scattered about the site are a few curious blocks in the south-eastern and south-western corners. They are round torus stones adorned with four slanting bands or fillets running round the body. As this type of torus moulding is not used in either of the bases, it is probable that it belonged to the string-course on the drum of the stupa.

There are fragments of trefoiled arches also, which contained images of the Buddha and Bodhisattvas. The large square structure to the south of the stupa is the rajavihara, or royal monastery. A flight of steps in the east wall gives access to one of its cells which served as a verandah. The monastery is a quadrangle of twenty-six cells enclosing a square courtyard which was originally paved with stone flags, some of which are extant. In front of the cells was a broad verandah, which was probably covered, the roof being supported by a colonnade which ran along the edge of the plinth. A flight of steps corresponding to the one mentioned above leads down to the courtyard.

Exactly opposite to this, in the middle of the west wall, are three cells preceded by a vestibule, which is built on a plinth projected into the courtyard. It is probable that these were the apartments occupied by the abbot of the monastery. Near a corner of it is a large stone trough, which may have served as a water reservoir for bathing purposes. A couple of stone drains passing underneath cells Nos. 18 and 21 (if we begin counting from the cell to the south of the entrance chamber) carry off the rain and other surplus water from the courtyard. Externally the plinth is about 10' high. In cell No. 25 (that is the one to the north of the entrance chamber) was found a small earthen jug which contained forty-four silver coins in excellent preservation.

They belonged to the time of kings Vinayaditya, Vigraha, and Durlabha. They are now exhibited in the Numismatic Section of the Srinagar Museum. The monastery was repaired at a subsequent period. The repairs are plainly distinguishable in the exterior of the wall on the eastern and western sides. The building next to it on the south side is the chaitya built by Lalitaditya. It stands on a double base of the usual type. A flight of steps on the east side leads to the entrance, which must originally have been covered by a large trefoil-arch, fragments of which are Iying about the site.

This building possesses some of the most massive blocks of stone that have ever been used in Kashmiri temples, and which compare favourably with those used in ancient Egyptian buildings. The floor of the sanctum is a single block 14' by 12' 6" by 5' 2". The sanctum is 27' square surrounded by a circumambulatory passage. It is probable that its ceiling was supported on four columns, the bases only of which survive at the four corners. The roof, which was probably supported on the massive stone walls of the pradakshina, may have been of the pyramidal type.

The courtyard is enclosed by a rubble-stone wall which has nothing remarkable about it. In front of the temple steps is the base of a column which probably supported the dhvaja, or banner, bearing the special emblem of the deity enshrined in the sanctuary. The flank walls of the stair were adorned with atlantes similar to those of the stupa. Near the chaitya is the foundation of a small building of the diaper-rubble style. While this Plateau was reserved for the erection of Buddhist buildings only, the other two were exclusively appropriated by Hindus.

Perhaps the arrangement was intentional, to avoid possible friction between the two powerful religious bodies.

On the karewa locally known as Gordan there are ruins of a Hindu temple which are probably all that remain of Lalitaditya's temple of Govardhanadhara. Crossing the ravine in which nestles the little village of Diwar- Yakmanpura, and ascending the Plateau opposite, are seen the immense ruins of two extraordinarily large temples - one of them has a peristyle larger than that of Martand - which may represent Lalitaditya's favourite shrines of Parihasakesava and Muktakesava.

PATAN

SUGANDHES'A TEMPLE

The Rajatarangini mentions the erection of three temples at Patan, which in ancient days was called S'ankarapurapattana, after the name of its founder, King S'ankaravarman (A.D. 883-902). Perhaps it would be well to remark here that vandalism of a serious kind had already begun in pre-Muslim times, as some of the materials used in the construction of these temples were removed from the older site of Parihasapura described above. The three temples named by the Kashmir chronicle are (1) S'ankaragauris'vara, (2) Sugandhesa, and (3) Ratnavardhanesa.

The first, identified with the larger temple near Patan, was built by the king himself, the second, which is the one nearer Srinagar, is named after Sugandha, his queen, and the third, of which no trace has so far been found, if we exclude the architectural fragments near the spring outside the dak bangalow, was built by Ratnavardhana, his minister. All three were dedicated to S'iva. The Sugandhesa temple does not differ materially from other temples of Kashmir. The shrine is 12' 7" square and has, as usual, a portico in front. It is open on one side only, and has trefoiled niches externally on the other sides. These niches contained images.

The temple stands on a double base, but it seems probable from the flank walls of the lower stair and the frieze of the lower base, in which the panels intended for sculpture decoration have been merely blocked out, but not carved, that the temple was never completed. The entrance to the courtyard is in the middle of the eastern wall of the peristyle, and consists, as usual, of two chambers with a partition wall and a doorway in the middle.

Among the architectural fragments lying loose on the site, the most noteworthy are (a) two fragments of fluted columns with their capitals, (b) two bracket capitals with voluted ends and carved figures of atlantes supporting the frieze above, (c) a huge stone belonging to the cornice of the temple, bearing rows of kirtimukhas (grinning lions' heads) and rosettes, and (d) a stone probably belonging to the partition wall of the entrance, having (1) two small trefoiled niches in which stand female figures wearing long garlands and (2) below them two rectangular niches, in one of which is an atlant seated between two lions facing the spectator, and in the other are two human-headed birds.

The cornice of the base of the peristyle is similar to that of the Avantisvami temple. The cells were preceded by a row of fluted columns, bases of some of which are in situ while those of others are scattered about in the courtyard. The attention of the visitor is called to the slots in the lower stones of the jambs of the cells. These are mortices for iron clamps which held pairs of stones together. Pieces of much-corroded iron are still extant in some of the mortices.

SANKARAGAURISVARA TEMPLE

Lower down is the larger temple built by the king himself. It is only an enlarged copy of the queen's temple. On account of the lack of proper facilities for drainage of rain water it has not been deemed advisable to excavate its courtyard. The peristyle, the temple-plinth, and a smaller shrine in the north-east corner, are therefore still underground. The rectangular path around the temple marks the position of the peristyle, tops of some columns of which are seen peeping out of the earth in the south-west corner. The square flower-bed with a projection on one side in the north-east corner of the courtyard coincides with the small shrine below.

The square space in the middle of the eastern path marks the position of the entrance. The temple itself is an imposing pile, though a great deal of its grandeur has been taken away by the concealment of its plinth. The cella is 17' square and the central stone of the floor measures 12' 6" by 10'. It has nine circular holes arranged in three rows. It is possible that these were mortices of tenons which held in position the pedestal of the idol. The left wall of the portico has a trefoiled niche which is divided into two panels. The lower and larger one contains a number of figures, of which the principal seems to be S'iva.

Above it, in the upper foil, is the squatting figure of the elephant-headed god, Ganesha, whose presence here would conclusively prove, even if there were any doubt about it, that the temple was dedicated to S'iva. The jambs of the recesses on the exterior of the temple have half-engaged columns which are decorated with well-executed geometrical and other patterns. Their capitals are surmounted by human-headed birds. A few yards to the north of the Patan dak bangalow has recently been excavated an old baoli whose waters are confined in three rectangular reservoirs which are connected with each other.

The one in the middle contains a miniature temple constructed originally of three stones. The top-stone is missing. It is 2' 8" square externally and is open on all four sides. The openings seem to have been closed originally with wooden doors. These little shrines belong to the time when the prosperity of the Hindus had waned, and they were not capable of devoting so much wealth to the glorification of their religion.

USHKAR AND BARAMULA

The village of Ushkar or Wushkur is situated at a distance of half a mile from the Baramula dak bangalow. The name is a corruption of Huvishkapura, which, according to Kalhana, was the name of a city founded by Huvishka, the great Kushan king in the second century A.D. It was a flourishing town in mediaeval times owing to its position on the principal trade-route between Kashmir and northwestern India. Lalitaditya built here a shrine of Vishnu named Muktasvamin and a large vihara with a stupa. Hsuan-tsang, the famous Chinese pilgrim who visited Kashmir in A.D. 631, entered the valley by the Baramula pass, and spent his first night at one of the monasteries here.

The reigning king accorded him a very hospitable welcome, sending his own mother and younger brother with chariots and horses to escort him to the capital. Of the monasteries and temples which Hsuan-tsang saw, and Kalhana mentions, none now remain above ground, except the ruins of a stupa and its surrounding wall, a few yards to the west of the village. On the analogy of style which is similar to that of the great stupa at Parihasapura, there can be little doubt that it is the same structure which the Kashmir chronicle states Lalitaditya built in the middle of the eighth century A.D. Only the lowest courses of its base are now in position.

An interesting fact about this stupa is that it seems to have been built over an older structure of nearly the same type, stones of which were found in situ when the silt round the base was removed some years ago. That structure may have belonged to Kushan times. This surmise is strengthened by the discovery outside the north-eastern corner of the surrounding wall, of eleven terracotta heads, besides a number of fragmentary limbs of images which display the unmistakable influence of the Gandhara School of the third and fourth century. These are now preserved in the Srinagar Museum.

a. Illustrates the head of a Bodhisattva. The unusually ornamental treatment of the hair in this fragment is noteworthy. The delicate features, rounded chin, and twisted, dandified locks secured by a beaded fillet placed sideways, make the face attractive in spite of the somewhat weary smile and the self-satisfied expression of the face.
b. The shaggy beard, close-pressed lips, knitted eyebrows, and furrowed forehead, of this Brahman ascetic are so

remarkably realistic that it would be difficult to imagine that the artist was not drawing a portrait from life. The hair is neatly brushed upwards and was probably gathered in a knot at the back of the head, where it was kept in position by an ornamental band. The ardent gaze and the prominent cheekbones are indicative of self-mortification.

c. This is one of the most beautiful heads found at Ushkar. The oval face, small nose, sensitive nostrils, soft delicate lips, plump rounded chin, hair smoothly combed back and falling in curly tresses on the shoulders, are all essentially feminine. She is an upasika, or female lay devotee. Her soft and wistful gaze, intensified by the upturned poise of the face, shows with what a feeling of devotion these feminine worshippers approached the Master.

d. This illustration represents the head of a contemplative young monk with shaven crown, high forehead, arched eyebrows, and large dreamy eyes. The remarkably high and narrow skull seems to be the result of lateral pressure, a practice which was once prevalent among certain tribes in Central Asia.

One of the large blocks of stones lying loose in the trench to the north of the stupa bears the Sarada letters he-sh-ka-ra incised upon its rough surface, a circumstance which proves that even in Lalitaditya's time the town was known by its colloquial name, though the dignified Sanskrit original remained in vogue in literature. Not the least interesting object here is the compact surrounding wall built of extremely small chips of stone in mud. The entrance to the courtyard must have been on the east side, opposite to the stairs of the stupa.

The lower portion of the wall is extraordinarily thick and served, no doubt, as plinth for a range of cells which ran along its entire length, the upper portion being utilised as their back wall. The foundations of the wall are pierced at intervals with openings for drains. Other objects of interest near by are two colossal S'iva-lingas erected at the two ends of the village. The town of Baramula, properly Varahamula, named after the Boar incarnation of Vishnu, was an important place in mediaeval times.

The temple of Adi-Varaha, "Primeval Boar," destroyed by Sikandar But-shikan, is said to have been one of the most splendid in Kashmir. Its site is identified, on the strength of local tradition, with the Kotitirtha situated half a mile below the bridge. A few architectural stones may still be seen lying about at this place. The only object of interest which it now contains is the large human-faced S'iva-linga. Further down is the site of the old watch-station, known as Drang, which name it has retained from very early times. It served the double purpose of a customs post and frontier outpost where traffic could be controlled and all suspicious characters apprehended.

FATHGARH

This is the name of the small village near the mouth of the Narvav valley. It is situated at a distance of nearly three miles from Baramula. It contains the ruins of a very large temple which presents several points of interest. Internally it is 28' 9" square. The greater part of the cella was occupied by a massive platform on which was placed a colossal S'iva-linga, a large fragment of which is lying there still. The platform was decorated with a torus moulding and the space around it was no doubt used as a pradakshina. Two fragments of the waterspout (pranali), which carried off the washings of the image, are also lying in the sanctum.

The front elevation of the platform is decorated with two rows of trefoiled niches, which were probably intended to contain lamps during the evening worship. A point of special interest about this temple is the arrangement of the ceiling. In other temples, as has been remarked above, the ceiling is either composed of overlapping stones which gradually lessen the span until it is sufficiently short to be covered by a single slab, usually circular, or it is straight-lined and triangular in section as at Narastan and Naranthal. Here both these arrangements have been discarded in favour of an elaborate system of corbelling.

A late memorial stele displaying very poor artistic skill has been discovered in the excavation of the cella. The lower panel contains a pair of clumsy human figures seated on stools facing each other. The upper one contains a trident. The dadoof the portico is adorned with rowof pedimented niches. The open doorway faces north-west and, like the closed recesses on the exterior of the other three sides, was covered by a large trefoiled arch surmounted by a pediment. Its pilasters are, as usual, adorned with half-engaged fluted columns. This temple has a particularly massive appearance and its thorough excavation is very desirable. In the south-east corner of the area is a late brick well.

NARANTHAL

This is the name of a village about two and a half miles below Baramula on the right bank of the river. On the old road to Muzaffarabad and situated at a short distance from the village is a small shrine which is said to have stood in a tank, though today it is on dry ground and no traces of a tank are visible. But there is a spring near by. Only the superstructure of the temple is above ground. It is built of plain blocks of slate which are now very much the worse for wear. There is only one arched entrance on the east side. Traces of a stone floor are visible inside. The second course from the top is formed of a single slab 4 1/2' square by 1 1/2' thick.

The interior is a square of 7 1/4' and is 9' 5" high. There is no ceiling. The topmost stone of the roof has a circular mortice in the centre which was originally intended to hold the finial which crowned the apex of the pyramid. The temple is probably of the late mediaeval era, not earlier than the twelfth century A.D., and perhaps much later.

BUNIAR

The temple of Buniar is situated on the Jhelum Valley road, two miles above Rampur. It is by far the best preserved of all the larger Kashmir temples. The gateway is a double-chambered structure faced on each open side by a trefoil arch surmounted by a steep pediment. The lintels of the closed arches are supported on pairs of columns which were originally fluted, though the weather has now left no trace of flutes. They have a double capital, the upper one being voluted on all four sides. The walls are externally surmounted by a cornice of kirti- mukhas, alternating with miniature trefoiled niches. Upon this rests the first course of the pyramidal roof.

The flights of steps-on the eastern and western sides respectively afford entrance to and exit from the entrance chamber. The one on the roadside is buried underground, but the inner stair has been excavated. It consists of seven steps flanked by sloping rails and upright side walls. Between this stair and the temple is a small stone platform which formed the lowermost course of the stepped base of a column (most probably a Garudadhvaja). The priest in charge of the temple has now placed in it a small stele of very crude workmanship and late date, which he has painted with vermilion. Another similar stele, still standing in the position in which it was found, is seen in front of the temple stair.

The temple itself stands on a double base, which is in every respect similar to other structures of its kind in Kashmir. A lofty trefoil arch, standing upon advanced pilasters and enclosing a rectangular entrance originally surmounted by an ornamental trefoil and steep pediment, gives access to the sanctum. The jambs of the entrance are adorned with half-engaged columns. The interior is a square of 14 feet. The pedestal of the image is placed on a broad platform. The original image, which seems to have been of Vishnu, is now replaced by small Siva-lingas originally brought from the bed of the river Narbada. The walls are covered with a coat of modern whitewash.

The string course from which the ceiling springs is still visible, but the ceiling itself which Bishop Cowie saw in 1865 and described as domical, has since either fallen down or been removed. It was, no doubt, similar to the ceilings of the larger temples at Wangath. Externally the only decorations are the trefoils of the recesses, their pediments, and the cornice of kirtimukhas and miniature trefoils from which the roof sprang. The quadrangle measures 145' by 119 1/2', and consists of fifty- three cells and the gateway. They are rectangular, 7' long by 4' broad.

Each cell has a single trefoiled entrance enclosed in a high- pitched pediment resting on half-engaged columns. These ranges of cells are preceded by a noble colonnade which stands on a base similar to that of the temple. A transverse beam connects the capitals of the columns with the roof of the cells. Over these beams rises the entablature, only one course of which, namely the frieze of miniature trefoils, is extant. In the centre of each range of cells, except, perhaps, the one in which the gateway stands, is an apartment of larger dimensions preceded by a pair of taller columns which are advanced about 4' from the rest of the peristyle.

The top course of the cells is also decorated in the same way as the frieze above. On the south side, projecting from the cornice of the upper base of the temple is the spout of the channel which carried off the washings of the image. It seems to have been shaped originally into a makara, or crocodile's head. Immediately below it is a huge water trough carved out of a single block of stone. The rain-water in the courtyard is carried off by a drain which runs under the south-eastern corner of the peristyle. In cell No. 11 of the north range, beginning the reckoning from the corner nearest the gateway, is the side entrance, which was then, as now, closed with a wooden door.

The monotony of the external face of the western wall is partially relieved by rows of small square projections. In its two corners are two cells opening outwards. Immediately outside the side-door mentioned above is a square structure built of plain blocks of stone. The middle portion of each of its four walls has fallen down, and the gaps have been filled in with small chips of stone built in mud. It is diflicult to surmise what was its original purpose.

DHATHAMANDIR OR THE BANDI TEMPLE

The temple known as Dhathamandir is situated on the Jhelum Valley cart road, midway between Rampur and Uri, about two miles below Mohora. The name signifies "ruined temple." The only material difference in style between this temple and the one at Buniar is that it does not possess any colonnade, and that the cells, which in the former are built of granite as the temple itself, are here built of kanjur, their plinth only being of limestone. The jambs of the cells were decorated with half-engaged columns, remnants of which may still be seen in the south-western corner of the peristyle.

The central shrine faces north-east, and is built of a very beautiful green limestone, which, curiously enough, seems to have been covered with a thick coat of lime plaster, decayed fragments of which are still clinging to various parts of the walls. The pedestal of the image is extant. There are two small shrines, replicas of the main building in the north-western corner of the courtyard. The bases of the columns which supported the trefoil arch of the gateway are still in situ.

Fragments of columns as well as their beautifully carved capitals are lying about in the compound and the area outside the gateway. On the hillside, a few yards to the south-east of the temple, are remains of two smaller shrines which, like the subsidiary temples in the courtyard, are replicas of the main temple.

FIROZPOR DRANG

Firozpor drang is a small village situated at a distance of a mile and a half from Tang Marg, at the spot where the Firozpornala issues from the mountains into the open ground. The latter part of the name preserves the memory of its ancient appellation Karkota-dranga. The term "dranga" was used in pre-Muslim times to indicate a frontier watch-station, established for the purpose of collecting customs duties and of generally safeguarding the frontier. Karkota-dranga (modern Firozpor) controlled the Tosamaidan route to Punch (ancient Parnotsa; Kashmiri Prunts).

The village contains the ruins of a small temple which was probably originally surrounded by a peristyle, no part of which, except the double-chambered gateway, is now extant above ground. The chief cause of the ruin of this temple seems to have been the unchecked growth of vegetation. Several walnut trees have taken root in the masonry, and are continuing the process of destruction. The temple faces north-east. The roof has fallen in, and has filled the whole cella with large boulders which have completely hidden the floor, and consequently made it impossible to ascertain to which particular god the shrine was dedicated. Internally it is 11' square.

The ceiling seems to have been of the Narastan type. The portico was surmounted by a trefoil-arch and a pediment of the usual type. Externally also this temple is similar to the Narastan temple, inasmuch as the corner pilasters have very slight projection and the trefoiled recesses on the sides are smaller than the arch of the portico. It stands on a base surmounted by a cyma recta moulding. Admission is gained by a flight of steps flanked by plain side-walls. The gateway measures 15' 6" square externally.

Ascending the spur, at whose foot these ruins are situated, we come to a very beautiful piece of open ground in the midst of dense forest. Among the trees at one corner of it are the scanty remains of the base of a small temple. The long lines of walling between the temple and the village are regarded by tradition as the ruins of the old watch-station.

MANASBAL

One of the most attractive places in the valley is the Manasbal Lake. Being absolutely free from disturbance of any kind, and nestling in an oval basin surrounded on all sides by hills and uplands, the lake is an ideal abode for the happy lotus-eater, who dreams away his days reclining under the shady chinar, and passes his evenings in watching the long streaks of moonlight flitting across the mirror-like surface of the water. Naturally, such a delightful spot would not have been overlooked either by the devout Hindu or the nature-adoring Mughal.

The former have left a small temple, now partially submerged during the greater part of the year. It is a very small structure, and only its two pyramidal roofs are visible in the driest seasons. The cornice of the lower roof, and the horizontal band which divides it from the upper storey, are decorated with series of dentils and metopes. Only the upper part of the pediment of the entrance is visible. It faces west. A few yards from the temple, up the hill, is a natural cavern of no particular interest. Further up is the Shahkul canal brought down from the Sindh River by Zain-ul-abidin.

On the south bank of the lake are ruins of a terraced Mughal garden, the construction of which is ascribed by tradition to Empress Nur Jahan. The garden, locally known as the Jarogha, is entirely in ruins, the only parts standing being the retaining walls and the corner bastions of the terraces. There are a number of sculptured stones, belonging to some Buddhist shrine, scattered about on top of the low ridge on the northern bank of the lake.

ANDARKOT

Near the entrance of the lake, on the left bank of the river, is the large village of Sumbal. At a distance of a mile from it is situated Andarkot, known originally by the name of Jayapura, the capital of King Jayapida. The site selected for the capital was in the midst of an extensive marsh, the drainage of which was so difficult a task that in Kalhana's time (twelfth century) it was believed that in the execution of his design the king had employed the services of rakshasas, "demons," whom his friend, King Vibhishana of Ceylon, had placed at his disposal. The ancient causeway which connects the island with the mainland of Sumbal is still the only means of communication in the rainy season, when the lowlands round about are covered with water.

There is not much left today of the Buddhist viharas and Hindu temples which are said to have been built here by Jayapida. Practically everything has been destroyed. The temple of Kes'ava is represented by a large heap of scorched and shapeless boulders. The only objects of interest are a couple of sculptured reliefs on two faces of the pilaster of the stair; and they too are woefully defaced. The relief on the flank depicts a four-armed Vishnu seated on a cushioned throne in what is technically known as the lalitasana (sportive attitude), while an attendant, probably a female, is standing on his left. The left foot of the god rests upon a small footstool.

His upper right hand holds a mace, and the lower one is placed in abhayamudra (pose of grantirig immunity from fear). He is profusely ornamented, and wears the mandaramala (garland - of celestial flowers). Under his throne are an atlant and some other indistinct figures. The relief on the front panel contains a group of three figures: Vishnu seated between his two consorts. The sculptures belong to about the seventh or eighth century A.D. Andarkot has a particularly sorrowful interest for the Hindus of Kashmir, for it was in the fort here that the last Hindu ruler, Queen Kotadevi, surrendered to her rebellious servant, Shah Mir, on certain stipulations which he did not fulfil afterwards.

THE WULAR LAKE

The ancient name of the Wular Lake was the Mahapadmasaras, (Lake of Mahapadma), the great Serpent Deity. Its modern name is probably derived from the Sanskrit ullola, the lake with the "high- leaping" waves. The historian Jonaraja states that King Zain-ul-abidin was anxious to build such a monument to his fame as had never been built by any king before. After much deliberation he decided to construct an island-palace in the middle of the Wular Lake, but he was so greatly impressed with the magnitude of the task that he sought the wise men of his time for advice regarding the ways and means of its accomplishment. They encouraged his efforts by narrating the following legend:

In ancient times there was a city at that very place where there is the lake nowadays. The city was presided over by the great snake deity, Mahapadma. But the lapse of time, and the security given by beneficent rule, brought in its train luxury and vice among the citizens, which grew with such alarming rapidity that Mahapadma resolved upon the destruction of the entire city, including its inhabitants. But, among the residents of the doomed city was a humble and virtuous potter, whom the deity resolved to spare. He appeared to him in a dream and, warning him of the impending fate of the city, told him to save himself. Next morning the potter related the warning to the citizens, but was laughed at for his pains.

As soon, therefore, as the potter left the city, the waters began to rise until the entire countryside was overwhelmed by one tremendous deluge. To quote from Jonaraja: "The terrified children who stood, at first when the water was low, at the feet of their mothers, soon, as the water began to rise higher, got into their laps, then clung to their breasts, next jumped upon their shoulders, and finally sat upon their heads, as if they were their embodied vital breaths. The flood covered the quaking limbs of women as if it were an affectionate lover embracing his beloved whose limbs are trembling with emotion."

After the Naga had thus wreaked his vengeance upon the sinful city, he established his permanent residence in the newly formed lake. "The Lord of the Snakes was in reality Kaliya, who, being trampled upon by the feet of Krishna, bore the mark of a lotus on his head, and from that time onwards bore the appellation of Mahapadma."

Zain-ul-abidin's wise men then wound up their story by the naive assurance that he, being an incarnation of Hari, could do as he pleased in the domain of his liege subject Mahapadma, and that his efforts would assuredly be crowned with success. He therefore set about vigorously for accomplishment of his purpose. Large cargo boats, which are still plentiful in Kashmir, were filled with boulders and sunk at the spot selected. The island was named Zainalanka after its builder, and still retains that name. The king built a small but very beautiful mosque at one corner of it, the ruins of which are still in existence.

It is built of large blocks of limestone, similar to those used in the mediaeval temples of Kashmir. Even the mouldings are those which are so common in the ancient Hindu temples. The principal decorative feature externally is a double row of trefoiled niches, which are flanked by pretty fluted columns surmounted by ribbed capitals. The lower row of niches stands on a quirked ovolo course, and is surmounted by a filleted torus. The corner pilasters have square filleted capitals. The two flank walls of the porch survive. The interior was paved with large stone flags. The floor was on a level with the filleted torus outside.

A large assortment of architectural fragments of Hindu temples, such as fluted columns, stones from pilasters, jambs, etc., are scattered round about the site, which tends to prove that there was once a Hindu temple also on the island. This hypothesis is further strengthened by the presence of a big Siva-linga, which is partly submerged, on the east side of the island. It is probable that the temple also was built by Zain-ul-abidin, for none of his successors on the Kashmir throne was capable of such a colossal task. There are indications to show that there were series of steps on all sides leading down to the water, though the principal landing seems to have been on the east side.

The only other structure on the island is a small domed chamber of brick masonry measuring 15' 7" square internally. This was also partly built of Hindu materials. The string-courses on top of the walls consist of projecting wooden beams. The entire surface of the chamber seems to have been coated with painted plaster. Externally the walls were adorned with shallow arched recesses which were originally covered with plaster. They were separated by glazed tiles. The square impressions of these tiles are visible on the plaster backing wherever it still adheres to the walls. Fragments of painted and glazed tiles are lying in the debris.

The structure seems to be a tomb, and is probably contemporary with the mosque. In 1874, Dr. Vincent-Smith discovered on this island a stone slab bearing a Persian inscription which mentioned the name of Zain-ul- abidin and contained the date A.H. 847 - A.D. 1442-43.

GARUR

On the north-eastern shore of the lake is situated the village of Garur. It contains a small mediaeval temple 4' 2" square internally, and 7' 3" high from basement to cornice. The roof has disappeared and the base is buried underground. The temple faces north-west and stands on the bank of a spring.

The steps which led down to the water are now missing. The absence of the external trefoil niches is remarkable. The roof was undoubtedly pedimented. There is a small pointed niche in each of these walls, which contains a sculptured relief. That on the back bears a three-headed Siva. The other two figures are too defaced to be identified with anything approaching certainty. The ceiling is built of overlapping stones.

WANGATH

The Srinagar-Sonamarg high roadl branches off at Wusan to the mountain village of Wangath and the long and narrow glen known to sportsmen by the name of Wangath Nala. The dense dark green forests of pine and fir which clothe the steep and in some places almost vertical hill-sides are favourite haunts of the bear in early autumn, when maize begins to ripen. The cow-track - for the Wangath road is nothing better - winds along the mountain spurs, always following the tortuous course of the Kanka-nadi torrent, whose white and foaming waters form a striking contrast to the sombre hue of the surrounding woods.

On all sides the view is bounded by long ranges of hills rising higher and still higher as they recede until they terminate in the bare, jagged, towering peaks of Tilail. An uphill trudge of eight or nine miles brings the jaded traveller to Narannag, the site of an interesting group of temples which are commonly known as the Wangath temples, though the village bearing the name "Wangath " is three miles distant. They are situated at the foot of the Butsher Mountain, whose extreme steepness and slipperiness have become proverbial, and have made it the terror and despair of Gangabal pilgrims.

Narannag is the modern name of ancient Sodaratirtha, which has been, since very early times, an important place of pilgrimage in Kashmir. The site probably owes its sanctity to the existence of a large spring, near which have been built two groups of temples belonging to the mediaeval era. All the temples are more or less in ruins, chiefly owing to the inroads of vegetation. The stone used is the greyish granite which is found in abundance at the place. The first group, that is the one nearer Wangath, comprises six temples situated within an enclosure wall. Judging by their positions, as they are by no means symmetrically disposed in relation to one another, and by the difference in their architectural details, it is probable that the various structures were built at different dates.

The principal temple is a square of 25', and, except in a few particulars, does not differ from other temples of Kashmir. The first point of departure from the usual style is the entrances. We have seen the temples of the vimana type, which have all the four sides open. But this one has two entrances opposite each other in the north-east and south-west sides. The second distinction is its domed ceiling; though there is no doubt that externally the roof was pyramidal. A large quantity of lime has been used in the masonry of the temple. The ceiling is built of circular courses of kanjur stone, and is crowned at the apex by a full-blown lotus. The dome springs from four large corner stones, which cut off the angles formed by the walls.

On two sides of the string-course upon which the dome rests are eight rectangular slots (four on each side), which seem to have been intended to hold the rafters of a canopy over the image. The interior measures 17' square. In the centre of the floor is a square space which is unpaved. It marks the site of the pedestal of the image. The mortices of the tenons of the doors can still be seen in both entrances. The two sides which are closed are decorated externally with square-topped recesses, each of which contains the pedestal of an image which was probably a replica of the one in the sanctum itself. The core of the roof consists of rubble-stone masonry in lime. This temple has been identified by Sir Aurel Stein with the Jyeshthega temple of Lalitaditya.

The small temple to the left possesses niches on three sides intended for images. Their pedestals with tenons are in situ. Part of the kanjur backing of the dome is intact on top of the walls. The temple immediately touching the porch of the preceding shrine is a single square structure, plain both internally and externally. One stone of the roof, which is the only one in situ, shows that the ceiling was not domical, but was built of overlapping stones. Immediately behind is the basement of another small temple. Its superstructure has fallen down.

Of the two temples behind, one has its entrance facing north-east, and the other faces south-east. The ceiling of the former was of the overlapping type while that of the latter was probably domical. Immediately to the left of the latter is the ruined plinth of another temple, smaller than any of those described above. The gateway of the enclosure is situated, curiously enough, at the north-west corner, and not in the middle of the wall, as is the case in other temples. It is, as usual, a two-chambered structure. In each chamber are the bases of two columns which supported the roof of the porch. Fragments of circular columns which stood on the bases- are laying strewn round about the site.

The retaining wall of the plinth on which this group of temples stands is built of closely packed pieces of slate, and in places where vegetation has not played havoc with it, it is very compact and beautiful. A broad causeway paved with huge blocks of granite leads to the second group of temples, situated about two hundred yards farther off. Between the two groups of temples are a number of structures which in themselves deserve to be classed into a third group. All of them have fallen down, but one, the base only of which is in existence, is unique in Kashmir. It appears to have been a spacious pillared hall or barahdari about loo' long by 67' broad.

The bases of the columns are in situ. They are eight in number on the longer side and four on the shorter. The staircase is built between the central pair of columns facing the first group of temples. The slots in the landing on the top of the stairs seem to have been intended for holding the posts of screens. The lower group of temples is likewise enclosed in a massive rectangular stone wall pierced by a two-chambered gateway. Inside the wall are half a dozen structures, all in ruined condition and partly buried under the ground. The largest temple has been identified by Sir Aurel Stein with that of Siva-Bhutesvara. Internally it is a square of 17', and was similar to the largest temple in the first group. The small temple to its right has a round-headed entrance.

There are two small shrines on its south, the first of which differs from all the structures at this site in that it is built of small pieces of slate in lime mortar, placed upon a granite base. The peculiar feature of the second is an immense rectangular stone trough carved out of a single gigantic block of granite. Among the objects lying scattered about the compound, the most noteworthy are two fragments, in the south-east corner of the quadrangle, of an octagonal pedestal of a S'iva-linga, and two stones in the same corner of the quadrangle, each decorated with a pair of remarkably well- executed geese.

The long raised line of brick masonry on the enclosure wall is the debris of the cellular quadrangle which usually surrounds the Kashmiri temple. Outside the north-western corner of the peristyle is the large spring, the real lodestone of the pilgrims, which was the occasion of all this magnificence. Its cool, delicious water, perhaps, contributed to some extent to its sanctity. The water issues out of the mountain side through the masonry walls of the tank. Slightly higher up, and more than half-buried under the ground, is a small temple whose double pyramidal roof is the only existing roof in the whole group of temples here.

This has been identified by Sir Aurel Stein with the temple of Bhairava, near which the turbulent baron Dhanva was decapitated for encroaching upon the lands and revenues of these temples. Before leaving the site, the visitor should not fail to observe the unusually massive stone retaining wall of this group of temples. The granite blocks are of so extraordinary a size and are so beautifully dressed and finely joined as to give the impression that their carvers regarded them more in the light of wooden beams than as close-grained intractable boulders to be chipped into shape with vigilant care and inexhaustible patience.

It is probable that this wall served the double purpose of protecting the temple enclosure from being overwhelmed by the debris of the hill above, and also as the back wall of the range of cells on this side. The site has from time immemorial enjoyed a very high degree of popular esteem, which remains unimpaired to this day, thanks to the pilgrims who, after consigning the ashes of their dead relatives to the Gangabal Lake, make it a point to offer worship here. The temples were endowed with extensive estates, and the priests in charge seem to have been a particularly influential body. In the later mediaeval period, after the death of Avantivarman, these temples shared the misfortunes which came upon Kashmir with ever-increasing violence.

The temple treasury was plundered by Bhadresvara, the minister of Samgramaraja (A.D. 1003-1028); a conflagration in the reign of Uchchala (A. D. 1101 - 1111) inflicted much damage upon the buildings; during the reign of Jayasimha (A.D. 1128-1155), Hayavadana, a rebel baron, had the temples " sacked by marauding hillmen." Śumanas, a brother of Rilhana, the minister of Jayasimha, built a matha or congregation hall here. It is possible that the pillared hall is this same matha. Further excavations may throw light upon the question.

8

Jammu, Kashmir and Ladakh Region

Ladakh Situated in the Indian state of Jammu and Kashmir between the Kunlun mountain range in the north and the main Great Himalayas to the south and is inhabited by people of Indo-Aryan and Tibetan descent, is one of the most sparsely populated regions in the area. Ladakh is renowned for its remote mountain beauty and culture. It is sometimes called "Little Tibet" as it has been strongly influenced by Tibetan culture. Historically, Ladakh was a Buddhist kingdom which included Baltistan and Aksai Chin which are now administered by Pakistan and China respectively.

It had a strategic location at the crossroads of major trade routes, but since the Chinese authorities closed the borders with Tibet and Central Asia in the 1960s, international trade has dwindled except for tourism. Since 1974 the Indian Government has successfully encouraged tourism in Ladakh. Ladakh has been a focal point of numerous wars between India and Pakistan and the Sino-Indian War of 1962. The Saltoro ridge in the Siachen glacier region is an active military zone even today. Today Ladakh consists of two districts - Leh and Kargil. The largest town in Ladakh is Leh.

A majority of Ladakhis are Tibetan Buddhists and the rest are mostly Shia Muslims. Some Ladakhi activists have in recent times called for Ladakh to be constituted as a union territory because of its religious and cultural differences with predominantly Muslim Kashmir. Ladakh constitutes the eastern-most part of the state of Jammu & Kashmir. This is one of the most breathtakingly beautiful parts of the state and its surreal landscape has often been termed as "moonscape". Ladakh covers about 117,000 square km and includes the Karakoram Range and the upper Indus River valley. Ladakh is one of the highest places on earth with average altitude being above 12,000 feet.

It hardly rains here because of the lofty surrounding mountain ranges. People live a very traditional life, herding sheep and yak, and growing barley near the river beds in summer. Most of the people here are Lamaistic Buddhist. Another section of people in the northern part of Ladakh, called Kargil, the people are mostly Shia Muslims. Neither the Shias nor the Buddhists support the militancy in the Valley. This spectacular place is connected by air to the regional capital, Leh. Road routes exist from Srinagar and Spiti (Himachal Pradesh). Rock carvings found in many parts of Ladakh showing that the area has been inhabited from Neolithic times. Ladakh's earliest inhabitants consisted of a mixed Indo-Aryan population of *Mons* and *Dards*, who find mention in the works of Herodotus, Nearchus, Megasthenes, Pliny, Ptolemy, and the geographical lists of the Puranas.

Around the 1st century, Ladakh was a part of the Kushana Empire. Buddhism spread into western Ladakh from Kashmir in the 2nd century when much of eastern Ladakh and western Tibet was still practising the Bon religion. The 7th century Buddhist traveler Xuanzang also describes the region in his accounts. In the 8th century, Ladakh was involved in the clash between Tibetan expansion pressing from the East and Chinese influence exerted from Central Asia through the passes. Suzerainty over Ladakh frequently changed hands between China and Tibet. In 842 Nyima-Gon, a Tibetan royal representative annexed Ladakh for himself after the break-up of the Tibetan empire, and founded a separate Ladakh dynasty.

During this period Ladakh acquired a predominantly Tibetan population. The dynasty spearheaded the "Second

Spreading of Buddhism" importing religious ideas from north-west India, particularly from Kashmir. Faced with the Islamic conquest of South Asia in the 13th century, Ladakh chose to seek and accept guidance in religious matters from Tibet. For nearly two centuries till about 1600, Ladakh was subject to raids and invasions from neighbouring Muslim states, which led to the partial conversion of Ladakhis to Islam.

King Bhagan reunited and strengthened Ladakh and founded the Namgyal dynasty which survives even today. The Namgyals repelled most Central Asian raiders and temporarily extended the kingdom as far as Nepal, in the face of concerted attempts to convert the region to Islam and destroy Buddhist artifacts. In the early 17th century efforts were made to restore destroyed artifacts and gompas, and the kingdom expanded into Zangskar and Spiti. Ladakh was, however defeated by the Mughals, who had already annexed Kashmir and Baltistan, but it retained its independence.

In the late 17th century, Ladakh sided with Bhutan in its dispute with Tibet, which resulted in an invasion by Tibet. Kashmiri help restored Ladakhi rule on the condition of that a mosque be built in Leh and that the Ladakhi king convert to Islam. The Treaty of Temisgam in 1684 settled the dispute between Tibet and Ladakh, but severely restricted Ladakh's independence. In 1834, the Dogras under Zorawar Singh, a general of Ranjit Singh invaded and annexed Ladakh. A Ladakhi rebellion in 1842 was crushed and Ladakh was incorporated into the Dogra state of Jammu and Kashmir.

The Namgyal family was given the *jagir* of Stok, which it nominally retains to this day. Starting from the 1850s, European influence increased in Ladakh - geologists, sportsmen and tourists started exploring Ladakh. In 1885, Leh became the headquarters of a mission of the Moravian Church. At the time of the partition of India in 1947, the Dogra ruler Maharaja Hari Singh was undecided whether to accede to the Indian Union or Pakistan. Eventually, the ruler signed the Instrument of Accession to India. Pakistani raiders had reached Ladakh and military operations were initiated to evict them.

The wartime conversion of the pony trail from Sonamarg to Zoji La by army engineers permitted tanks to move up and successfully capture the pass. The advance continued and Dras, Kargil and Leh were liberated and Ladakh cleared of the infiltrators. In 1949, China closed the border between Nubra and Xinjiang, blocking old trade routes. In 1955 China began to build roads connecting Xinjiang and Tibet through this area. It also built the Karakoram highway jointly with Pakistan. India built the Srinagar-Leh Highway during this period, cutting the journey time between Srinagar to Leh from 16 days to two.

The entire state of Jammu and Kashmir continues to be the subject of a territorial dispute between India on the one hand and Pakistan and China on the other. Kargil was an area of conflict in the wars of 1947, 1965, 1971 and the focal point of a potential nuclear conflict during the Kargil War in 1999. The Kargil War of 1999, codenamed 'Operation Vijay' by the Indian Army, saw infiltration by Pakistani troops into parts of Western Ladakh, namely Kargil, Dras, Mushkoh, Batalik and Chorbatla, overlooking key locations on the Srinagar-Leh highway. Extensive operations were launched in high altitudes by the Indian Army with considerable artillery and air force support. Pakistani troops were evicted from the Indian side of the Line of Control which the Indian Government ordered was to be respected and which was not crossed by Indian troops.

The Siachen glacier area in the north-east corner of Ladakh is the venue of a continuing military standoff since 1984 between India and Pakistan and the highest battleground in the world. The dispute arose because on non-demarcation of the boundary in the 1972 Simla Agreement beyond a point NJ 9842. Oropolitics by Pakistan and cartographic aggression by the United States Defense Mapping Agency in 1957 was eventually followed by a race to occupy the heights of the Saltoro Ridge which borders the Siachen glacier. Since then strategic points on the glacier are occupied by both sides, with the Indians having a clear strategic advantage.

The Ladakh region was bifurcated into Kargil and Leh districts in 1979. In 1989, there were violent riots between Buddhists and Muslims. Following demands for autonomy from the Kashmiri dominated state government; the Ladakh Autonomous Hill Development Council was created in 1993. Information on Ladakh before the birth of the kingdom (10th century) is scarce. The earliest layer in the population of Ladakh was probably composed of the Dardis. Herodotus mentions twice a people called Dadikai, first along with the Gandarioi, and again in the catalogue of king Xerxes's army invading Greece.

Herodotus also mentions the gold-digging ants of Central Asia, which is also later mentioned in connection with the Dardi people by Nearchus, the admiral of Alexander, and Megasthenes. In the 1st century, Pliny the Elder repeats that the Dards are great producers of gold. Herrmann brings arguments to show that the tale ultimately goes back to a hazy knowledge of gold-washing in Ladakh and Baltistan. Ptolemy situates the Daradrai on the upper reaches of the Indus, and the names Darada is used in the geographical lists of the Puranas.

The first glimpse of political history is found in the Kharosthi inscription of Uvima Kavthisa discovered near the *K'a-la-rtse* bridge on the Indus, showing that in around the 1st century, Ladakh was a part of the Kushana empire. A few other short Brahmi and Kharosthi inscriptions have been found in Ladakh. The Chinese pilgrim monk, Xuanzang, c. 634 CE, describes a journey from *Chuluduo* (Kûluta, Kulu) to *Luohuluo* (Lahul), then goes on saying that: "From here the road, leading to the north, for over one thousand eight hundred or nine hundred *li* by perilous paths and over mountains and valleys, takes one to the country of Lâhul.

Going further to the north over two thousand li along a route full of difficulties and obstacles, in cold winds and wafting snowflakes, one could reach the country of Marsa (also known as Sanbohe)." The kingdom of *Moluosuo*, or *Mar-sa*, would seem to be synonymous with *Mar-yul*, a common name for Ladakh. Elsewhere, the text remarks that *Mo-lo-so*, also called *San-po-ho* borders with *Suvarnagotra* or *Suvarnabhumi* (Land of Gold), identical with the Kingdom of Women (*Strirajya*). According to Tucci, the *Zan-zun* kingdom, or at least its southern districts were known by this name by the 7th century Indians.

In the 8th century, Ladakh was involved in the clash between Tibetan expansion pressing from the East, and Chinese influence exerted from Central Asia through the passes. In 634/5 Zangzung acknowledged Tibetan suzernaity for the first time, and in 653 a Tibetan commissioner (*mnan*) was appointed there. Regular administration was introduced in 662, and a unsuccessful rebellion broke out in 677. In 719 a census was taken, and in 724 the administration was reorganized. In 737, the Tibetans launched an attack against the king of Bru-za (Gilgit), who asked for Chinese help, but was ultimately forced to pay homage to Tibet.

In 747, the hold of Tibet was loosened by the campaign of General Gao Xianshi, who tried to re-open the direct communications between Central Asia and Kashmir. After Xianshi's defeat against the Qarluqs and Arabs on the Talas river (751), Chinese influence decrease rapidly and Tibetan influence resumed. The geographical treatise *Hudud-al-Alam* (982) mentions Bolorian (Bolor = Bolu, Baltistan) Tibet, where people are chiefly merchants and live in huts. Nestorian crosses, apparently due to Sogdian Christian merchants found in Drangtse is an evidence of the importance of trade in this region. After the collapse of the Tibetan monarchy in 842, Tibetan suzerainty vanished quickly.

THE FIRST DYNASTY

After the break-up of the Tibetan empire in 842, Nyima-Gon, a representative of the ancient Tibetan royal house founded the first Ladakh dynasty. Nyima-Gon's kingdom had its centre well to the east of present-day Ladakh. This was the period in which Ladakh underwent Tibetanization, eventually making Ladakh a country inhabited by a mixed population, the predominant racial strain of which was Tibetan. However, soon after the conquest, the dynasty, intent on establishing Buddhism, looked not to Tibet, but to north-west India, particularly Kashmir.

This has been termed the Second Spreading of Buddhism in the region (the first one being in Tibet proper.) Little is known about the early kings of Nyima-Gon's dynasty. The fifth king in line has a Sanskrit name Utpala, who conquered Kulu, Mustang, and parts of Baltistan. Around the 13th century, due to political developments, India ceased having anything to offer from a Buddhist point of view, and Ladakh began to seek and accept guidance in religious matters from Tibet.

THE NAMGYAL DYNASTY

The Namgyal dynasty of Ladakh was founded by Bhagan, a Basgo king, who reunited Ladakh by overthrowing the king of Leh. He took on the surname Namgyal (meaning victorious) and founded a new dynasty which still survives today. King Tashi Namgyal (1555-1575) successfully managed to repel most Central Asian raiders, and built a royal fort on the top of the Namgyal Peak. Tsewang Namgyal temporarily extended his kingdom as far as Nepal.

During the reign of Jamyang Namgyal, concerted efforts were made to convert Ladakh to Islam and destruction of Buddhist artefacts. Today, few gompas exist from before this period. Sengge Namgyal (r. 1616-1642), known as the 'lion' king made efforts to restore Ladakh to its old glory by an ambitious and energetic building programme including the Leh palace and the rebuilding of several gompas, the most famous of which are Hemis and Hanle.

He expanded the kingdom into Zanskar and Spiti, but was defeated by the Mughals, who had already occupied Kashmir and Baltistan. His son Deldan Namgyal (1642-1694) had to placate the Mughal emperor Aurangzeb by building a mosque in Leh. However, he successfully defeated the Mughal army in Baltistan. He sided with Bhutan in a religious dispute between Tibet and Bhutan, which resulted in an attempted invasion by the Fifth Dalai Lama. Kashmiri help restored Ladakhi rule at a price - the building of a mosque in Leh and the conversion of the Ladakhi king to Islam. Also, all of Ladakh's valuable pashmina wool had to go to Kashmir. The Treaty of Temisgam in 1684 settled the dispute between Tibet and Ladakh, but its independence was seriously restricted.

By the beginning of the 19th century, the Mughal Empire had collapsed, and Sikh rule had been established in Punjab and Kashmir. However the Dogra region of Jammu remained under its Rajput rulers, the greatest of whom was Maharaja Gulab Singh-his General Zorawar Singh, invaded Ladakh in 1834. King Tshespal Namgyal was dethroned and exiled to Stok.

Continual raids on Ladakh by the plundering Muslim states of Central Asia lead to the weakening and partial conversion of Ladakh. Ladakh was divided, with Lower Ladakh ruled by King Takpabum from Basgo and Temisgam, and Upper Ladakh by King Takbumde from Leh and Shey. Bhagan, a later Basgo king reunited Ladakh by overthrowing the king of Leh. He took on the surname Namgyal (meaning victorious) and founded a new dynasty which still survives today. King Tashi Namgyal (1555-1575) successfully managed to repel most Central Asian raiders, and built a royal fort on the top of the Namgyal Peak. Tsewang Namgyal temporarily extended his kingdom as far as Nepal.

During the reign of Jamyang Namgyal, concerted efforts were made to convert Ladakh to Islam and destruction of Buddhist artifacts. Today, few gompas exist from before this period. Sengge Namgyal (1616-1642), known as the 'lion' king made efforts to restore Ladakh to its old glory by an ambitious and energetic building programme which rebuilt several gompas, the most famous of which is Hemis. He expanded the kingdom into Zanskar and Spiti, but was defeated by the Mughals, who had already occupied Kashmir and Baltistan. His son Deldan Namgyal (1642-1694) had to placate the Mughal emperor Aurangzeb by building a mosque in Leh. However; he successfully defeated the Mughal army in Baltistan.

MODERN TIMES

By the beginning of the 19th century, the Mughal Empire had collapsed, and Sikh rule had been established in Punjab and Kashmir. However the Dogra region of Jammu remained under its Rajput rulers, the greatest of whom was Maharaja Gulab Singh whose General Zorawar Singh invaded Ladakh in 1834. King Tshespal Namgyal was dethroned and exiled to Stok. Ladakh came under Dogra rule and was incorporated into the state of Jammu and Kashmir in 1846. It still maintained considerable autonomy and relations with Tibet. In 1947, partition left Ladakh a part of the Indian state of Jammu and Kashmir, to be administered from Srinagar. In 1948, Pakistani raiders invaded Ladakh and occupied Kargil and Zanskar, reaching within 30km of Leh.

Reinforcement troops were sent in by air, and a battalion of Gurkhas made its way slowly to Leh on foot from south. Kargil was a scene of fighting again in 1965, 1971, and 1999. In 1949, China closed the border between Nubra and Sinkiang, blocking the 1000-year old trade route from India to Central Asia. In 1950, China invaded Tibet, and thousands of Tibetans, including the Dalai Lama sought refuge in India. In 1962, China occupied Aksai Chin, and promptly built roads connecting Sinkiang and Tibet, and the Karakoram Highway, jointly with Pakistan. India built the Srinagar-Leh highway during this period, cutting the journey time between Srinagar to Leh from 16 days to two.

Simultaneously, China closed the Ladakh-Tibet border, ending the 700-year old Ladakh-Tibet relationship. Since the early 1960s the number of immigrants from Tibet (including Changpa nomads) has increased as they flee the occupation of their homeland by the Chinese. Today, Leh has some 3,500 refugees from Tibet. They hold no passports, only customs papers. Some Tibetan refugees in Ladakh claim dual Tibetan/Indian citizenship, although their Indian citizenship is unofficial. Since partition Ladakh has been governed by the State government based in Srinagar, never to the complete satisfaction of the Ladakhis, who demand that Ladakh be directly governed from New Delhi as a Union Territory.

They allege continued apathy, Muslim bias, and corruption of the state government as reasons for their demands. In 1989, there were violent riots between Buddhists and Muslims, provoking the Ladakh Buddhist Council to call for a social and economic boycott of Muslims, which was lifted in 1992. In October 1993, the Indian government and the State government agreed to grant Ladakh the status of Autonomous Hill Council. In 1995, the Ladakh Autonomous Hill Development Council was created.

GEOGRAPHY OF LADAKH

Ladakh is the highest plateau of the Indian state of Kashmir with much of it being over 3,000 m (9,800 ft). It spans the Himalayan and Karakoram mountain ranges and the upper Indus River valley. Historically, the region included the Baltistan (Baltiyul) valleys, the Indus Valley, the remote Zangskar, Lahaul and Spiti to the south, Ngari including the Rudok region and Guge in the east, Aksai Chin in the east, and Nubra valley to the north over Khardung La in the Ladakh mountain range. Contemporary Ladakh borders Tibet to the east, the Lahaul and Spiti to the south, the Vale of Kashmir, Jammu and Baltiyul regions to the west, and the trans-Kunlun territory of East Turkistan in Central Asia on the other side of the Kunlun range across the Karakoram Pass in the far north.

Running southwest to northeast, the Altyn Tagh converges with the Kunlun range in Kashmir which runs southeast to northwest forming a "V" shape which converges at Pulu. The geographical divide between Ladakh in the highlands of Kashmir and the Tibetan Plateau commences in the vicinity of Pulu and continues southwards along the intricate maze of ridges situated east of Rudok, wherein are situated Aling Kangri and Mavang Kangri and culminates in the vicinity of Mayum La. Before partition, Baltistan (now under Pakistani administration) was a district in Ladakh. Skardu was the winter capital of Ladakh while Leh was the summer capital.

The mountain ranges in this region were formed over a period of 45 million years by the folding of the Indian plate into the more stationary Eurasian Plate. The drift continues, causing frequent earthquakes in the Himalayan region. The peaks in the Ladakh range are at a medium altitude close to the Zoji-la (5,000–5,500 m or 16,000–18,050 ft), and increase towards south-east, reaching a climax in the twin summits of Nun-Kun (7000 m or 23,000 ft). The Suru and Zangskar valleys form a great trough enclosed by the Himalayas and the Zangskar range. Rangdum is the highest inhabited region in the Suru valley, after which the valley rises to 4,400 m (14,436 ft) at Pensi-la, the gateway to Zangskar.

Kargil, the only town in the Suru valley, is the second most important town in Ladakh. It was an important staging post on the routes of the trade caravans before 1947, being more or less equidistant, at about 230 kilometres from Srinagar, Leh, Skardu, and Padum. The Zangskar valley lies in the troughs of the Stod and the Lungnak rivers. The region experiences heavy snowfall; the Pensi-la is open only between June and mid-October. Dras and the Mushkoh Valley form the western extremity of Ladakh.

The Indus River is the backbone of Ladakh. Most major historical and current towns - Shey, Leh, Basgo, and Tingmosgang (but not Kargil), are situated close to the Indus River. After the Indo-Pakistani War of 1947, the stretch of the Indus flowing through Ladakh is the only part of this river, which is greatly venerated in the Hindu religion and culture, which still flows through India. The Siachen Glacier is located in the eastern Karakoram Range in the Himalaya Mountains along the disputed India-Pakistan border. The Karakoram Range forms a great watershed that separates China from the Indian subcontinent and is sometimes called the "Third Pole."

The glacier lies between the Saltoro Ridge immediately to the west and the main Karakoram Range to the east. At 70 km long, it is the longest glacier in the Karakoram and second-longest in the world's non-polar areas. It falls from an altitude of 5,753 m (18,875 ft) above sea level at its source at Indira Col (pass) on the China border down to 3,620 m (11,875 ft) at its snout. The passes and some dominating heights on the Saltoro ridge, which has a crestline having heights from 5,450 to 7,720 m (17,880 to 25,330 feet) are occupied by troops on both sides.

Saser Kangri is the highest peak in the Saser Muztagh, the easternmost subrange of the Karakoram Range in India, Saser Kangri I having an altitude of 7,672 m (25,171 ft). The Ladakh range has no major peaks; its average height is a little less than 6,000 m (19,700 ft), and few of its passes are less than 5,000 m (16,400 ft). The Pangong range runs parallel to the Ladakh range about 100 km northwest from Chushul, along the southern shore of the Pangong Lake. Its highest range is 6,700 m (22,000 ft), and the northern slopes are heavily glaciated. The region comprising the valley of Shayok and Nubra Rivers is known as Nubra.

The Karakoram Range in Ladakh is not as mighty as in Baltistan and North of the Karakoram lies the Kunlun. Thus, between Leh and eastern Central Asia, there is a triple barrier - Ladakh range, Karakoram Range, and Kunlun. Nevertheless, a major trade route was established between Leh and Yarkand. Ladakh is a high altitude desert as the Himalayas create a rain shadow, denying entry to monsoon clouds. The main source of water is the winter snowfall on the mountains. Recent flooding of the Indus River in the region has been attributed either to abnormal rain patterns, or the retreating of glaciers, both of which might be linked to global warming.

The Leh Nutrition Project, headed by Chewang Norphel, also known as the 'Glacier Man', currently creates artificial glaciers as one solution for this problem. The regions on the north flank of the Himalayas - Dras, the Suru valley and Zangskar - experience heavy snowfall and remain virtually cut off from the rest of the country for several months in the year. Summers are short, though they are long enough to grow crops in the lower reaches of the Suru valley. The summer weather is dry and pleasant. Temperature ranges are from -3 to 30 °C in summer and from -20 to 15 °C in winter. There is little moisture to temper the effects of rarefied air. Ladakh lies in the *Very High Damage Risk* cyclone zone.

Ladakh is the highest altitude plateau region in India (much of it being over 3,000 m), straddling the Himalayan and Karakorum Mountain ranges and the upper Indus River valley. The mountain ranges in this region were formed over a period of 45 million years by the folding of the Indian Plate into the stationary landmass of Asia. While the Himalayas were formed from the base material of the Indian plate, the Zanskar Range consists of layers of sediment from the ocean floor, and the Ladakh Range of granite was born of the immense heat generated by the friction between the two plates.

In Ladakh, the suture zone between the continental masses runs a little to the south of the Indus Valley. The drift continues and is the cause of the frequent earthquakes in the Himalayan region. Crossing the Himalayas by the dip of the Zoji-la, the crest-line of the range remains at a relatively modest level, the highest peaks near the pass being little more than 5000-5500 m above sea level. South-east of Zoji-la the scale increases, reaching a climax in the mighty massif of Nun-Kun, with two summits over 7000 m.

The Suru and Zanskar valleys form a great trough at the foot of the northern, heavily glaciated flank of the Himalayas, while opposite rise the mountains of the Zanskar range. The Suru River forms the western and northern boundary of the Zanskar range. The Suru, after receiving the combined waters of the Dras and Shingo Rivers a short distance north of Kargil, joins the Indus at Marol in Baltistan, which is now on the Pakistan side of the Line of Control. Rangdum Monastery and the attendant village of Julidok is the last inhabited region in the Suru valley; it is also the destination of the nomadic herdspeople called Bakarwals, who trek up every summer from the Jammu region.

From Rangdum the valley rises to 4400 metres at the Pensi-la, the gateway into Zanskar. Kargil, the only town in the Suru valley, was an important staging post on the routes of the trade caravans before 1947, being more or less equidistant, at about 230 kilometres from Srinagar, Leh, Skardo, and Padum. Rangdum though on the northern side of the Pensi-la, is regarded as socially and culturally part of Zangskar rather than of Suru. Zanskar consists of troughs of two rivers, the Stod (Doda) and the Lungnak (Tsarap Lingti). One of the Lungnak's main tributaries rises as the Tsarap far away to the east in Rupshu.

A little away north of Bara-lacha-la it is joined by the Lingti and another tributary; it then flows north-west before turning abruptly south through a gorge and past Phugtal Gompa to join the Kargyak River descending from Shingo-la, that goes into Himachal Pradesh. The Stod carries meltwater of the Drang-drung glacier below the Pensi-la, and flows down a broad open valley, approaching the Lungnak. As the Zangskar river, their united waters flow northwards through a gorge in the Zanskar range, to join the Indus at Nyemo in Central Ladakh. Zanskar suffers heavy snowfall, and the Pensi-la opens only in June and is blocked again in mid-October. The entire valley is virtually treeless.

The Indus River is the backbone of Ladakh - all the major places historically and currently, Shey, Leh, Basgo, and Tingmosgang, are situated close to the river. The Ladakh range has no major peaks; its average height is a little less than 6000 metres, and few of its passes are less than 5000 m. Within Ladakh it forms the northern boundary wall of the Indus valley, though when the river enters Ladakh at Demchok, some 250 km south-east of Leh, it is actually flowing along the foot of the northern flank of these granite mountains, which it crosses by a great gorge close to its confluence with the Hanle river. The Pang-gong range runs parallel to the Ladakh range some 100 km northwest from Chushul, along the southern shore of the Pang-gong Lake.

It is divided from the main range by the Tangtse River. Its highest range is 6700 m, and the northern slopes are heavily glaciated. The Shyok River rises just below the Karakoram Pass. The region comprising the valley of Shyok and Nubra Rivers is known as Nubra. The Karakoram Range in Ladakh is not as mighty as in Baltistan. The massifs to the north and east of the Nubra-Siachan line include the Apsarasas group (highest point 7245 m), the Rimo group (highest point 7385 m) and the Teram Kangri group (highest point 7464 m), together with Mamostong Kangri (7526m) and Singhi Kangri (7751 m.) North of the Karakoram lay the Kun-lun mountains.

Thus, between Leh and eastern Central Asia, there is a triple barrier - Ladakh range, Karakoram Range, and Kun-lun. Nevertheless, a major trade route was established between Leh and Yarkand. The enormous mass of the Himalayas creates a rain shadow, denying entry to the moisture-laden clouds of the Indian monsoon. Ladakh is thus, a high altitude desert. The main source of water is the winter snowfall on the mountains. The regions on the north flank of the Himalayas - Dras, the Suru valley and Zanskar - experience heavy snowfall and remain virtually cut off from the rest of the country for several months in the year. Summers are short, although long enough to grow crops.

The proportion of oxygen is less than in many other places at a comparable altitude because of lack of vegetation. There is little moisture to temper the effects of rarefied air. Naked barley (Urdu: *grim*), normal barley and wheat are the staple crops all over Ladakh, along with mustard (for oil), lentils and other pulses, and vegetables. The extreme limit of cultivation is at Korzok near Tso-Moriri Lake, at 4600 m, said to be the highest fields in the world.

Historic Ladakh consists of a number of distinct areas (mainly under Indian rule), including the fairly populous main Indus valley, the more remote Zanskar (in the south) and Nubra valleys (to the north over Khardung La in the Ladakh mountain range, a high motorable pass at 5,359 metres (17,580 ft)), the almost deserted Aksai Chin (under Chinese rule) and the predominantly Shi'ite Muslim Kargil and Suru valley areas in the west (Kargil being the second most important town in Ladakh).

The Baltistan and Skardu / Skardo area, under Pakistani rule and entirely Muslim, used to be included in what is geographically referred to as Ladakh. Before partition, Baltistan was one of the districts of Ladakh. Skardo was the winter capital of Ladakh while Leh was the summer capital. People of Baltistan and Ladakh speak very similar languages closely related to Tibetan. The wildlife of this region was first studied by Ferdinand Stoliczka, an Austrian-Czech palaeontologist, who carried out a massive expedition in the region in the 1870s. Vegetation is extremely sparse in Ladakh except along streambeds and wetlands, on high slopes, and in irrigated places.

The fauna of Ladakh have much in common with that of Central Asia in general and that of the Tibetan Plateau in particular. Exceptions to this are the birds, many of which migrate from the warmer parts of India to spend the summer in Ladakh. For such an arid area, Ladakh has a great diversity of birds - a total of 225 species have been recorded. Many species of finches, robins, redstarts (like the Black Redstart) and the Hoopoe are common in summer. The Brown-headed Gull is seen in summer on the river Indus and on some lakes of the Changthang. Resident water-birds include the Brahminy duck also known as the Ruddy Sheldrake and the Bar-headed Goose.

The Black-necked Crane, a rare species found scattered in the Tibetan plateau, is also found in parts of Ladakh. Other birds include the Raven, Red-billed Chough, Tibetan Snowcock and Chukar. The Lammergeier and the Golden Eagle are common raptors here. The Bharal or "blue sheep" is the most abundant mountain ungulate in the Ladakh region. However it is not found in some parts of Zangskar and Sham areas.. The Asiatic ibex is a very elegant mountain goat that is distributed in western part of Ladakh. It is the second most abundant mountain ungulate in the region with a population of about 6000 individuals. It is adapted to rugged areas where it easily climbs when threatened.

The Ladakh Urial is another unique mountain sheep that inhabits the mountains of Ladakh. The population is however declining, and presently there are not more 3000 individuals left in Ladakh. Urial is endemic to Ladakh, where it is distributed only along two major river valleys: Indus and Shayok. The animal is often persecuted by farmers whose crops are allegedly damaged by the animal. The population of this animal declined precipitously in the last century due to indiscriminate shooting by hunters along the Leh-Srinagar highway. The Tibetan argali or Nyan is the largest wild sheep in the world, standing 3.5 to 4 feet at the shoulder with the horn measuring 90-100 cm. It is distributed on the Tibetan plateau and its marginal mountains encompassing a total area of 2.5 million km^2.

There is only a small population of about 400 animals in Ladakh. The animal prefers open and rolling terrain as it runs, unlike wild goats that climb into steep cliffs, to escape from predators. The endangered Tibetan Antelope, (Commonly known as *chiru* or Ladakhi *tsos*) has traditionally been hunted for its wool, shahtoosh, which is the finest natural fiber and thus valued for its light weight and warmth status symbol. The fiber is smuggled into Kashmir and woven into exquisite shawls by Kashmiri workers. Ladakh is also home to the Tibetan Gazelle, which inhabits the vast rangelands in eastern Ladakh bordering Tibet.

The *Kiang*, or Tibetan Wild Ass, is common in the grasslands of Changthang, numbering about 2,500 individuals. These animals are in conflict with the nomadic people of Changthang who held the Kiang responsible for pasture degradation. There are about 200 Snow Leopards in Ladakh. The Hemis High Altitude National Park in central Ladakh is especially a good habitat for this predator as it has abundant prey populations. The Eurasian lynx is another rare cat that preys on smaller herbivores in Ladakh. It is mostly found in Nubra, Changthang and Zangskar.

The Pallas's cat, which looks somewhat like a house cat, is very rare in Ladakh and not much is known about the species. The Tibetan Wolf, which sometimes preys on the livestock of the Ladakhis, is the most persecuted amongst the predators. There are also a few brown bears in the Suru valley and the area around Dras. The Tibetan Sand Fox has recently been discovered in this region. Among smaller animals, marmots, hares, and several types of pika and vole are common. The ibex (Ladakhi: *skin*) is found in high craggy terrain of Europe, North Africa and Asia, and numbers several thousand in Ladakh: trekkers often spot them.

The Bharal or "blue sheep" (*napo*) is even more common, ranging in the Himalayas from Ladakh east as far as Sikkim. The Tibetan Urial sheep (*shapo*) is a rare goat found at lower elevations, mostly in river valleys, and therefore is often directly in competition with domesticated animals. They are now rare, numbering about one thousand. The Tibetan Argali sheep (*nyan*) is a relative of the Marco Polo sheep of the Pamirs. Impressive animals with huge horizontal curving horns, they are extremely rare in Ladakh, numbering only a couple hundred, but they do have a wide range throughout mountainous areas of the Chinese Provinces of Xinjiang, Qinghai, and Gansu.

The habitat of the extremely rare Tibetan Gazelle (*gowa*) is near the Tibetan border in southeastern Ladakh. The musk deer (*lhawa*) has not been seen in Ladakh for decades if not generations. The Tibetan Antelope, (Ladakhi: *tsos*, Indian English *chiru*) is also endangered. Early in the 20th century the *chiru* was seen in herds of thousands, surviving on remarkably sparse vegetation, but they are vanishingly rare now. It has been hunted for its fine under-wool (Urdu: *shahtoosh*, Ladakhi: *tsoskul*), which must be pulled out by hand, a process done after the animal is killed. This *shahtoosh* is valued in South Asia for its light weight and warmth, but more than anything else, as a status symbol.

Owning or trading in *shahtoosh* is now illegal in most countries. The Tibetan Wild Ass (Ladakhi: *kyang*) is one animal that visitors can expect to see from the comfort of a vehicle, if they take a jeep tour on the Changthang. Favouring the rolling grasslands of this area, their natural curiosity makes them fairly easy to spot, despite the relatively low numbers, about 1500 individuals. The Snow Leopard (Ladakhi: *shan*) once ranged throughout the Himalaya, Tibet, and as far as the Sayan mountains on the Mongolian-Russian border; and in elevation from 1800 m to 5400 m. They are extremely shy and hard to spot, and as such not well known.

It is believed there are about 200 in Ladakh. While tourists are unlikely to see leopards themselves, during winter the footprints and other marks are not uncommon. Other cats in Ladakh are even rarer than the snow leopard: the Lynx (*ee*), numbering only a few individuals, and the Pallas's cat, which looks somewhat like a house cat. The Tibetan Wolf (*shangku*) is the greatest threat to the livestock of the Ladakhis and as such is the most persecuted. There are only about 300 wolves left in Ladakh. There are also a very few *brown bears* (*drenmo / tret*) in the Suru valley and the area around Dras.

The red fox is common, and Tibetan Sand Fox has recently been discovered in this region (both: *watse*). Among smaller animals, marmots (Ladakhi: *pheya*) are common; you can even sometimes see them from the road, although they do not look very different from the marmots common to other mountainous areas of the world. There are also plenty of hares (*ribong*), and several types of voles and pika (both: *rdzabra / zabra*).

GOVERNMENT AND POLITICS

Ladakh district was a district of the Jammu and Kashmir state of India until 1 July 1979 when it was divided into Leh district and Kargil district. Each of these districts is governed by a Ladakh Autonomous Hill Development Council, which is based on the pattern of the Darjeeling Gorkha Autonomous Hill Council. These councils were created as a compromise solution to the demands of Ladakhi people to make Leh a union territory.

In October 1993, the Indian government and the State government agreed to grant each district of Ladakh the status of Autonomous Hill Council. This agreement was given effect by the Ladakh Autonomous Hill Development Council Act, 1995. The council came into being with the holding of elections in Leh District on August 28, 1995. The inaugural meeting of the council was held at Leh on September 3, 1995. Kargil followed Leh's footsteps in July 2003, when the Ladakh Autonomous Hill Development Council - Kargil was established. The council works with village panchayats to take decisions on economic development, healthcare, education, land use, taxation, and local governance which are further reviewed at the Block Headquarters in the presence of the Chief Executive Councilor and Executive Councilors.

The government of Jammu and Kashmir looks after law and order, judicial system, communications and the higher education in the region. Ladakh sends one member (MP) to the lower house of the Indian parliament the Lok Sabha. The current MP from Ladakh in the current Lok Sabha is Thupstan Chhewang of the Ladakh Union Territory Front (LUTF). Although on the whole there has been religious harmony in Ladakh, religion has tended to get politicized in the last few decades. As early as 1931, Kashmiri neo-Buddhists founded the Kashmir Raj Bodhi Mahasabha that led to some sense of separateness from the Muslims.

The bifurcation of the region into Muslim majority Kargil district and Buddhist majority Leh district in 1979 again brought the communal question into fore. The Buddhists in Ladakh accused the overwhelmingly Muslim state government of continued apathy, corruption and a bias in favour of Muslims. On these grounds, they demanded union territory status for Ladakh. In 1989, there were violent riots between Buddhists and Muslims, provoking the Ladakh Buddhist Association to call for a social and economic boycott of Muslims which went on for three years before being lifted in 1992. The Ladakh Union Territory Front (LUTF), which controls the Ladakh Autonomous Hill Development Council - Leh, demands union territory status for Ladakh.

ECONOMY

For centuries, Ladakh enjoyed a stable and self-reliant agricultural economy based on growing barley, wheat and peas, and keeping livestock, especially yak, cows, dzos (yak-cow cross breed), sheep and goats. At altitudes of 3,000 to 4,300 m (10,000 to 14,000 ft), the growing season is only a few months long every year, similar to the northern countries of the world. Animals are scarce and water is in short supply. The Ladakhis developed a small-scale farming system adapted to this unique environment. The land is irrigated by a system of channels which funnel water from the ice and snow of the mountains.

The principal crops are barley and wheat. Rice was previously a luxury in the Ladakhi diet, but, subsidised by the government, has now become a cheap staple. At lower elevations fruit is grown, while the high altitude Rupshu region is the preserve of nomadic herders. In the past, surplus produce was traded for tea, sugar, salt and other items. Two items for export are apricots and pashmina. Currently, the largest commercially sold agricultural product is vegetables, sold in large amounts to the Indian army as well as in the local market.

Production remains mainly in the hands of small-landowners who work their own land, often with the help of migrant labourers from Nepal. Naked barley (Ladakhi: *nas*, Urdu: *grim*) was traditionally a staple crop all over Ladakh. Growing times vary considerably with altitude. The extreme limit of cultivation is at Korzok, on the Tso-moriri lake, at 4,600 m (15,100 ft), which are widely considered to be the highest fields in the world.

In the past Ladakh's geographical position at the crossroads of some of the most important trade routes in Asia was exploited to the full. Ladakhis collected tax on goods that crossed their kingdom from Turkestan, Tibet, Punjab, Kashmir and Baltistan. A minority of Ladakhi people were also employed as merchants and caravan traders, facilitating trade in textiles, carpets, dyestuffs and narcotics between Punjab and Xinjiang. However, since the Chinese Government closed the borders with Tibet and Central Asia, this international trade has completely dried up.

Since 1974, the Indian Government has encouraged a shift in trekking and other tourist activities from the troubled Kashmir region to the relatively unaffected areas of Ladakh. Although tourism employs only 4% of Ladakh's working population, it now accounts for 50% of the region's GNP.

Extensive government employment and large-scale infrastructure projects - including, crucially, road links - have helped consolidate the new economy and create an urban alternative to farming. Subsidised food, government jobs, tourism industry, and new infrastructure have accelerated a mass migration from the farms into Leh town.

Adventure tourism in Ladakh started in the 19th century. By the turn of the 20th century, it was not uncommon for British officials to undertake the 14-day trek from Srinagar to Leh as part of their annual leave. Agencies were set up in Srinagar and Shimla specialising in sports-related activities - hunting, fishing and trekking. This era is recorded in Arthur Neves *The Tourist's Guide to Kashmir, Ladakh and Skardo*, first published in 1911. Today, about 30,000 tourists visit Ladakh every year. Among the popular places of tourist interest include Leh, Drass valley, Suru valley, Kargil, Zangskar, Zangla, Rangdum, Padum, Phugthal, Sani, Stongdey, Shyok Valley, Sankoo, Salt Valley and several popular trek routes like Manali to Ladakh, the Nubra valley, the Indus valley etc.

TRANSPORT

There are about 1,800 km (1,100 mi) of roads in Ladakh of which 800 km (500 mi) are surfaced. The majority of roads in Ladakh are looked after by the Border Roads Organisation. Ladakh was the connection point between Central Asia and South Asia when the Silk Road was in use. The sixty-day journey on the *Ladakh route* connecting Amritsar and Yarkand through eleven passes was frequently undertaken by traders till the third quarter of the 19th century. Another common route in regular use was the Kalimpong route between Leh and Lhasa via Gartok, the administrative centre of western Tibet. Gartok could be reached either straight up the Indus in winter, or through either the Taglang la or the Chang la.

Beyond Gartok, the Cherko la brought travelers to the Manasarovar and Rakshastal lakes, and then to Barka, which is connected to the main Lhasa road. These traditional routes have been closed since the Ladakh-Tibet border has been sealed by the Chinese government. Other routes connected Ladakh to Hunza and Chitral but as with the previous case, there is currently no border crossing between Ladakh and Pakistan. In present times, the only two land routes to Ladakh in use are from Srinagar and Manali. Travelers from Srinagar start their journey from Sonamarg, over the Zoji La pass (3,450 m, 11,320 ft) via Dras and Kargil (2,750 m, 9,022 ft) passing through Namika la (3,700 m, 12,140 ft) and Fatu la (4,100 m, 13,450 ft.)

This has been the main traditional gateway to Ladakh since historical times and is now open to traffic from April or May until November or December every year. However, with the rise of militancy in Kashmir, the main corridor to the area has shifted from the Srinagar-Kargil-Leh route via Zoji la to the high altitude Manali-Leh Highway from Himachal Pradesh. The highway crosses four passes, Rohtang la (3,978 m, 13,050 ft), Baralacha la (4,892 m, 16,050 ft), Lungalacha la (5,059 m, 16,600 ft) and Taglang la (5,325 m, 17,470 ft), and is open only between May and November when snow is cleared from the road.

Buses run from Leh to the surrounding villages. The Manali-Leh-Srinagar road makes up about half of the road network, the remainder being spurs off it. Ladakh is criss-crossed by a complex network of mountain trails which, even today provides the only link to most of the valleys, villages and high pastures. For the traveler with a number of months it is possible to trek from one end of Ladakh to the other, or even from places in Himachal Pradesh.

The large number of trails and the limited number of roads allows one to string together routes that have road access often enough to restock supplies, but avoid walking on motor roads almost entirely. There is one airport in Leh, from which there are multiple daily flights to Delhi on Jet Airways, Air Deccan, and Indian, and weekly flights to Srinagar and Jammu. There are two airstrips at Daulat Beg Oldie and Fukche for military transport.

DEMOGRAPHICS

Ladakh has a population of about 260,000 which is a blend of many different races, predominantly the Tibetans, Mons and the Dards. People of Dard descent predominate in Dras and Dha-Hanu areas. The residents of Dha-Hanu, known as Brokpa, are followers of Tibetan Buddhism and have preserved much of their original Dardic traditions and customs. The Dards around Dras, however, have converted to Islam and have been strongly influenced by their Kashmiri neighbours. The Mons are descendants of earlier Indian settlers in Ladakh. They work as musicians, blacksmiths and carpenters.

Unlike the rest of Jammu and Kashmir which is mainly Islamic, most Ladakhis in Leh District as well as Zangskar Valley of Kargil District are Tibetan Buddhist, while most of the people in the rest of Kargil District are Shia Muslims. There are sizeable minorities of Buddhists in Kargil District and of Shia Muslims in Leh District. There are some Sunni Muslims of Kashmiri descent in Leh and Kargil towns, and also Padum in Zangskar. There are a few families of Ladakhi Christians, who converted in the 19th century. Among descendants of immigrants, there are small numbers of followers of Hinduism, Sikhism, and the Bon religion.

Most Buddhists follow the tantric form of Buddhism known as Vajrayana Buddhism. Shias are mostly found among the Balti and Burig people. Ladakhis are generally of Tibetan descent with some Dardic and Mon admixture. The Changpa nomads who live in the Rupshu plateau are more closely related to Tibetans. Since the early 1960s nomad numbers have increased as Chang Thang nomads from across the border flee Chinese-ruled Tibet. There are about 3,500 Tibetan refugees from all parts of Tibet in Leh District. However, since 2000 some nomads, notably most of the community of Kharnak, have abandoned the nomadic life and settled in Leh town.

Muslim Arghons, descendants of Kashmiri or Central Asian merchants and Ladakhi women, mainly live in Leh and Kargil towns. Like other Ladakhis, the Baltis of Kargil, Nubra, Suru Valley and Baltistan show strong Tibetan links in their appearance and language, and were Buddhists until recent times. The principal language of Ladakh is Ladakhi, a Tibetan dialect. Educated Ladakhis usually know Hindi/Urdu and often English. Within Ladakh, there is a range of dialects, so that the language of the Chang-pa people may differ markedly from that of the Purig-pa in Kargil, or the Zangskaris, but they are all mutually comprehensible.

Due to its position on important trade routes, the racial composition as well as the language of Leh is enriched with foreign influences. Traditionally, Ladakhi had no written form distinct from classical Tibetan, but recently a number of Ladakhi writers have started using the Tibetan script to write the colloquial tongue. Administrative work and education are carried out in English, although Urdu was used to a great extent in the past and has been decreasing since the 1980s. The Total Birth Rate in 2001 was 22.44, while it was 21.44 for Muslims and 24.46 for Buddhists. Brokpas had the highest TBR at 27.17 and Arghuns had the lowest at 14.25. TFR was 2.69 with 1.3 in Leh and 3.4 in Kargil. For Buddhists it was 2.79 and for Muslims it was 2.66. Baltis had a TFR of 3.12 and Arghuns had a TFR of 1.66.

The Total Death Rate was 15.69, with Muslims having 16.37 and Buddhists having 14.32. Highest was for Brokpas at 21.74 and lowest was for Bodhs at 14.32. The sex ratio for Leh district has declined from 1011 females per 1000 males in 1951 to 805 in 2001, while for Kargil district, it has declined from 970 to 901. The urban sex ratio in both the districts is about 640. The adult sex ratio reflects large numbers of (mostly male) seasonal and migrant labourers and merchants. About 84% of Ladakh's population lives in villages. The average annual population growth rate from 1981–2001 was 2.75% in Leh District and 2.83% in Kargil district.

CULTURE

Ladakhi culture is similar to Tibetan culture. Ladakhi food has much in common with Tibetan food, the most prominent foods being *thukpa,* noodle soup; and *tsampa,* known in Ladakhi as *ngampe*, roasted barley flour. Eatable without cooking, tsampa makes useful, if dull trekking food. A dish that is strictly Ladakhi is *skyu*, a heavy pasta dish with root vegetables. As Ladakh moves toward a cash-based economy, foods from the plains of India are becoming more common. Like in other parts of Central Asia, tea in Ladakh is traditionally made with strong green tea, butter, and salt; it is mixed in a large churn and known as *gurgur cha*, after the sound it makes when mixed.

Sweet tea (*cha ngarmo*) is common now, made in the Indian style with milk and sugar. Most surplus barley produced is fermented into *chang*, an alcoholic beverage drunk especially on festive occasions. The architecture of Ladakh contains Tibetan and Indian influences, and monastic architecture reflects a deeply Buddhist approach. The Buddhist wheel, along with two dragons, is a common feature on every gompa (including the likes of Lamayuru, Likir, Thikse, Hemis, Alchi and Ridzong Gompas). Many houses and monasteries are built on elevated, sunny sites facing south, and in the past were made of rocks, earth and wood, but are now more often concrete frames filled in with stones or adobes.

The music of Ladakhi Buddhist monastic festivals, like Tibetan music, often involves religious chanting in Tibetan or Sanskrit, as an integral part of the religion. These chants are complex, often recitations of sacred texts or in celebration of various festivals. Yang chanting, performed without metrical timing, is accompanied by resonant drums and low, sustained syllables. Religious mask dances are an important part of Ladakh's cultural life. Hemis monastery, a leading centre of the Drukpa tradition of Buddhism, holds an annual masked dance festival, as do all major Ladakhi monasteries.

The dances typically narrate a story of fight between good and evil, ending with the eventual victory of the former. Weaving is an important part of traditional life in eastern Ladakh. Both women and men weave, on different looms. Typical costumes include *gonchas* of velvet, elaborately embroidered waistcoats and boots, and hats. The Ladakh

Festival is held every year from 1st to September 15. Performers adorned with gold and silver ornaments and turquoise headgear throng the streets. Monks wear colourful masks and dance to the rhythm of cymbals, flutes and trumpets. The Yak, Lion and Tashispa dances depict the many legends and fables of Ladakh. Buddhist monasteries sporting prayer flags, display of 'thankas', archery competitions, a mock marriage, and horse-polo are the some highlights of this festival.

The most popular sport in Ladakh now is ice hockey, which is played only on natural ice in January. Cricket is also very popular. Archery is a traditional sport in Ladakh, and many villages still hold archery festivals, which are as much about traditional dancing, drinking and gambling as about the sport. The sport is conducted with strict etiquette, to the accompaniment of the music of *surna* and *daman* (shenai and drum). Polo, the other traditional sport of Ladakh is indigenous to Baltistan and Gilgit, and was probably introduced into Ladakh in the mid-17th century by King Singge Namgyal, whose mother was a Balti princess.

A feature of Ladakhi society that distinguishes it from the rest of the state is the high status and relative emancipation enjoyed by women compared to other rural parts of India. Fraternal polyandry and inheritance by primogeniture were common in Ladakh until the early 1940s when these were made illegal by the government of Jammu and Kashmir, although they still exist in some areas. Another custom was known as *khang-bu*, or 'little house', in which the elders of a family, as soon as the eldest son has sufficiently matured, retire from participation in affairs, and taking only enough of the property for their sustenance, yield the headship of the family to him.

Tibetan medicine has been the traditional health system of Ladakh for over a thousand years. This school of traditional healing contains elements of Ayurveda and Chinese medicine, combined with the philosophy and cosmology of Tibetan Buddhism. For centuries, the only medical system which was accessible to the people has been the 'amchi' who are traditional doctors following the Tibetan medical tradition. 'Amchi' medicine is still an important component of public health to this day, especially in remote areas.

A number of programmes by the government, local and international organisations are underway to develop and rejuvenate this traditional system of healing. Efforts are on to preserve the intellectual property rights of 'amchi' medicine for the people of Ladakh. Government has also been trying to promote the Seabuckthorn in form of juice and jam, as it is believed to possess many medicinal properties. It is also seen as a means of providing employment to the various self help groups in rural Ladakh.

There are many [NGOs] which are actively working to improve the life in Ladakh like [LEDeG], [Leho], [Leh Nutrition project], Women's alliance etc. [LEDeG] has been working actively since 1971 by installing Hydraulic rams to improve the water supply in the region. It has also been successful in setting up hydro power projects in the otherwise energy starved region.

EDUCATION

According to the 2001 census, the overall literacy rate in Leh District is 62% (72% for males and 50% for females), and 58% in Kargil District (74% for males and 41% for females). Traditionally there was little or nothing by way of formal education except in the monasteries. Usually, one son from every family was obliged to master the Tibetan script in order to read the holy books. The Moravian Mission opened a school in Leh in October 1889, and the *Wazir-i Wazarat* of Baltistan and Ladakh ordered that every family with more than one child should send one of them to school.

This order met with great resistance from the local people who feared that the children would be forced to convert to Christianity. The school taught Tibetan, Urdu, English, and Geography, Sciences, Nature study, Arithmetic, Geometry and Bible study. The school is still in existence today. The first local school to provide western education was opened by a local

Society called "Lamdon Social Welfare Society" in 1973. Later with support from HH Dalai Lama, and some international organisations, the school has grown to accommodate approximately two thousand pupils in several branches. The school prides itself in preserving Ladakhi tradition and culture.

The Druk White Lotus School, under the guidance of His Holiness Gyalwang Drukpa, spiritual head of the Drukpa Order (the dominant Buddhist sect in Ladakh and traditionally, the state religion of Ladakh) located in Shey is another school which aims at helping to maintain the cultural traditions of Ladakh. Schools are well distributed throughout Ladakh, but 75% of them provide only primary education. 65% of the children attend school, but absenteeism of both students and teachers remains high. In both districts the failure rate at school-leaving level (class X) had for many years been around 85–95%, while of those managing to scrape through, barely half succeeded in qualifying for college entrance (class XII.)

Before 1993, students were taught in Urdu until they were 14, after which the medium of instruction shifted to English. In 1994 the Students' Educational and Cultural Movement of Ladakh (SECMOL) launched 'Operation New Hope' (ONH), a campaign to provide 'culturally appropriate and locally relevant education' and make government schools more functional and effective. The ONH works with the government, the NGOs, the teachers and the village communities. By 2001, ONH principles were being implemented in all the government schools of Leh District, and the matriculation exam pass rate had risen to 50%. A government degree college has been opened in Leh, enabling students to pursue higher education without having to leave Ladakh.

LEH

Leh has for centuries been an important stopover on trade routes along the Indus Valley between Tibet to the east, Kashmir to the west and also between India and China. The main goods carried were salt, grain, *pashm* or cashmere wool, *charas* or cannabis resin) from the Tarim Basin, indigo, silk yarn and Banaras brocade. Although there are a few indications that the Chinese knew of a trade route through Ladakh to India as early as the Kushan period (1st to 3rd centuries CE), and certainly by Tang dynasty, little is actually known of the history of the region until the formation of the kingdom towards the end of the 10th century by the Tibetan prince, *Skyid lde nyima gon* (or *Nyima gon*), a grandson of the anti-Buddhist Tibetan king, Langdarma (r. circa 838 to 841 CE).

He conquered Western Tibet although his army originally numbered only 300 men. Several towns and castles are said to have been founded by Nyima gon and he apparently ordered the construction of the main sculptures at Shey. "In an inscription he says he had them made for the religious benefit of of the *Tsanpo* (the dynastical name of his father and ancestors), and of all the people of *Ngaris* (Western Tibet). This show that already in this generation Langdarma's opposition to Buddhism had disappeared." Shey, just 15 km east of modern Leh was the ancient seat of the Ladakhi kings.

Several trade routes have traditionally converged on Leh, from all four directions. The most direct route was the one the modern highway follows from the Punjab via Mandi, the Kulu valley, over the Rohtang Pass, through Lahaul and on to the Indus Valley, and then down river to Leh. The route from Srinigar was roughly the same as the road that today crosses the *Zoji La* (pass) to Kargil, and then up the Indus Valley to Leh. From Baltistan there were two difficult routes: the main on ran up the Shyok Valley from the Indus, over a pass and then down the Hanu River to the Indus again below Khalsi (Khalatse). The other ran from Skardu straight up the Indus to Kargil and on to Leh. Then, there were both the summer and winter routes from Leh to Yarkand across the Karakorum. Finally, there were a couple of possible routes from Leh to Lhasa.

The first recorded royal residence in Ladakh, built at the top of the high Namgyal ('Victory') Peak overlooking the present palace and town, is the now-ruined fort and the *gon-khang* (Temple of the Guardian Divinities) built by King Tashi Namgyal. Tashi Namgyal is known to have ruled during the final quarter of the 16th century CE. The Namgyal or Tsemo

Gompa (= 'Red Gompa'. Also, *dGon-pa-so-ma* = 'New Monastery') is temple is the main Buddhist centre in Leh. There are some older walls of fortifications behind it which Francke reported used to be known as the "Dard Castle." If it was indeed built by Dards, it must pre-date the establishment of Tibetan rulers in Ladakh, over a thousand years ago.

Below this are the Chamba (Byams-pa, *i.e.*, Maitreya) and Chenresi (sPyan-ras-gzigs, i.e. Avalokiteshvara) monasteries which are of uncertain date. The royal palace, known as Leh Palace was built by King Sengge Namgyal (1612-1642), presumably between the period when the Portuguese Jesuit priest, Francisco de Azevado, visited Leh in 1631, and made no mention of it, and Sengge Namgyal's death in 1642. The Leh Palace is nine storeys high; the upper floors accommodated the royal family, the stables and store rooms are located in the lower floors. The palace was abandoned when Kashmiri forces besieged it in the mid-19th century. The royal family moved their premises south to their current home in Stok Palace on the southern bank of the Indus.

COEXISTENCE WITH RELIGIONS OTHER THAN BUDDHISM

Since the eighth century people belonging to different religions, particularly Buddhism and Islam have been living in harmony in Leh. They coexisted from the time of early period of Namgyal dynasty and there has been no mention of any conflict between them. But with the opening of Ladakh to the outside world and politics creeping into peaceful Ladakhi society, the issue of religion has emerged and stained this long tradition of coexistence and co-evolution.

In recent times, relations between the Buddhist and Muslim communities soured due the petty conflicts motivated by political interest. With the visit of the Dalai Lama in August 2003 and his strong appeal to the masses regarding religious pluralism and peaceful coexistence, the situation has ameliorated and normalcy has been restored. Thus, Ladakh resumed its age-old tradition of cohesiveness.

During the reign of Delegs Namgyal (1660-1685), the Nawab of Kashmir, which was then a province in the Mogul Empire, arranged for the Mongol army to (temporarily) leave Ladakh (but returned later. As payment for assisting Delegs Namgyal, the Nawab made a number of onerous demands. One of the least was to build a large Sunni Muslim mosque in Leh at the upper end of the bazaar in Leh, below the Leh Palace. This was apparently not the first mosque in Leh; there are two smaller ones which are said to be older. The mosque reflects a mixture of Islamic and Tibetan architecture and can accommodate more than 500 people.

Besides these two communities, there are people living in the region who belong to different religions like Christianity, Hinduism, and Sikhism. And they too live in harmony and form a vital part of the society. The small Christian community in Leh is descendants of converts from Tibetan Buddhism by German Moravian missionaries who established a church at Keylong in Lahaul in the 1860s, and were allowed to open another mission in Leh in 1885 and had a sub branch in Khalatse. They stayed open until Indian Independence in 1947. In spite of their successful medical and educational activities, they made only a few converts.

GEOGRAPHY

Average annual rainfall is only 90 mm (3½ inches). The temperature can range from "28 °C (-18.4°F) in winter to 33°C (91.4°F) in summer. The principal access roads include the 434 km Srinagar-Leh highway which connects Leh with Srinagar and the 473 km Leh-Manali Highway which connects Manali with Leh. Both roads are open only on a seasonal basis. Although the access roads from India are often blocked by snow in winter, the local roads in the Indus Valley usually remain open due to the low level of precipitation and snowfall.

CLIMATE

Leh has a cold, arid climate with long, harsh winters from October to early March, with minimum temperatures well below freezing for most of the winter. The city gets occasional snowfall during winter. The weather in the remaining months is generally fine.

AGRICULTURE

Although Leh is only about 400 metres higher, it means that only one crop a year can be grown there, while two can be grown at Khalatse. By the time crops are being sown at Leh in late May, they are already half-grown at Khalatse. The main crop is *grim* (naked barley - *Hordeum vulgare* L. var. *nudum* Hook. f., which is an ancient form of domesticated barley with an easier to remove hull) - from which tsampa, the staple food in Ladakh, is made).

DEMOGRAPHICS

According to the 2001 Census, 77.3 % of Leh District's population is Buddhist, 13.8 % Muslim, 8.2% Hindu and 0.8% others. The Muslim presence dates back to the annexation of Ladakh by Kashmir, after the Fifth Dalai Lama attempted to invade Ladakh from Tibet. Since then, there has been further migration from the Kashmir Valley due firstly to trade and latterly with the transfer of tourism from the Kashmir Valley to Ladakh. As of 2001 India census, Leh town had a population of 27,513.

Males constitute 61% of the population and females 39%, due to a large presence of non-local labourers, traders and government employees. Leh has an average literacy rate of 75%, higher than the national average of 59.5%: male literacy is 82%, and female literacy is 65%. In Leh, 9% of the population is under 6 years of age. The total population of Leh district is 1.17 lacs (117,000) people.

TOPOGRAPHY

The district is the northern as well as the eastern most part of J&K State. It is linked with the Kashmir valley by the Zojila (10,098 feet) pass and forms part of the outer Himalayas. It is one of the highest regions of the earth (altitude 8,800 feet to 18,000 feet approx.) with mountains running along parallel ranges. The climate is very cold and in winter, temperatures dip to minus 40 degrees Centigrade.

The district is bounded by the international border or Line of Actual Control with China in the north and east, and with Pakistan Occupied Kashmir in the north. The geographical area of the district is 45,110 sq. km. with Leh as the district Headquarters. The district has two assembly constituencies, namely Nobra and Leh and five blocks namely, Leh, Khaisi, Nobra, Nyoma and Durbuk. The literacy rate is 24.18 per cent - male 35.37 per cent and female 11.77 per cent.

Important places:

Hemis Gumpa (36 kms. south of Leh)

Tsemo Gumpa (known for Chamba Buddha statue)

Mashro Gumpa

Chemmrey Gumpa

Alchie Gumpa

Lomayuru Gumpa (oldest monastry in the distt.)

Likir Gumpa

Shey Palaces & monastry

Spituk monastry

Thiksay & Sankar monastery

Leh monastery

Leh Khar Palace

Leh mosque (in main Bazar)

POLITICAL SCENARIO

The Congress is the main political party and its candidates won the Leh assembly seat in the 1977, 1983 and 1987 assembly elections. Tsering Samphal, ex-MLA of Congress, won from Leh assembly constituency in the 1987 elections and is the most important political figure of the district. Buddhists constitute more than 80 per cent of the district population and the Ladakh Buddhist Association has been agitating for district Autonomy. Consequently, the Ladakh Autonomous Hill Development

Council (LAHDC) was constituted and elections to this body were held on 28 Aug, 1995.

The newly elected and nominated members of the LAHDC took oath on 3 September 1995. P. Namgyal (Ex-MP, Congress), Stanzin Chamba Gambo (Head Lama), Thupsten Chhewang (Executive Counsellor) are the important political figures in the district. Chantan Namgyal (NCF) and Tsering Doiji Larook (Congress) won the Assembly elections. P.Namgyal was elected to the Lok Sabha in 1996, while Agha Sayeed Hussain (NC/F) was elected to the Lok Sabha elections in 1998. Militancy has not established roots in the district.

KARGIL

TOPOGRAPHY

Kargil town is located at a distance of 204 km from Srinagar, almost midway on the Srinagar-leh National Highway. Most of the villages of the district are located at an average height of 10,000 feet above sea level. It shares the Line of Control (LoC) with POK in the north and borders with Leh in the east and the Kashmir valley in the west. The geographical area of the district is 14,036 sq kms. The district has two tehsils as well as two assembly constituencies, namely Kargil and Zanskar. The climate is very cold and in winter, the highway is blocked for more than six months from Dec. to June every year. The snowfall around Zojila passand Drass region is very heavy. The literacy rate is 17.06 per cent - male 29-49 per cent and female 3.21 per cent.

ECONOMY

Agriculture is the main occupation and about 91per cent of the population is engaged in it. Wheat and millet are the major crops. Though the district is devoid of industrial units, the development of handicraft has added to jobs and income. The Baltel-Kargil road, linking Kargil with Srinagar is the life-line of the district with the construction of the 230 kms. Kargil-Padam and Bodh Khushboochaktan road are in progress.

Tourism is being promoted as an industry after Ladakh was opened to foreign tourists in 1974. Horticulture and forestry are being given special attention. Co-operative movement is also active in the district.

POLITICAL SCENARIO

Shia Muslims constitute more than 78 per cent of the population and the NC (F) is the most influential party here. Its candidate Qamar Alt, NC (F) won the seat in 1987. However, younger generation of Shias feel discriminated in matters of employment, and they have rallied under the banner of 'Imam Khomeim Memorial Trust' which has been fanning anti-India feelings. Commander Hassan (Ind.), Kachru Ali Mohd. (Congress, ex-Deputy Minister) are prominent political leaders. Kamar Ali Akhoon and Haji Md. Abbas (both NCF) won the Assembly elections in 1996.

The Kargil War, also known as the Kargil conflict, was an armed conflict between India and Pakistan that took place between May and July 1999 in the Kargil district of Kashmir. The cause of the war was the infiltration of Pakistani soldiers and Kashmiri militants into positions on the Indian side of the Line of Control (LOC), which serves as the *de facto* border between the two states. During and directly after the war, Pakistan blamed the fighting entirely on independent Kashmiri insurgents, but documents left behind by casualties and later statements by Pakistan's Prime Minister and Chief of Army Staff showed involvement of Pakistani paramilitary forces, led by General Ashraf Rashid.

The Indian Army, later on supported by the Indian Air Force, attacked the Pakistani positions and, with international diplomatic support, eventually forced withdrawal of the Pakistani forces across the LOC. The war is one of the most recent examples of high altitude warfare in mountainous terrain, which posed significant logistical problems for the combating sides. This was only the second direct ground war between any two countries after they had developed nuclear weapons, after the Sino-Soviet border conflict of 1969; it is also the most recent. (India and Pakistan both test-detonated fission devices in May 1998, though the first Indian nuclear test was conducted in 1974.)

The conflict led to heightened tension between the two nations and increased defence spending by India. In Pakistan, the aftermath caused instability of the government and the economy, and, on October 12, 1999, a *coup d'etat* by the military placed army chief Pervez Musharraf in power. Before the Partition of India in 1947, Kargil was part of the Baltistan district of Ladakh, a sparsely populated region with diverse linguistic, ethnic and religious groups, living in isolated valleys separated by some of the world's highest mountains. The First Kashmir War (1947–48) concluded with the Line of Control (LOC) bisecting the Baltistan district, with the town and district of Kargil lying on the Indian side in the Ladakh subdivision of the Indian state of Jammu and Kashmir.

After Pakistan's defeat in the Indo-Pakistani War of 1971, the two nations signed the Simla Agreement promising not to engage in armed conflict with respect to that boundary. The town of Kargil is located 205 km (120 miles) from Srinagar, facing the Northern Areas across the LOC. Like other areas in the Himalayas, Kargil has a temperate climate. Summers are cool with frigid nights, while winters are long and chilly with temperatures often dropping to "48 °C ("54 °F). An Indian national highway (NH 1) connecting Srinagar to Leh cuts through Kargil. The area that witnessed the infiltration and fighting is a 160 km long stretch of ridges overlooking this highway.

The military outposts on the ridges above the highway were generally around 5,000 metres (16,000 ft) high, with a few as high as 5,485 metres (18,000 ft). Apart from the district capital, Kargil, the populated areas near the front line in the conflict included the Mushko Valley and the town of Drass, southwest of Kargil, as well as the Batalik sector and other areas, northeast of Kargil. One of the reasons why Kargil was targeted was that the terrain surrounding it, lent itself to pre-emptive seizure of unoccupied military positions. With tactically vital features and well-prepared defensive posts atop the peaks, a defender of the high ground would enjoy advantages akin to a fortress.

Any attack to dislodge a defender from high ground in mountain warfare requires a far higher ratio of attackers to defenders, and the difficulties would be exacerbated by the high altitude and freezing temperatures. Kargil was also just 173 km (108 mi) from the Pakistani-controlled town of Skardu, which was capable of providing logistical and artillery support to Pakistani combatants. After the Indo-Pakistani War of 1971, there had been a long period with relatively few direct armed conflicts involving the military forces of the two neighbors - notwithstanding the efforts of both nations to control the Siachen Glacier by establishing military outposts on the surrounding mountains ridges and the resulting military skirmishes in the 1980s.

During the 1990s, however, escalating tensions and conflict due to separatist activities in Kashmir, some supported by Pakistan, as well as the conducting of nuclear tests by both countries in 1998, and led to an increasingly belligerent atmosphere. In an attempt to defuse the situation, both countries signed the Lahore Declaration in February 1999, promising to provide a peaceful and bilateral solution to the Kashmir conflict. During the winter of 1998 -1999, some elements of the Military of Pakistan were covertly training and sending Pakistani troops and paramilitary forces, some allegedly in the guise of *Mujahideen*, into territory on the Indian side of the LOC.

The infiltration was code named "Operation Badr"; its aim was to sever the link between Kashmir and Ladakh, and cause Indian forces to withdraw from the Siachen Glacier, thus forcing India to negotiate a settlement of the broader Kashmir dispute. Pakistan also believed that any tension in the region would internationalise the Kashmir issue, helping it to secure a speedy resolution. Yet another goal may have been to boost the morale of the decade-long rebellion in Indian Administered Kashmir by taking a proactive role. Some writers have speculated that the operation's objective may also have been as retaliation for India's Operation Meghdoot in 1984 that seized much of Siachen Glacier.

According to India's then Army Chief Ved Prakash Malik, and many other scholars, much of the background planning, including construction of logistical supply routes, had been undertaken much earlier. On several occasions during the 1980s and 1990s, the army had given Pakistani leaders (namely Zia ul Haq and Benazir Bhutto) similar proposals for infiltration into the Kargil region, but the plans had been shelved for fear of drawing the nations into all-out war. Some analysts believe that the blueprint of attack was reactivated soon after Pervez Musharraf was appointed chief of army staff in October 1998.

After the war, Nawaz Sharif, Prime Minister of Pakistan during the Kargil conflict, claimed that he was unaware of the plans, and that he first learned about the situation when he received an urgent phone call from Atal Bihari Vajpayee, his counterpart in India. Sharif attributed the plan to Musharraf and "just two or three of his cronies", a view shared by some Pakistani writers who have stated that only four generals, including Musharraf, knew of the plan. Musharraf, however, asserted that Sharif had been briefed on the Kargil operation 15 days ahead of Vajpayee's journey to Lahore on February 20.

WAR PROGRESS

There were three major phases to the Kargil War. First, Pakistan infiltrated forces into the Indian-controlled section of Kashmir and occupied strategic locations enabling it to control NH1. The next stage consisted of India discovering the infiltration and mobilizing forces to respond to it. The final stage involved major battles by Indian and Pakistani forces resulting in India capturing positions held by Pakistani forces and the withdrawal of Pakistani forces back across the Line of Control.

OCCUPATION BY PAKISTAN

During the winter season, due to extreme cold in the mountainous areas of Kashmir, it was a common practice for both the Indian and Pakistan Armies to abandon some forward posts on their respective sides of the LOC and to reduce patrolling of areas that may be avenues of infiltration. When weather conditions became less severe, forward posts would be reoccupied and patrolling resumed. During February 1999, the Pakistan Army began to re-occupy the posts it had abandoned on its side of the LOC in the Kargil region, but also sent forces to occupy some posts on the Indian side of the LOC.

Troops from the elite Special Services Group as well as four to seven battalions of the Northern Light Infantry (a paramilitary regiment not part of the regular Pakistani army at that time) covertly and overtly set up bases on the vantage points of the Indian-controlled region. According to some reports, these Pakistani forces were backed by Kashmiri guerrillas and Afghan mercenaries. Pakistani intrusions took place in the heights of the lower Mushkoh valley, along the Marpo La ridgeline in Dras, in Kaksar near Kargil, in the Batalik sector east of the Indus River, on the heights above of the Chorbatla sector where the LOC turns north and in the Turtok sector south of the Siachen area.

INDIA DISCOVERS INFILTRATION AND MOBILIZES

Initially, these incursions were not detected for a number of reasons: Indian patrols were not sent into some of the areas infiltrated by the Pakistani forces and heavy artillery fire by Pakistan in some areas provided cover for the infiltrators. But by the second week of May, the ambushing of an Indian patrol team led by Capt Saurabh Kalia, who acted on a tip-off by a local shepherd in the Batalik sector, led to the exposure of the infiltration. Initially, with little knowledge of the nature or extent of the encroachment, the Indian troops in the area assumed that the infiltrators were jihadis and claimed that they would evict them within a few days.

Subsequent discovery of infiltration elsewhere along the LOC, and the difference in tactics employed by the infiltrators, caused the Indian army to realize that the plan of attack was on a much bigger scale. The total area seized by the ingress is generally accepted to between 130 km^2 - 200 km^2; Musharraf, however, stated that 500 square miles (1,300 km^2) of Indian Territory was occupied. The Government of India responded with Operation Vijay, a mobilisation of 200,000 Indian troops. However, because of the nature of the terrain, division and corps operations could not be mounted; subsequent fighting was conducted mostly at the regimental or battalion level.

In effect, two divisions of the Indian Army, numbering 20,000, plus several thousand from the Paramilitary forces of India and the air force were deployed in the conflict zone. The total number of Indian soldiers that were involved in the military operation on the Kargil-Drass sector was thus close to 30,000. The number of infiltrators, including those providing logistical backup, has been put at approximately 5,000 at the height of the conflict. This figure includes troops from Pakistan-administered Kashmir who provided additional artillery support.

The Indian Air Force launched Operation Safed Sagar in support of the mobilization of Indian land forces, but its effectiveness during the war was limited by the high altitude and weather conditions, which in turn limited bomb loads and the number of airstrips that could be used. The Indian Navy also readied itself for an attempted blockade of Pakistani ports (primarily Karachi port) to cut off supply routes. Later, the then-Prime Minister of Pakistan Nawaz Sharif disclosed that Pakistan was left with just six days of fuel to sustain itself if a full-fledged war had broken out.

INDIA ATTACKS PAKISTANI POSITIONS

The terrain of Kashmir is mountainous and at high altitudes; even the best roads, such as National Highway No. 1 (NH 1) from Leh to Srinagar, are only two lanes. The rough terrain and narrow roads slowed traffic, and the high altitude, which affected the ability of aircraft to carry loads, made control of NH 1A (the actual stretch of the highway which was under Pakistani fire) a priority for India. From their observation posts, the Pakistani forces had a clear line-of-sight to lay down indirect artillery fire on NH 1A, inflicting heavy casualties on the Indians. This was a serious problem for the Indian Army as the highway was its main logistical and supply route. The Pakistani shelling of the arterial road posed the threat of Leh being cut off, though an alternative (and longer) road to Leh existed via Himachal Pradesh.

The infiltrators, apart from being equipped with small arms and grenade launchers, were also armed with mortars, artillery and anti-aircraft guns. Many posts were also heavily mined, with India later stating to having recovered more than 8,000 anti-personnel mines according to an ICBL report. Pakistan's reconnaissance was done through unmanned aerial vehicles and AN/TPQ-36 Firefinder radars supplied by the US. The initial Indian attacks were aimed at controlling the hills overlooking NH 1A, with high priority being given to the stretches of the highway near the town of Kargil.

The majority of posts along the Line of Control were adjacent to the highway, and therefore the recapture of nearly every infiltrated post increased both the territorial gains and the security of the highway. The protection of this route and the recapture of the forward posts were thus ongoing objectives throughout the war. The Indian Army's first priority was to recapture peaks that were in the immediate vicinity of NH1a. This resulted in Indian troops first targeting the Tiger Hill and Tololing complex in Dras, which dominated the Srinagar-Leh route. This was soon followed by the Batalik-Turtok sub-sector which provided access to Siachen Glacier.

Some of the peaks that were of vital strategic importance to the Pakistani defensive troops were Point 4590 and Point 5353. While 4590 was the nearest point that had a view of NH1a, point 5353 was the highest feature in the Dras sector, allowing the Pakistani troops to observe NH1A. The recapture of Point 4590 by Indian troops on June 14 was significant, notwithstanding the fact that Point 4590 resulting in the Indian Army suffering the most casualties in a single battle during the conflict. Though most of the posts in the vicinity of the highway were cleared by mid-June, some parts of the highway near Drass witnessed sporadic shelling until the end of the war.

Once India regained control of the hills overlooking NH 1A, the Indian Army turned to driving the invading force back across the Line of Control. The Battle of Tololing, among other assaults, slowly tilted the combat in India's favor. The Pakistani troops at Tololing were aided by Pakistani fighters from Kashmir. Some of the posts put up a stiff resistance, including Tiger Hill (Point 5140) that fell only later in the war. Indian troops found well-entrenched Pakistani soldiers at Tiger Hill, and both sides suffered heavy casualties. After a final assault on the peak in which 10 Pakistani soldiers and 5 Indian soldiers were killed, Tiger Hill finally fell.

A few of the assaults occurred atop hitherto unheard of peaks – most of them unnamed with only Point numbers to differentiate them – which witnessed fierce hand to hand combat. As the operation was fully underway, about 250 artillery guns were brought in to clear the infiltrators in the posts that were in the line-of-sight. The Bofors field howitzer (infamous in India due to the Bofors scandal) played a vital role, with Indian gunners making maximum use of the terrain that assisted such an attack. However, its success was limited elsewhere due to the lack of space and depth to deploy the Bofors gun.

It was in this type of terrain that aerial attacks were used with limited effectiveness. The IAF lost a MiG-27 strike aircraft which it attributed to an engine failure as well as a MiG-21 fighter which was shot down by Pakistan; Pakistan said it shot down both jets after they crossed into its territory and one Mi-8 helicopters to Stinger SAMs. During attacks the IAF used laser-guided bombs to destroy well-entrenched positions of the Pakistani forces. On May 27 1999, Flt. Lt. Nachiketa developed engine trouble in the Batalik sector and bailed out of his craft. Sqn Ldr Ajay Ahuja went out of his way to locate his comrade but was shot down using a shoulder-fired Stinger missile. According to reports, he had bailed out of his stricken plane safely but was apparently killed by his captors as his body was returned riddled with bullet wounds.

In many vital points, neither artillery nor air power could dislodge the outposts manned by the Pakistani soldiers, who were out of visible range. The Indian Army mounted some direct frontal ground assaults which were slow and took a heavy toll given the steep ascent that had to be made on peaks as high as 18,000 feet (5,500 m). Since any daylight attack would be suicidal, all the advances had to be made under the cover of darkness, escalating the risk of freezing. Accounting for the wind chill factor, the temperatures were often as low as "11 °C to "15 °C (12 °F to 5 °F) near the mountain tops.

Based on military tactics, much of the costly frontal assaults by the Indians could have been avoided if the Indian Military had chosen to blockade the supply route of the opposing force, virtually creating a siege. Such a move would have involved the Indian troops crossing the LoC as well as initiating aerial attacks on Pakistan soil, a manoeuvre India was not willing to exercise fearing an expansion of the theatre of war and reducing international support for its cause. Two months into the conflict, Indian troops had slowly retaken most of the ridges they had lost; according to official count, an estimated 75%–80% of the intruded area and nearly all high ground were back under Indian control.

WITHDRAWAL AND FINAL BATTLES

As Pakistan found itself struggling, the Pakistan army had covertly planned a nuclear strike on India, the news of which alarmed U.S. President Bill Clinton, resulting in a stern warning to Nawaz Sharif. Following the Washington accord on July 4, where Sharif agreed to withdraw Pakistani troops, most of the fighting came to a gradual halt, but some Pakistani forces remained in positions on the Indian side of the LOC. In addition, the United Jihad Council (an umbrella for all extremist groups) rejected Pakistan's plan for a climb-down, instead deciding to fight on.

The Indian army launched its final attacks in the last week of July; as soon as the Drass subsector had been cleared of Pakistani forces, the fighting ceased on July 26. The day has since been marked as *Kargil Vijay Diwas* (Kargil Victory Day) in India. By the end of the war, India had resumed control of all territory south and east of the Line of Control, as was established in July 1972 as per the Shimla Accord.

WORLD OPINION

Pakistan was criticised by other countries for allowing its paramilitary forces and insurgents to cross the Line of Control. Pakistan's primary diplomatic response, one of plausible deniability linking the incursion to what it officially termed as "Kashmiri freedom fighters", was in the end not successful. Veteran analysts argued that the battle was fought at heights where only seasoned troops could survive, so poorly equipped freedom fighters would neither have the ability nor the wherewithal to seize land and defend it. Moreover, while the army had initially denied the involvement of its troops in the intrusion, two soldiers were awarded the Nishan-E-Haider (Pakistan's highest military honour).

Another 90 soldiers were also given gallantry awards, most of them posthumously, confirming Pakistan's role in the episode. India also released taped phone conversations between the Army Chief and a senior Pakistani general where the latter is recorded saying: "the scruff of [the militants] necks is in our hands," although Pakistan dismissed it as a "total fabrication". Concurrently, Pakistan made several contradicting statements, confirming its role in Kargil, when it defended the incursions saying that the LOC itself was disputed. Pakistan also attempted to internationalize the Kashmir issue, by linking the crisis in Kargil to the larger Kashmir conflict but, such a diplomatic stance found few backers on the world stage.

As the Indian counter-attacks picked up momentum, Pakistani Prime Minister Nawaz Sharif flew to meet U.S. president Bill Clinton on July 4 to obtain support from the United States. Clinton rebuked Sharif, however, and asked him to use his contacts to rein in the militants and withdraw Pakistani soldiers from Indian Territory. Clinton would later reveal in his autobiography that "Sharif's moves were perplexing" since the Indian prime minister had travelled to

Lahore to promote bilateral talks aimed at resolving the Kashmir problem and "by crossing the Line of Control, Pakistan had wrecked the [bilateral] talks." On the other hand, he applauded Indian restraint for not crossing the LoC and escalating the conflict into an all-out war.

G8 nations supported India and condemned the Pakistani violation of the LOC at the Cologne summit. The European Union also opposed Pakistan's violation of the LOC. China, a long-time ally of Pakistan, did not intervene in Pakistan's favour, insisting on a pullout of forces to the LoC and settling border issues peacefully. Other organizations like the ASEAN Regional Forum too supported India's stand on the inviolability of the LOC. Faced with growing international pressure, Sharif managed to pull back the remaining soldiers from Indian Territory. The joint statement issued by Clinton and Sharif conveyed the need to respect the Line of Control and resume bilateral talks as the best forum to resolve all disputes.

GALLANTRY AWARDS

A number of Indian soldiers earned awards for gallantry during the campaign.

Grenadier Yogendra Singh Yadav, 18 Grenadiers, Param Vir Chakra, Posthumously, but it was his namesake that had been slain in the mission while he was recuperating in a hospital.

Lieutenant Manoj Kumar Pandey, 1/11 Gorkha Rifles, Param Vir Chakra, Posthumous.

Captain Vikram Batra, 13 JAK Rifles, Param Vir Chakra, Posthumous.

Rifleman Sanjay Kumar, 13 JAK Rifles, Param Vir Chakra, Posthumous.

IMPACT AND INFLUENCE OF MEDIA

The Kargil War was significant for the impact and influence of the mass media on public opinion in both nations.

Coming at a time of exploding growth in electronic journalism in India, the Kargil news stories and war footage were often telecast live on TV, and many websites provided in-depth analysis of the war. The conflict became the first "live" war in South Asia; it was given such detailed media coverage that one effect was the drumming up of jingoistic feelings. The conflict soon turned into a news propaganda war. Press briefings by government officials of each nation produced such conflicting claims and counterclaims that an outside observer listening to both Indian and Pakistani coverage would wonder whether they were describing the same conflict.

The Indian government placed a temporary news embargo on information from Pakistan, banning the telecast of the state-run Pakistani channel PTV and blocking access to online editions of the *Dawn* newspaper. The Pakistani media criticized this apparent curbing of freedom of the press in India, while India media claimed it was in the interest of national security. The Indian government ran advertisements in foreign publications including *The Times* and *The Washington Post* detailing Pakistan's role in supporting extremists in Kashmir in an attempt to garner political support for its position. As the war progressed, media coverage of the conflict was more intense in India than in Pakistan.

Many Indian channels showed images from the battle zone in a style reminiscent of CNN's coverage of the Gulf War (one of the shells fired by Pakistan troops even hit a Doordarshan transmission centre in Kargil while coverage continued). Reasons for India's increased coverage included the greater number of privately owned electronic media in India compared to Pakistan and relatively greater transparency in the Indian media. At a seminar in Karachi, Pakistani journalists agreed that while the Indian government had taken the press and the people into its confidence, Pakistan had not.

The print media in India and abroad was largely sympathetic to the Indian cause, with editorials in newspapers based in the west and other neutral countries observing that Pakistan was largely responsible for the conflict. Some analysts believe that Indian media, which was both larger in number and more credible, may have acted as a force multiplier for the Indian military operation in Kargil and served as a morale booster. As the fighting intensified, the Pakistani version of events found little backing on the world stage. This helped India gain valuable diplomatic recognition for its position.

WMDS AND THE NUCLEAR FACTOR

Since Pakistan and India each had weapons of mass destruction, many in the international community were concerned that if the Kargil conflict intensified, it could lead to nuclear war. Both countries had tested their nuclear capability in 1998 (India conducted its first test in 1974 while it was Pakistan's first-ever nuclear test). Many pundits believed the tests to be an indication of the escalating stakes in the scenario in South Asia. When the Kargil conflict started just a year after the nuclear tests, many nations desired to end it before it intensified.

International concerns increased when Pakistani foreign secretary Shamshad Ahmad made a statement on May 31 warning that an escalation of the limited conflict could lead Pakistan to use "any weapon" in its arsenal. This was immediately interpreted as a threat of nuclear retaliation by Pakistan in the event of an extended war, and the belief was reinforced when the leader of Pakistan's senate noted, "The purpose of developing weapons becomes meaningless if they are not used when they are needed." Many such ambiguous statements from officials of both countries were viewed as warnings of an impending nuclear crisis where the combatants would consider use of their limited nuclear arsenals in 'tactical' nuclear warfare in the belief that it would not have ended in mutual assured destruction, as could have occurred in a nuclear conflict between the United States and the USSR.

Some experts believe that following nuclear tests in 1998, the Pakistani military was emboldened by its nuclear deterrent to markedly increase coercion against India. The nature of the India-Pakistan conflict took a more sinister turn when the U.S.

received intelligence that Pakistani nuclear warheads were being moved towards the border. Bill Clinton tried to dissuade Pakistan Prime Minister Nawaz Sharif from nuclear brinkmanship, even threatening Pakistan of dire consequences.

According to a White House official, Sharif seemed to be genuinely surprised by this supposed missile movement and responded that India was probably planning the same. In an article in May 2000, Dr Sanjay Badri-Maharaj claimed that India too had readied at least five nuclear-tipped ballistic missiles, but could not back up this claim with any official proof. Sensing a deteriorating military scenario, diplomatic isolation, and the risks of a larger conventional and nuclear war, Sharif ordered the Pakistani army to vacate the Kargil heights. He later claimed in his official biography that General Pervez Musharraf had moved nuclear warheads without informing him.

Recently however, Pervez Musharraf revealed in his memoirs that Pakistan's nuclear delivery system was not operational during the Kargil war; something that would have put Pakistan under serious disadvantage if the conflict went nuclear. The threat of WMD included chemical and even biological weapons. Pakistan accused India of using chemical weapons and incendiary weapons such as napalm against the Kashmiri fighters. India, on the other hand, showcased a cache of gas masks, among other firearms, as proof that Pakistan may have been prepared to use non-conventional weapons. The US official and the OPCW determined that Pakistani allegations of India using banned chemicals in its bombs were unfounded.

AFTERMATH

India

From the end of the war until February 2000, the Indian stock market rose by over 30%. The next Indian national budget included major increases in military spending. There was a surge in patriotism, with many celebrities expressing their support for the Kargil cause. Indians were angered by media reports of the death of pilot Ajay Ahuja, especially after Indian authorities reported that Ahuja had been murdered and his body mutilated by Pakistani troops. The war had produced higher than expected fatalities for the Indian military, with a sizeable percentage of them including newly commissioned officers. One month after conclusion of the Kargil war, the Atlantique Incident - where a Pakistan Navy plane was shot down by India - briefly reignited fears of a conflict between the two countries.

After the war, the Indian government severed ties with Pakistan and increased defence preparedness. India increased its defence budget as it sought to acquire more state of the art equipment. Media reported about military procurement irregularities and criticism of intelligence agencies like RAW, which failed to predict the intrusions or the identity/number of infiltrators during the war. An internal assessment report by the armed forces, published in an Indian magazine, showed several other failings, including "a sense of complacency" and being "unprepared for a conventional war" on the presumption that nuclearism would sustain peace.

It also highlighted the lapses in command and control, the insufficient troop levels and the dearth of large-calibre guns like the Bofors. In 2006, retired Air Chief Marshal, A.Y. Tipnis, alleged that the Indian Army did not fully inform the government about the intrusions, adding that the army Chief Ved Prakash Malik was initially reluctant to use the full strike capability of the Indian Air Force, instead requesting only helicopter gunship support. Soon after the conflict, India also decided to complete the project - previously stalled by Pakistan - to fence the entire LOC.

The end of the Kargil conflict was followed by the 13th Indian General Elections to the Lok Sabha, which gave a decisive mandate to the NDA government. It was re-elected to power in September–October 1999 with a majority of 303 seats out of 545 in the Lok Sabha. On the diplomatic front, Indo-U.S. relations improved, as the United States appreciated Indian attempts to restrict the conflict to a limited geographic area. Relations with Israel – which had discreetly aided India with ordnance supply and matériel such as unmanned aerial vehicles and laser-guided bombs, as well as satellite imagery – also were bolstered.

Kargil Review Committee

Soon after the war the Atal Behari Vajpayee government set up an an inquiry into its causes and to analyze perceived Indian intelligence failures. The high-powered committee was chaired by eminent strategic affairs analyst K. Subrahmanyam and given powers to interview anyone with current or past associations with Indian security, including former Prime Ministers. The committee's final report (also referred to as the 'Subrahmanyam Report') led to a large-scale restructuring of Indian Intelligence. It, however, came in for heavy criticism in the Indian media for its perceived avoidance of assigning specific responsibility for failures over detecting the Kargil intrusions.

The Committee was also embroiled in controversy for indicting Brigadier Surinder Singh of the Indian Army for his failure to report enemy intrusions in time, and for his subsequent conduct. Many press reports questioned or contradicted this finding and claimed that Singh had in fact issued early warnings that were ignored by senior Army commanders and, ultimately, higher government functionaries.

In a departure from the norm the final report was published and made publicly available. Some chapters and all annexures, however, were deemed to contain classified information by the government and not released. K. Subrahmanyam later wrote that the annexures contained information on the development of India's nuclear weapons program and the roles played by Prime Ministers Rajiv Gandhi, P. V. Narasimha Rao and V P Singh.

Pakistan

Faced with the possibility of international isolation, the already fragile Pakistani economy was weakened further. The morale of Pakistani forces after the withdrawal declined as many units of the Northern Light Infantry suffered heavy casualties. The government refused to acknowledge the dead bodies of many officers, an issue that provoked outrage and protests in the Northern Areas. Pakistan initially did not acknowledge many of its casualties, but Sharif later said that over 4,000 Pakistani troops were killed in the operation and that Pakistan had lost the conflict.

Responding to this, Pakistan President Pervez Musharraf said, "It hurts me when an ex-premier undermines his own forces," and claimed that Indian casualties were more than that of Pakistan. Many in Pakistan had expected a victory over the Indian military based on Pakistani official reports on the war, but were dismayed by the turn of events and questioned the eventual retreat. The military leadership is believed to have felt let down by the prime minister's decision to withdraw the remaining fighters. However, some authors, including ex-CENTCOM Commander Anthony Zinni, and ex-PM Nawaz Sharif, state that it was General Musharraf who requested Sharif to withdraw the Pakistani troops.

With Sharif placing the onus of the Kargil attacks squarely on the army chief Pervez Musharraf, there was an atmosphere of uneasiness between the two. On October 12, 1999, General Musharraf staged a bloodless *coup d'état*, ousting Nawaz Sharif. Benazir Bhutto, an opposition leader and former prime minister, called the Kargil War "Pakistan's greatest blunder". Many ex-officials of the military and the ISI (Pakistan's principal intelligence agency) also believed that "Kargil was a waste of time" and "could not have resulted in any advantage" on the larger issue of Kashmir.

A retired Pakistani Army General, Lt Gen Ali Kuli Khan, lambasted the war as "a disaster bigger than the East Pakistan tragedy", adding that the plan was "flawed in terms of its conception, tactical planning and execution" that ended in "sacrificing so many soldiers." The Pakistani media criticized the whole plan and the eventual climbdown from the Kargil heights since there were no gains to show for the loss of lives and it only resulted in international condemnation.

Despite calls by many, no public commission of inquiry was set up in Pakistan to investigate the people responsible for initiating the conflict. The PML (N) published a white paper in 2006, which stated that Nawaz Sharif constituted an inquiry committee that recommended a court martial for General Pervez Musharraf, but Musharraf "stole the report" after toppling the government, to save him. The report also claims that India knew about the plan 11 months before its launch, enabling a complete victory for India on military, diplomatic and economic fronts.

A statement in June, 2008 by a former army corps commander of Pakistan that Sharif "was never briefed by the army" on the Kargil attack, reignited the demand for a probe of the episode by legal and political groups. Though the Kargil conflict had brought the Kashmir dispute into international focus – which was one of the aims of Pakistan – it had done so in negative circumstances that eroded its credibility, since the infiltration came just after a peace process between the two countries was underway. The sanctity of the LOC too received international recognition.

President Clinton's move to ask Islamabad to withdraw hundreds of armed militants from Indian-administered Kashmir was viewed by many in Pakistan as indicative of a clear shift in US policy against Pakistan. After the war, a few changes were made to the Pakistan army. In recognition of the Northern Light Infantry's performance in the war - which even drew praise from a retired Indian Lt. General - the regiment was incorporated into the regular army. The war showed that despite a tactically sound plan that had the element of surprise, little groundwork had been done to gauge the politico-diplomatic ramifications.

And like previous unsuccessful infiltrations attempts, such as *Operation Gibraltar*, which sparked the 1965 war, there was little coordination or information sharing among the branches of the Pakistan military. One U.S. Intelligence study is reported to have stated that Kargil was yet another example of Pakistan's (lack of) grand strategy, repeating the follies of the previous wars.

Casualties

Casualties for both sides were heavy. Pakistani claims gave two figures. The figure of 357 soldiers dead was challenged by some Pakistani officials, who claimed that 4,000 Pakistani soldiers were killed in the conflict. Pakistan also confirmed that more than 665 Pakistani troops were wounded and 8 were captured. According to India, Indian losses stand at 527 soldiers killed, 1,363 wounded, and 1 captured. Pakistan army losses have been difficult to determine, partly because Pakistan has not published an official casualties list. The US Department of State had made an early, partial estimate of close to 700 fatalities. According to numbers stated by Nawaz Sharif there weie 4,000+ fatalities. His party Pakistan Muslim League (N) in its "white paper" on the war mentioned that more than 3,000 *Mujahideens*, officers and soldiers were killed.

Another major Pakistani political party, the PPP, also says that "thousands" of soldiers and irregulars died. Indian estimates stand at 1,042 Pakistani soldiers killed. Musharraf, in his Hindi version of his memoirs, titled "Agnipath", differs from all the estimates stating that 357 troops were killed with a further 665 wounded. Apart from General Musharraf's figure on the number of Pakistanis wounded, the number of people injured in the Pakistan camp is not yet fully known. One Indian Pilot was officially captured during the fighting, while there were eight Pakistani soldiers who were captured during the fighting, and were repatriated on 13 August 1999.

KARGIL WAR IN THE ARTS

The brief conflict provided considerable dramatic material for filmmakers and authors in India. Some documentaries which were shot on the subject were used by the ruling party coalition, led by BJP, in furthering its election campaign that immediately followed the war. The following is a list of the major films and dramas on the subject.

LOC: Kargil (2003), a Hindi movie which depicts many incidents from the war was one of the longest in Indian movie history, running for more than four hours.

Lakshya (2004), another Hindi movie portraying a fictionalised account of the conflict. Movie critics have generally appreciated the realistic portrayal of characters. The film also received good reviews in Pakistan because it portrays both sides fairly.

Sainika (2002), the Kannada film directed by Mahesh Sukhdhare depicted the life of a soldier with Kargil war as one of the events starring C.P.Yogishwar, Sakshi Shivanand.

Dhoop (2003), directed by national award winner Ashwini Chaudhary, which depicted the life of Anuj Nayyar's parents after his death. Anuj Nayyar was a captain in the Indian army and was awarded Maha Vir Chakra posthumously. Om Puri plays the role of S.K. Nayyar, Anuj's father.

Mission Fateh - Real Stories of Kargil Heroes, a TV series telecast on Sahara channel chronicling the Indian Army's missions.

Fifty Day War - A theatrical production on the war, the title indicating the length of the Kargil conflict. This was claimed to be the biggest production of its kind in Asia, involving real aircraft and explosions in an outdoor setting.

Kurukshetra (2008) - A Malayalam film directed by a former Indian Army Major - major Ravi (Retd) based on his actual experience of Kargil War.

Many other movies like *Tango Charlie* drew heavily upon the Kargil episode, which still continues to be a plot for mainstream movies with a Malayalam movie *Keerthi Chakra*. The impact of the war in the sporting arena was also visible during the India-Pakistan clash in the 1999 Cricket World Cup, which coincided with the Kargil timeline. The game witnessed heightened passions and was one of the most viewed matches in the tournament.

INFLUENCE OF MILITANCY

Though there is no local militancy, Pakistan has twice tried to push in militants into the area. Both times the militants were pushed back. Jammu and Kashmir is one of the most famous and popular tourist destinations in India. The state is referred to as the "Paradise on Earth" and out of the state`s total population, a major portion lives in the villages. The villages of Jammu and Kashmir are colourful and picturesque and their wonderful scenic beauty attracts numerous tourists every year. The people in the villages live in unity and there is a great harmony found in all sphere of the village society in Jammu and Kashmir. The residents in the villages of Jammu and Kashmir follow various religious philosophies and also speak different languages.

The three major religious communities living in the villages of Jammu and Kashmir include Muslims, Hindus and Buddhists. The Muslims are in majority in the Kashmir region whereas Hinduism is the principal religion in the Jammu region. In the Ladakh region of the state, the major religious community is the Buddhists. Apart from these three religions, there is also a group of people known as Dogras. They mainly live in the villages of Jammu and follow Hinduism. However, a few of them also follow Islam. Urdu is the official language of Jammu and Kashmir, as it is spoken by most people in the villages of Jammu and Kashmir. Besides Urdu, the other languages spoken in the villages include Kashmiri, Ladakhi and Dogri. Dogri is actually the language of Dogra group of people and it was accepted as a national language of India in 2003.

The villages of Jammu and Kashmir have an impressive educational scenario. The state governmental authorities have established many schools at the primary and secondary levels in the villages of Jammu and Kashmir. The children begin their educational career from the village primary schools and then pursue higher education in the colleges and universities, mostly located in the urban areas of the state. Though the literacy rate is impressive, the governmental authorities have taken several initiatives to further improve the educational status. Agriculture is the principal occupation in the villages of Jammu and Kashmir. A majority of the total population of the state is engaged in agricultural activities and they cultivate many crops throughout the year.

The major crops cultivated in the villages of Jammu and Kashmir include Rice, Wheat, Maize, Tobacco, Rape seed, mustard, linseed, toria, cotton seed, Pulses, Saffron, Amarnath (Ganhar), etc. The villagers in the state also produce the fruits like apples, pears, cherries, plums, grapes, pomegranates, mulberry, peaches, apricots, walnuts, almonds, etc. in good quantity. The valley of Kashmir is quite famous for the cultivation of potatoes, turnips, carrots, spinach, tomatoes, cabbage, cauliflowers, radish, onions, lotus-stalk, brinjal, gourd and bitter gourd etc. as well.

Among all the crops cultivated in Jammu and Kashmir, Saffron is undoubtedly the most important one. Kashmir is one of the very few places in the world where Saffron is cultivated and the Kashmiri saffron is world famous for its great quality. Tourism is another major occupation of people in the villages of Jammu and Kashmir. As the state is world famous for its pictorial locations and great scenic beauty, many people are involved with the tourism sector to earn their livelihoods. The people work as tourist guides, run different types of business in the popular tourist spots and also provide lodging facilities to the tourists.

Apart from agriculture and tourism, handicrafts and textiles are the other major occupations of people in the villages of Jammu and Kashmir. The villagers produce numerous unique and extraordinary arts and crafts items like Carpets, Namdas, Papier Mache, Chain Stitch and Crewel Furnishings, Silks, Tweeks, Pherans, Shawls, Basketry, Walnut Wood, Copper, Silverware, etc. Many people in the villages of Jammu and Kashmir are also involved with the industries like Minerals, Gems and Jewellery, Floriculture, Horticulture, Electronic industry, etc.

The villages of Jammu and Kashmir are quite famous all over India and also in abroad for their diverse culture. The villages in the three regions of the state like Jammu, Kashmir and Ladakh have different culture and traditions and each of them are rich in their own way. Though the people follow different customs, all of them have love, affection and tolerance in common. The simplicity of the Kashmiri people is the most unique feature of their lifestyle. All the people in the villages of Jammu and Kashmir celebrate various religious and social fairs and festivals together, no matter which religious path they follow. The major religious festivals of the state include Eid-ul-Fitr, Eid-ul-Azha, Muharram, Diwali, Holi, Dussehra, Navaratri, Ramnavami, Maha Shivratri, Basant Panchami, Buddha Purnima, etc.

Apart from the religious festivals, there are also many social and cultural festivals celebrated in the villages of Jammu and Kashmir. These fairs and festivals include Lohri, Purmandal Mela, Bahu Mela, Chaitre Chandesh, Sindhu Darshan, The Ladakh Festival, Jhiri Mela, Hemis Festival, Amarnath Yatra, Mansar Food and Craft Mela, Spitok Gutor Zanskar, Dosmochey, Matho Nagrang, Stok Guru Tsechu, Phyang Tsedup, Yuru Kabgyat, Ph-Yang Tsedup, Korzok Gustor, Dak-Thok Tse-Chu, Shachukul Gustor, Thiksay Gustor, Chemrey Angchok, Galdan Namchot, etc.

The people in the villages of Jammu and Kashmir also enjoy various winter sports. During the religious and social festivals, the people in the villages of Jammu and Kashmir love to wear their traditional attires and also perform various traditional music and dance. The males wear the clothes like Kurta Pyjama in summers and woolen clothes in winters. They wear a kind of an overcoat called Pheran over Kurta. Most women in the villages wear Salwar Kamiz and Burqha (veil) in both summers and winters. They also wear Pheran during winters. Apart from wearing the traditional attires, the people in the villages of Jammu and Kashmir also perform various traditional music, dance and theatre forms that include Kud, Heren, Fumenie and Jagarana, Bakh/Gwatri/Kark/Masade, Gwatri, Karak, Benthe, Bhand Pather, Chakri, Sufiana Music, Marriage songs and dance (wedding dance), Jabro, Alley Yate, etc.

The villages of Jammu and Kashmir have a varied, diversified and unique cultural blend that has made the state distinct from the rest of the country. The multifaceted ethical and social entities living in the villages of the state rightly represent the real essence of India, "unity in diversity". The different cultural forms found in the villages of Jammu and Kashmir like fair and festivals, rites and rituals, art and architecture, language and mountains, seer and sagas, etc. are indeed a great treat for the tourists. The princely state of Jammu & Kashmir acceded to the Dominion of India in 1947 through an instrument of accession beween India and the Maharaja Hari Singh of J&K. At that time the areas of Jammu, Kashmir and Ladakh were a part of J&K though the three regions were geographically, culturally and linguistically different.

Over the years, Jammu and Ladakh regions that form a major portion of the area of J&K wish to unconditionally integerate with the Indian nation and for all practical purposes consider themselves as Indians. Despite discrimination agenda of the majority population of the state, they do not have a sense of alienatation. On the contrary, the Kashmir region that has the political power; thanks to faulty delimitation in its favour, feels alienated. It is still undecided and looks towards independence or acession with Pakistan rather than with India.

Their indecision has resulted in the sufferings of the other two regions of the sate as the world and Indian nation considers Kashmir more important despite being of no consequence (has a small area, much smaller than the area of J&K under Pakistani control and an indecisive population whose leaders are emotionally inclined towards Pakistan but want facilities generated by the Indian nation). The national level Indian leaders and the media are so awed by Kashmir that their every action conciously or sub-consciously works for winning their favour. The evidence to that may be gathered from everyday happenings.

The role of Kashmiri leaders during Shri Amarnath Shrine Board land issue, including those of the so called Kashmir based mainstream political parties has vindicated the stand that there is no hope for the people of Jammu province to get justice in the present political set up where Jammu province remains as a part of Jammu and Kashmir State. This is borne by the fact of resorting to 62 days of an unprecedented & unique massive agitation by the people of Jammu region to have this trivial matter settled.

The communal, parochial and anti – Jammu mind set of the Kashmiri leadership would in no case allow Jammu to get its due representation and share in the State Assembly, the State Government services, in the matter of development & in selection to professional institutions. The problems of displaced persons of 1947 from the Pakistan occupied part of Jammu and Kashmir and from Chhamb in 1965, 1971 or of those of West Pakistan refugees have not been addressed so far & are not going to be addressed by any of the Kashmir dominated Govt. because of its communal and prejudicial perceptions.

The worry of the people of Jammu province is that Kashmiri leadership by its calculated and mischievous designs is bent upon eroding and finishing their geographical, political and cultural identity. They are trying to create communal divide among the people of Jammu province, making all efforts to create a Kashmir like situation in Jammu province and then separate whole of Jammu and Kashmir from India. The people of Jammu province have been subjected to political neglect and worst kind of discrimination and have become practically slaves in the hands of Kashmir rulers. This region possesses almost 50% of the state's population and an area 1.7 times of the Kashmir Valley, and it is of difficult and inaccessible terrain.

The region deserves more seats in the state assembly than valley. With 37 seats in the state assembly on an average one assembly segment represents 710 sq. Km area with 73 thousands voters in Jammu province, whereas in Kashmir it has 346 sq. Km area and 55 thousand voters. In the Civil Secretariat, representation of the people of Jammu province is less than 15% & only about 25% in the total state government services. The problem of unemployment in Jammu province is far more acute than that in the valley. Out of total unemployed youth in the state about 70% belong to this region.

Jammu province contributes over 70% to the state's revenue whereas it gets only 20-30% of the total allocation for development. Hardly 10% of funds available from the Government of India have so far been spent in the development works in Jammu province. Tourism; Handicrafts & Horticulture in Jammu province have remained deliberately neglected so that the region does not become a competitor to the valley. The Governments lead by Mufti and Ghulam Nabi Azad which boast of equitable treatment for all the regions did not play a fair game with Jammu province. Road network of Jammu province is about 24 % against 55% in the Valley.

Expenditure on the road network in Jammu province in the 8th and 9th plan remained 14,418 lac and 29,238 lac where it is 24,722lac and 40,368 lac for the Valley. This is in spite of the fact that Jammu has 170 times more area than the valley and the difficult hilly terrain in Jammu province needs more expenditure for the construction of roads.

The Tourism budget of 2007 shows that Jammu got 4 crore against 20 crore allocated for the valley, i.e. only 16.66 per cent. Total expenditure on Irrigation schemes incurred in Jammu province, where a major portion of the area is 'KANDI'; in the 8th and 9th plan is only 6118 lac and 8705 lac where as it is 10,297 lac and 15,944 lac in Kashmir where the major portion of land is flat & its water table is very high. In Horticulture too about 90% expenditure was made in the valley in the 8th and 9th plans & only 10% in Jammu region.

It is asserted that the division of Jammu and Kashmir State into three states of Jammu, Ladakh and Kashmir alongwith the creation of a Union Territory in the Valley for the Kashmir Pandits, Kashmiri Sikhs and other communities like Gujjars and Shia Muslims of Kashmir Valley is the requirement of the day. This division of Jammu and Kashmir State is essential because of the following reasons: -

The anti- Jammu, anti-Ladakh policies and communal and secessionist mindset of the Kashmir leadership coupled with the appeasement policy towards the Kashmiri Muslim leadership pursued by the Government of India and the other national political parties shall not allow Jammu and Ladakh to get justice and their due share in the present political structure in Jammu and Kashmir State. The writ of the Kashmiri leaders shall always run the state. The aspirations of the people of the other two regions shall always be sacrificed and the people of these regions shall be forced to accept the type of the political structure that the Kashmiri leadership proposes, even if that may be Azadi, Self Rule or Greater Autonomy.

The union of Jammu, Kashmir and Ladakh regions is an unnatural wedlock that took place during Maharaja Gulab Singh reign under the Amritsar Treaty of 1846. All the three regions have their own distinct identity and personality since times immemorial. All the three regions have different political, linguistic, social and cultural perceptions. The interests, aspirations and needs of these regions are conflicting and mutually exclusive. The nature has also separated these regions and has provided distinct geographical identities. Jammu is separated from the Kashmir Valley by Pirpanjal range where as Kashmir Valley is separated from the Ladakh region by Zanskar ranges.

This division of Jammu and Kashmir State shall be an instrument in fulfilling the aspirations of all the regions and communities of the state and shall provide them the opportunity to form the Government of their choice and develop and progress as per their aspirations in a democratic and secular country as the India is.

The division shall free the people of Jammu & Ladakh regions from the domination of fundamentalist, communal and secessionist leadership of the Kashmir valley and the secular traditions and secular ethos will be allowed to flourish there.

The secessionist elements shall remain confined within the Kashmir Valley and other areas of the present Jammu and Kashmir State can be insulated from their influence and propaganda.

The identity of each region shall be protected. It may be mentioned that the identities of Jammu and Ladakh regions are under constant threats of elimination due to the Kashmiri influence and domination.

There shall be no complaint of discriminatory treatment against any region or community. The present alienations of the people of the three regions among themselves shall vanish and good understanding and friendly relationship shall develop after the division of the state.

This present agitation has given the opportunity to the people of Jammu province to assert their will & also bring to the forefront the discrimination they have faced since the last 61 years. It is a massive demonstration of the will of the people of Jammu region irrespective of the religion and the area to which they belong to. It gave a clear signal to the Kashmir leadership and to the power that at Delhi that people of Jammu region should not be taken for granted & their aspirations can no longer be neglected to appease the secessionist forces of the valley.

In case the old exercise of appeasing the Kashmiris at the cost of the people of Jammu region is repeated the people of Jammu region shall respond with heightened protests and demonstrations. It should also be understood the massive participation of the people in the present agitation and their unique support is an out burst of these people & they want freedom - Azadi from the Kashmir domination now. With Jammu and Ladakh happy being a part of the Indian nation, does plebiscite has any relevance. Lets analyse. Recent events indicate that the issue of plebiscite continues to haunt Kashmiris and many well-meaning people from other parts of India as a means to satisfy the majority population of Jammu and Kashmir.

The "Azadi" march and frequent references to collection of a sizable number of Muslims in Srinagar at Idgah are being taken as an indication that the demand for a plebiscite reflects the aspirations of a sizable majority of the state's population consisting of Jammu, Ladakh and Kashmir. On the other hand, the well meaning Indians including leading journalists feel that India stands on a morally weak ground by insisting on the Simla Agreement of July 2nd 1972 and rejecting a referendum. They also feel that this is the only way for the people of J&K

to articulate their right to self-determination. However, Kashmiris in Srinagar city and few journalists calling for a plebiscite in J&K does not mean that the plebiscite is an easy and a viable option. The discussion below shall clearly indicate that the concept has lost its meaning with the passage of time.

The U.N. resolutions passed in 1948 calling for a referendum were meant to apply to the whole of the former kingdom of Jammu and Kashmir, as it existed with Maharaja Hari Singh. Presently, that area is divided between India, Pakistan and China. To manage a referendum within the populations of areas being controlled by two nations other than India seems a distant dream. Discussing the population aspect of the area with India, in the event of a referendum being held only in J&K with India, we must realize that it consists of Jammu, Ladakh and Kashmir with a religious mix of populations. Contrary to normal national belief, Jammu & Kashmir is not a state where only Kashmiri Muslims live. It is a multi-ethnic, multi-religious state with 64% Muslims, 33% Hindus, and 3% Buddhists, Sikhs, Christians and others.

At the outset, 36% population (33+3) is already wedded to the Indian nation. The three regions are also culturally and geographically distinct and have different aspirations. Further analysis indicates that fifteen per cent of the state's Muslims live in the provinces of Jammu and Ladakh; being non-Kashmiris, they stand behind J&K's association with India. This makes it about 51% of the total population of the sate. Of the state's 49% who reside in the Kashmir province, about 13% are Shia Muslims. Shia Muslims do not wish to have anything to do with Sunni-dominated Pakistan, knowing full well the fate that awaits them there.

This is also true of the Shias of Kargil who know of the poverty and degradation experienced by their ethnic siblings in Baltistan, a part of Pakistan occupied Kashmir referred to as the "Northern Areas". Moreover, 14% of the people in Kashmir province are the pastoral nomadic Gujar and Bakarwal people. They are strong supporters of association with India. As far as non-Muslim groups are concerned there is no reason for them to even think about living outside multi-religious and secular India. We should also not forget the modern secular Muslim from Kashmir who wants to be a citizen of a modern democracy with unparalleled opportunities rather choosing the concept of a failed nation. So a plebiscite loses its meaning, even it is supposedly conducted in the J&K with India.

As far as the slogan of Azadi goes, according to the UN Resolution, the choice does not exist at all. The people were to be given the choice between acceding to India or Pakistan, but not of independence or Azadi. The resolution also required that Pakistan withdraw its troops first from its side of the region, followed by the bulk of the Indian forces, before a plebiscite were held, the willingness of that Pakistan has never expressed. Pakistan has also never mentioned the issue of plebiscite.

As per a Dr. Syed Nazir Gilani in an article *Thoughts on Plebiscite March* recently, "...Kashmiri leaders to ask the Government of Pakistan why did it fail to raise the Kashmir question at the UN for 30 years and 9 months, that is, from 5 November 1965 to 15 September 1996, when it attracted rule 11 of procedure rules of UN Security Council and was clubbed with 50 other items for deletion. Kashmir is no more on UN Security Council agenda in the manner in which it continued to be for 48 years from 6 January 1948 to 15 September 1996.

It is now subject to an annual reminder..... Kashmiri leaders who opted to sell General Musharraf's 4-point formula and on 18 August 2008 had the cheek to lead the 'Plebiscite March' in Srinagar have to explain the valiant and trusting people, as to why General Musharraf skipped any reference to self-determination while he addressed the 61st Session of the UN General Assembly on 19 September 2006. Musharraf's sales persons are answerable to the people as to why their regular host in cash and kind in Delhi, Riaz Mohammad Khan, foreign secretary, again betrayed the Constitution of Pakistan, the trust of the people of Kashmir and UN Charter obligations and did not make any reference to self-determination of the people of Kashmir while he addressed the 62nd Session of the UN General Assembly on 2 October 2007." In all, the concept clearly has no meaning in Jammu and Ladakh and shall lose its shine in the valley also.

It has been 56 days since the people of Jammu started agitating for restoration of land to the Shri Amarnath Shrine Board. After all what the Jammu people are asking for is just 800 kanals of land and that too is to be used for a period of only 2 months. This piece of land is situated at an altitude of almost 10,000 feet above the sea level. Is it too much, that the Govt. of India is unable to give when we have thousands of acres of land being illegally occupied by Mosques, Temples and Gurudwaras throughout the country. Are the people of Jammu asking for too much, when the Government of India does so much for Haj pilgrims? Mind you no country in the world (including the Muslim states including Pakistan) subsidizes the Haj pilgrimage, the way it is done in India. But we have no objection to that. We feel if the government can afford it, it should be continued.

The common man on the streets of Jammu is asking; why the Govt of India is so afraid of the separatists that it is unable to give the Jammu people their due. After all the people of Jammu are protesting with tricolour in their hands and shouting slogans like Bharata Mata ki jai and Vande Mataram. Contrast this to whatever is happening in the valley where the Indian tricolour is burnt, Pakistani flag is raised and the security forces are told to look the other way. The government of India is giving the impression that it can bend to any degree to accommodate the seditionist and anti national elements in the valley but it would not accede to any of the legitimate demands of the people of Jammu.

This means that anti nationals are held at a premium and the patriots are to be sneered at. Nationalist is communal and sedition is secular. There is increasingly a feeling getting generated among the youth of Jammu that this government listens only when you kick it in the back. You make a slogan of separate Dograland and start burning the tricolour and then this government as well as the pseudo-secular media shall start listening to your problems. This happened in Assam where the minority-ism of the centre culminated in the formation of ULFA and the demand for a separate ASSAM nation. What the government is doing is going to result in some sort of counter militancy in Jammu region and this would be a situation which would be impossible even for a country like India to handle.

And what the so called journalistic brains are doing in Delhi, sitting in their drawing rooms. They want the Kashmiris to be given what they want. What they do not realize is that the Kashmiris have got much more than what they deserved without contributing in any way to the nation has been feeding them for the past 61 years The so called intelligentsia backed by the government of India played into the hands of the separatists and the valley centric politicians by pandering to the boogey of economic blockade. These brains could not see the actual game of the seditionists of trying to divert the attention from the just agitation of the people of Jammu and allowed them to hijack the international media attention to the cause of so called azaadi.

These no-brainers fail to see that they are marginalizing the pro-India forces in the valley. The Government of India has always sided with the anti-nationals at the cost of patriotic forces everywhere be it in the valley or Jammu or elsewhere in the country. It should be made very clear to the anti-India forces that people of India are not going to cede even a single inch of its territory. Yes, we can facilitate the migration of pro-Pakistani elements to Pakistan or so called Azad Kashmir, but then they shall not be allowed to return. The seditionist elements in the valley and elsewhere should be dealt with sternly.

Now coming to the solution of the problem:

Immediately restore the land to the Shri Amarnath Shrine Board. The land should be diverted to the Shrine board for constructing temporary structures for usage for 3 months during the Amarnath yatra. For the rest of the year nobody should be allowed to use this land.

Immediate steps should be taken to redress the grievances of the people of Jammu region who have been continuously been discriminated against by the Kashmiris with active connivance of all the central governments.

The permanent solution to the Jammu and Kashmir problem should be sought within the provisions of the constitution of India after taking the interests of the people of Jammu and Ladakh into consideration. The two options could be-

- Separate Jammu and Ladakh regions from the valley by creating Jammu state and Ladakh Union territory. The division should be on the present administrative lines, and
- Restructuring on Jammu and Ladakh should not be allowed. The Kashmir valley could be given some more autonomy including free trade across the border with POK, but the integrity of India should be ensured. Section 370 should be abolished. An area directly administered by the government of India should be reserved in the valley for the Kashmiri pandits. The Govt. of India should be responsible for their safety.

Remove 370

Conduct fresh delimitation based on the latest figures available with the Election commission taking both the population asw ell as the area of the three regions into account. Make regional councils having constitutional guarantees from the Govt. of India. The regional councils should be Ladakh, Kashmir (minus Baramulla), Pahari (Poonch, Rajouri and Baramulla), Chenab valley (Districts of Udhampur, Doda minus Bhaderwah, Ramban, Kishtawar and Reasi), Jammu (Jammu and Samba), Kathua (Including Bhaderwah tehsil). All funds from the centre should go directly to these councils and the councils should be encouraged for devolution of power as per the Panchayati Raj. This is the only way of keeping the state of J&K together.

In any case the deleterious effect of the valley politics should not be allowed in the Jammu and Ladakh regions. It should be made clear to the people of Kashmir, that in case they want to stay in India they have to abide by the law of the land and that they shall not be allowed to create fundamentalist mess in Jammu and Ladakh regions. Today, most of us are seeking the answer to the same question in our minds. What shall be result of this agitation that has been going on for over one and a half month in Jammu? While seeking solutions to the Amarnath land row, naturally we also seek a solution that is permanent to other related issues. We seek the analysis of what went wrong when J&K acceded to India after India's independence in 1947?

Sometimes we blame the Maharaja who did not accede to the Indian nation in the first go and waited for Pakistan to attack J&K and enter Kashmir? We also tend to put the blame on Nehru, habitually calling it a Nehruvian blunder? As the Amarnath land row paved path for larger issues, the current situation in Jammu and Kashmir gradually turned into a divide of Jammu vs Kashmir. Sixty-one years of patience, effort, expenses, army, blood, love and hatred; here we are, if not back to where we started then not very far away from it also. Often repeated issues like relevance of article 370, absence of delimitation in J&K, the Kashmiri leaders demand of plebiscite come to the fore.

Article 370 of our constitution restrains the legitimacy of any law enacted by the parliament unless the state government ratifies it though with an exception of defence, foreign policy and communication. J&K state is the only one in India to have its own Constitution and the President of India cannot issue directions to the state government in exercise of the executive power of the Union as he can in every other state. All Kashmiris are Indian citizens but Indians are not necessarily Kashmiri citizens and keeping in view the instrument of accession cannot own any property in J&K. The delimitation process shall give the leverage to Jammu area on the assembly seats front but the demand is always ignored.

The promise of plebiscite that the Indian nation promised and through which, the Kashmiri leaders feel shall get the right of self determination has not been addressed to. While the

Indian nations spend so much on other fronts like money; Sanghvi writes in HT (17th Aug, 2008), "Then, there is the money. Bihar gets per capita central assistance of Rs 876 per year. Kashmir gets over ten times more: Rs 9,754 per year. While in Bihar and other states, this assistance is mainly in the forms of loans to the state; in Kashmir 90 per cent is an outright grant.

The Indian taxpayer meets Kashmir's entire Five Year Plan expenditure. In addition, New Delhi keeps throwing more and more money at the state: in 2004, the Prime Minister gave Kashmir another $ 5 billion for development." While most of the money is siphoned off to the valley, Jammu region has born it all by meekly shouting, "Foul". India has tried so far and sought integration of Kashmir with India, even at the cost of overlooking aspirations of the people of Jammu region. But Kashmiris through their leaders whether elected or not have nevertheless demanded azaadi. If there are people who do not subscribe to this idea, they have not voiced their opinion so far, suggesting acceptance to this idea.

It is time that the Indian nation as a whole thinks on this issue and discusses the subjects that have been considered a taboo so far. Plebiscite, if it was not held so far may be held now. Let us also overlook the part of Kashmir that the Pakistan occupies as it is not under the control of this nation. The choices as also suggested by Swaminathan (TOI, 17th August, 2008), are three: independence, union with Pakistan, and union with India. Whatever decision the Kashmir valley takes, it will be its own and after that it shall be responsible for its plight. Jammu will definitely opt to stay with India, and probably Ladakh too.

The dissident voices will be settled for once and all. Also, voices of those who do not have the courage to come out in the open shall also get manifested. Ladakh – 'the Land of Passes' (*La*-passes, *dakh*-land) is the largest in area when compared to the three main regions of the Jammu & Kashmir State viz., Jammu, Kashmir and Ladakh. This region falls under the districts of Ladakh and Kargil. The most striking feature of Ladakh region is the mountain ranges that stretch from the southeast to the northeast. Although most of Ladakh is mountainous, there are many valleys lying in the lap of the mountain ranges such as the Great Himalayan range, the Zanskar range, the Ladakh range and the Karakoram Range.

As like all other high altitude mountainous region, Ladakh is sparsely populated (*ca.* 1, 50,000) i.e., only two persons/km^2, although life is difficult at high altitudes (2,900-5,900 metres), yet both man and wildlife survive here comfortably as revealed by the rich diversity of wildlife. The Ladakh landscape is characterized by snow-clad mountains, treeless arctic deserts and a few narrow fertile valleys, some of them breathtakingly beautiful. With the advent of summer, a miraculous change occurs when life-sustaining vegetation lends color to an otherwise bleak landscape. Ladakh is a large barren but beautiful region of intense sunlight and clear unpolluted air. The temperature in summer may rise up to 37°C, but may also drop to -40°C degrees in winter. Dras in Kargil district experiences the lowest winter temperatures. There is very low rainfall in the region is about 92 mm/annum because it is situated in the rain shadow region of the Greater Himalayas. Most of the water source is the frozen snow or ice.

The Fauna of Ladakh is a mixture of Palearctic and Oriented regions and comprises mostly of mammals and birds. Ladakh has poor representation of reptiles and amphibians. The mammalian fauna comprises mainly of ungulates, rodents and carnivores. Ladakh is well recognized for its mountain ungulate diversity. Information on the status and distribution of these mountain ungulates in Ladakh are presented below.

The most notable animal of the Ladakh, Tibet and adjacent parts of central Asia is the Wild Yak. It is a large animal weighting about a ton. It has long black hair, which is tinged with gray at the muzzle. The horns are curved and long which may grow up to 75 cm in length. The wild yak, which moves in herds, spends the summer at great heights and descends to lower altitudes in winter. Prior to 1962, the Wild Yak was distributed in plang darpo and kuenlum into Tibet westwards in Ladakh. As per the local people, the animals were found near Pangong Lake, Changchenmo Valley, Tsoogsalu, Daulat Beg Olde and Chushul areas.

Since then, their distribution range has drastically shrunken and number has greatly declined due to massive hunting. There were no official reports on the presence of Wild Yak in Ladakh for the last thirty years. A survey was conducted by a team of six members in the Karakoram Range of (a corridor between India & China) Changchenmo Valley, North-East of Ladakh during July-August 1996 in order to confirm the presence of Wild Yak. About 300 km were covered during surveys of which 170 km were by vehicle and the rest on foot. One male was sighted at Satlung Yogma and herd of 47 Yaks were sighted at Satlung Parma area in the Karakoram Range, Changchenmo Valley. This survey confirmed the presence of Wild Yak in this area.

The *Chiru* or Tibetan antelope (Tsoros-Ladakhi) - is a valuable species that inhabits high altitudes of Ladakh. It is slender but stout looking due to the thick coat of interwoven pale-brown hair. The color varies from season to season and from individual to individual. They roam the eastern fringe of Ladakh and inhabit Aksaichin and Tibetan plateau above 5,000 metres. Their horns measure up to 70 cm and are black having knots indicating the animal's age. In case of male front legs has a strip of black or dark brownish in colour The *Chiru* is persecuted in large numbers for the sake of under fleece-shahtoosh- from which the famous shahtoosh shawls or 'ring shawls' are made. Hardly a pound of under fleece is obtained from one animal. These shawls are the highly priced, softest and warmest quality product.

It was reported that the Tibetan antelope was extinct as no reports of sightings were made during the period 1960-1990. In 1984, the *Chiru* were reported to occur in the Aksai chin and Tibetan plateau. The *Chiru* are migratory and come in to Indian Territory in the Changchenmo valley and DBO during summer. In 1991, the Indian Army reported the presence of *Chiru* in DBO (Daulat Beg Olde) falling in the Karakoram

Wildlife Sanctuary located along the border with China. In 1994, Mr. N.A. Kitchloo, Wildlife Warden, Leh, deputed a survey team of 9 person headed by Mr. Amchuk, R.O. to DBO and reported the sighting of *Chiru*.

The *Chiru* population was estimated to be between 250 and 300. In India, the *Chiru* is found in the Changchenmo DBO (Daulat Beg Olde) valley of northern Ladakh between 3,700-5,500 metres from where it crosses from Tibet through Lanak La (pass) at the head of the valley. After this survey, it was certain that the animal is not killed in the Indian Territory i.e., DBO and Changchenmo – a fact supplemented by the security forces as well. In Ladakh, the illegal trade was reportedly carried out through the border of Changthang. No trade is reported from DBO and Changchenmo valley where the animals are found at present in Ladakh, the reason being that the area is not inhabited up to at least 180 km from Phobrang village to, Changchenmo and silk head to DBO (Daulat Beg Olde).

The population of *Chiru* has declined drastically by excessive poaching and disturbance of its natural habitats in Tibet as has been reported by various agencies. These animals come into this area during summer season (May to September) and they migrate to the lower elevations across the international border to winter. They breed there in November – December and the young ones are born in May which is followed by their migration to higher elevations. The *Chiru* is a ruminant and feeds mostly during early mornings and late evenings especially along grassy edges and glacial streams. During day, it spends resting and before resting it first digs or scraps shallow pit in sand/ gravel and lies in side for concealment.

When ever any reference is made to Jammu & Kashmir State of India (Princely State of Maharaja Hari Singh), this day, it is so casually taken as a simple reference to Kashmir Valley only. Where as Kashmir Valley is just one of the arms of the "J&K Triangle". In view of mass migration of Hindu from Valley after 1989 a fair picture of population of J&K can be had only from 1981 census. Population of Kashmir, Jammu and

Ladakh Regions was 3134909, 2718113 and 134372 respectably and the present area of Kashmir, Jammu and Ladakh Regions is 15948 sq km, 26293 sq km and 96701 sq km respectably. Kashmir Valley came with Jammu State only in 1846.

The separatists do not have any public display or settlement in Jammu Region. There is another small triangle with in Kashmir Valley with one arm as total Pro accession elements, the other being of groups like PDP/ Moulvi Farooq/ Shabir Shah/ ANC and the third one of the JKLF/ direct foreign aided and abetted separatists/ Jamaat e Islami etc; and the innocent confused masses are suffocating in the core of Valley triangle. Indian Government has been working with a policy that looks only at Valley and appeasement of Kashmiri majority community. Some pro India Kashmiri leaders did sermon that it is better question the intentions of GOI for obtaining favours and attention.

What ever may be the occasion what ever may be the reference, what matters is who is saying what and in what atmosphere. Rather there is a need to first take to the way "J&K should be seen this day". The Indian as well as local Kashmiri leadership has this day landed itself in a situation where the vote race in Kashmir can not be easily won with out talking of alleged injustice done to Kashmiries since 1947 by India. Jammu and Ladakh Regions have so far been not given legitimate weightage. People of Kashmir Valley have regularly questioned the intentions of Bharat Sarkar and GOI has been extending all first favors to Valley.

J&K TRIANGLE TODAY

The base of the J&K Triangle is Jammu Region. Ladakh Region is area wise the largest region of Jammu & Kashmir.But Jammu region could be called the largest economic cum civic region of J&K. It has about 70% more area than Kashmir valley and has a well distributed population mix; and has most of the commercial forest wealth and hydel power potential. The Hindu and Muslim of Jammu region have so far not raised any religion based ambitions and even during the times (before

Oct 1947) of Hari Singh majority did not endorse the two nation theory and had more affinity towards Congress.

Linguistic segments of Jammu Province were/ are more near to each other and muslims of region are more near to Dogra and Punjabi traditions.No party or group of this arm (Jammu Region) have so far raised significant voice against the 1947 accession nor any group has publically carried pro Pakistan activity. No doubt the Valley centric main stream political parties (even Congress) have attempted religious cards for votes in belts of Doda, Rajouri, Poonch (Jammu region) but anti India cards have not worked in this region. In 2004 Madan Lal Sharma got elected from Jammu Poonch Rajouri and Lal Singh from the Kathua Udhampur Doda Lok Sabha segments.

In the past from both these segments BJP candidates have been sent to Lok Sabha. National Conference that totally holds to 1947 Accession of J&K with India has a strong footing in Jammu Region because of commitment of Dr. Farooq Abdullah to Indian Nationality. Jammu Region has another face as well that has remained unknown to the out side world. Over 90% of October 1947 Displaced persons from Pakistan Occupied J&K are in Jammu region. Similarly 99% of the refugees who came to J&K (India) from West Pakistan are also in Jammu region. Demands have been raised from Jammu Region for dividing J&K into three parts, the State of Jammu (10 districts), the State of Kashmir (10 districts) and Union Territory of Ladakh (2 districts).

Some of the Kashmiri separatist leaders are attempting to divide the people of (Muslim majority areas in Jammu Region) and if taken lightly they may succeed to communalize some areas as they did in valley against Kashmiri Pundits. The Left arm of the triangle is Kashmir Valley. Kashmir Valley has always been the center of political controversies. The separatist / anti India / confusing view points have been allowed to grow in Kashmir valley.The recent unmindful handling of Shri Amarnath Shrine Board land case by Ghulam Nabi Azad Government, handing over the issue to separatist elements by the J&K People's Democratic Party leadership (MUFTI); and the National Conference leadership too not outrightly speaking against the separatist slogans in Kashmir Valley clearly support the inference.

The Valley of today is practically free of the Hindu population. Local Hindu from Kashmir Valley is ousted from valley for over 20 years. They form about 7 lac of the J&K Population at today's standards. Migrant Kashmiri do not want Pakistan but demand a separate STATE for Kashmir Hindu (Panun Kashmir) out of Kashmir Valley.

Broadly the political groups in valley could be classified in four: Those who hold to 1947 Accession in totality. National Conference (Farooq Abdullah) could be undoubtedly counted in this. Mufti has to remain in race with National Conference in painting Kashmiri Muslims as more special subjects of State. Hence PDP explores indirect methods to exploit Kashmiri Muslims by suggesting even what appear negating the Accession. But it is sure that Mufti Sayeed/his party can not dare to defy the 1947 accession. Though National Conference forms the 2/3rd of this arm (Valley Arm) and holds fast to Indian nationality, still as on date under the circumstances that Indian leadership has made J&K to land in, a small part of the "third arm" (separatists/their over ground supporters) have gained some notorious fame. It needs careful handling.

The leaders like Mirwaiz Omar Farooq (Awami Action Committee), Maulana Abbas Ansari (*Ittihad ul Musilimeen*), Bilal Gani Lone (*Peoples Conference*), Sajjad Ahd Lone (*Peoples Conference*), Prof Abdul Ghani Bhat (*Muslim Conference*), S. Hameed (*Peoples League*), Shabir Ahmd Shah (*J&K Demcratic Freedom Party*), Ghulam M. Shah (*Awami National Conference*), Mohd Yusaf Tarigami (*CPI -M*) will have to be put in a proper place (but their place is surely not any where near to *National Conference*).

Most of them have been made to survive comfortably raising anti Accession slogans. But they well know in their hearts that they can not win a place for J&K (Kashmir Valley) outside India nor can they survive honourably in Pakistan (but still since they are supported in cash by the enemies of India and anti India stance is on date more paying for them they would keep on black mailing weak governments at Delhi by approaching foreign organizations like OIC). Sayeed Ali Shah Geeli and his Jamaat e Islami wants Kashmir to go with Pakistan and declare that they will vote for Pakistan if there is plebiscite. The Yasin Malik (JKLF) lead Jammu Kashmir Liberation Front (earlier Kashmir Liberation Front) started with independent State of Kashmir only and now is for Independent Jammu & Kashmir and asks for Pakistan to also vacate POK).

Mirwaiz Moulvi Farooq lead group limited geographically in Srinagar is not clear in the ideology except that they talk of Kashmiriat and rights of Kashmiri. It is certain that the day the so called united separatists / anti Accession elements / Hurriryat etc come on a local democratic platform, they will split since they have only anti India agenda as a uniting force.The pro separatist leaders in valley will keep on cashing till the miss informed innocent masses and new youth of Kashmiri Muslims is attended from very near by the main stream parties by working on ground. The innocent masses need be informed about he wrongs of the information so far passed on as well the unknown goods of the Indian nationality.

Of course return of Hindu to Valley is must for reconstruction since problem is not economic. Since the anti propaganda has consumed 50 years for setting roots in Kashmir Valley, the corrections would also take atleast 5 years of sincere work. The right Arm of the J&K Triangle is the Ladakh region. This is smallest population wise and largest area wise. This region has majority of the population in Budhists and the Shia Muslims. This region has never disputed the 1947 accession of J&K with India and has never substantially provided cadres to the separatist. The pro India and pro accession people of this region have grievances against Government of India for giving more attention to Kashmir Valley in comparison to Ladakh Region. They are judiciously demanding settlement in a Union Territory status.

Bibliography

Ananya Jahanara Ka | bir.*Territory of Desire: Representing the Valley of Kashmir*: University of Minnesota Press, March 2009.

Ashley J. Tellis, C. Christine Fair and Jamison Jo Medby. *Limited Conflict Under the Nuclear Umbrella: Indian and Pakistani Lessons from the Kargil Crisis*: RAND, 2001.

Chitralekha Zutshi. *Languages of Belonging: Islam, Regional Identity, and the Making of Kashmir*: Oxford University Press, 2004.

Constantina Rhodes Bailly. *Shaiva Devotional Songs of Kashmir*: SUNY Press, 1987.

Howard S. Brembeck. *In Search of the Fourth Freedom: University* of Notre Dame Press, 2000.

Iffat Sana Malik.*Kashmir: Domestic Insurgency, International Dispute*: Oxford University Press, 2002.

Itty Abraham. *South Asian Cultures of the Bomb: Atomic Publics and the State in India and Pakistan*: Indiana University Press, 2009.

Jean-Marie Lafont. *Maharaja Ranjit Singh: Lord of the Five Rivers*: Oxford University Press, 2002.

Jonathan S. Addleton. *Some Far and Distant Place: Muslim-Christian Encounters Viewed through the Eyes of a Child*: University of Georgia Press, 2002.

Kaul Suvir. *Partitions of Memory*: Indiana University Press, 2002.

Kavita Daiya.*Violent Belongings: Partition, Gender, and*

National Culture in Postcolonial India:Temple University Press, 2008.

Mridu Rai. *Hindu Rulers, Muslim Subjects: Islam, Rights, and the History of Kashmir*: Princeton University Press, 2004.

Owen Bennett Jones. *Pakistan: Eye of the Storm*: Yale University Press, 2002.

Paul R. Brass.*The Production of Hindu-Muslim Violence in Contemporary India*: University of Washington Press, 2003.

Pervaiz Iqbal Cheema. *The Armed Forces of Pakistan*: New York University Press, 2003.

Prem Shankar Jha. *Kashmir, 1947: Rival Versions of History*: Oxford University Press, 1996.

R. S. P. Bates and E. H. N. Lowther. *Breeding Birds of Kashmir*: Oxford University Press, 1952.

Rafiq Dossani and Henry Rowen. *Prospects for Peace in South Asia*:Stanford University Press, 2005.

Ravina Aggarwal. *Beyond Lines of Control: Performance and Politics on the Disputed Borders of Ladakh, India*: Duke University Press, 2004.

Robert A. Huttenback. *Kashmir and the British Raj 1847-1947*: Oxford University Press, 2005.

Samina Ahmd, David Cortright. *Pakistan and the Bomb*: University of Notre Dame Press, 1997.

Sten Widmalm.*Kashmir in Comparative Perspective: Democracy and Violent Separatism in India:* Oxford University Press, 2006.

Stephen P. Cohen. *The Idea of Pakistan*: Brookings Institution Press, 2004.

Strobe Talbott. *Engaging India: Diplomacy, Democracy, and the Bomb*: Brookings Institution Press, 2004.

Sudha Koul. *The Tiger Ladies: A Memoir of Kashmir*: Beacon Press, 2002.

Sumantra Bose. *Kashmir: Roots of Conflict, Paths to Peace*: Harvard University Press, 2003.

Sumantra Bose.*Contested Lands: Israel-Palestine, Kashmir, Bosnia, Cyprus, and Sri Lanka*:Harvard University Press, 2007.

Sumit Ganguly and Devin T. Hagerty. *Fearful Symmetry: India-Pakistan Crises in the Shadow of Nuclear Weapons*:University of Washington Press, 2005.

Sumit Ganguly. *Conflict Unending: India-Pakistan Tensions Since 1947* : Columbia University Press, 2002.

Sumit Ganguly.*The Crisis in Kashmir: Portents of War, Hopes of Peace*:Woodrow Wilson Center Press and Cambridge University Press, 1997.

T. N. Madan. *Family and Kinship: A Study of the Pandits of Rural Kashmir*: Oxford University Press, 2002.

Urvashi Butalia. *The Other Side of Silence: Voices from the Partition of India:* Duke University Press, 2000.

Index

G

H

I

J

K

L

M

N

O

P